Imagination

Imagination

Mary Warnock

Essay Index

UNIVERSITY OF CALIFORNIA PRESS
Berkeley and Los Angeles

University of California Press
Berkeley and Los Angeles, California

ISBN: 0-520-03115-6
Library of Congress Catalog Card Number: 75-22663

Printed in Great Britain

Contents

Preface

Imagination is a vast subject, and it may seem rash to treat of it in a relatively small book. But I do not wish to apologize for this too abjectly. For I have not tried to cover all possible aspects of the subject, nor have I aimed to present a complete theory of imagination, either philosophical or aesthetic. The book may be regarded rather as the record of an experiment, which I hope it may be, to some extent, instructive to follow through its various steps. I have tried to trace a single thread which runs through different accounts of imagination, and different instances of its exercise, and the experiment has been to see whether certain features of imagination would emerge as essential and as universal, if the thread could, as I hoped, be followed.

Chronologically, my thread is picked up first in Hume's *Treatise of Human Nature*, though this is a somewhat arbitrary choice. (I certainly do not wish to suggest that Hume invented out of nothing the concept of imagination which he discussed.) It is then followed through Kant to Coleridge and Wordsworth, and into the twentieth century, by way of phenomenology, to Wittgenstein, Ryle and Sartre. But I have not been primarily concerned with the influences of one thinker, or one user, on another. The connexions are conceptual rather than causal.

I have long believed and still believe that, if only one could understand imagination, one would understand a great deal both about perception, and about pleasure and other values. I have also come very strongly to believe that it is the cultivation of imagination which should be the chief aim of education, and in which our present systems of education most conspicuously fail, where they do fail. This book is not the proper place to justify this belief or even to explain it in detail. Nevertheless, my hope is that by bringing out the connexions between certain different functions of imagination, I may also suggest why it is that in education we have a duty to educate the imagination above all else. For we use imagination in our ordinary perception of the world. This perception cannot be separated from interpretation. Interpretation can be common to everyone, and in this sense ordinary, or it can be inventive, personal and revolutionary. So imagination is necessary, I have suggested, to enable us to recognize things in the world as familiar, to take for granted features of the world which we need to take for granted and rely on, if we are to go about our ordinary business; but it is also necessary if we are to see the world as significant of something unfamiliar, if we are ever to treat the objects of perception as symbolizing or suggesting things other than themselves. The thread I have tried to trace thus leads from our commonplace perceptual experience to our most outlandish interpretations. And I have tried to show that the connexion between these two extremes can come only by way of the concept of imagination as *that which creates mental images*, perhaps the most ordinary sense of the word 'imagination' that there is.

For a long time, and very vaguely, I believed that Coleridge possessed the secret of the kind of understanding of imagination that I sought, and that it was contained both in his theory and in his practice. Alas, I have given up this faith. But the connexion between perception and recognizable flights of creative imagination *is* to be found in Coleridge, and still more clearly in Wordsworth. I have tried among other things to bring both Wordsworth and Coleridge into a framework of professionally philosophical thinking, about the very subject matter with which they were concerned, as poets.

In attempting this, I claim no originality. I acknowledge many debts which indeed it will be obvious that I have incurred. But there are certain debts which must be acknowledged. The first is to Geoffrey Grigson, whose anthology, *The Romantics*,[1] was a revelation, in my school days, of a kind of intensity of perceptual experience which it is still part of my main interest to try to account for. Apart from that, my greatest debt is to Peter Strawson, whose article 'Imagination and Perception', appearing in a volume of lectures delivered at Amherst in 1968–9 (*Experience and Theory*, 1970), made it seem that my projected thread-tracing

[1] Routledge, 1942.

might possibly be philosophically respectable, even if I have failed to make it so in the end. I am also deeply indebted to Oscar Wood who read my manuscript, and saved me from numerous mistakes; and finally I must record my gratitude to the Principal and Fellows of Lady Margaret Hall who, by electing me to the Talbot Research Fellowship, presented me with far more time for reading and writing than I should ever have been able to find for myself.

MARY WARNOCK

PART I

Imagination and Perception

Hume and Kant

The concept of imagination which is going to be my concern in the following pages can be seen in its first form in Hume's *Treatise of Human Nature*. But Hume was by no means wholly an innovator. He wrote in a tradition of empiricist thought which included Locke and Berkeley, and which in a way had its starting point further afield in Descartes. It was, above all, Descartes who set philosophy in the habit of raising the question 'what are we aware of?' in a general form, and of answering that we are aware of *the content of our consciousness*. It seemed self-evidently obvious to philosophers after Descartes, however critical they may have been of the details of his solutions, that in order to answer questions about knowledge, belief, perception, or indeed about causation and substance, one had to turn one's attention inwards, and examine the objects of one's consciousness. These objects were, generally speaking, mental objects or *ideas*. Thus, for these philosophers there was always one problem which had to be solved, above all others, namely the problem of the relation between ideas in my head and things which are apparently not in my head but in the outside world. I *seem* to perceive the world. But, in another sense, Descartes had taught that what I perceive is my own ideas. How are these two perceptions related?

Locke, writing in 1690,[1] introduced the word 'idea' in this way: 'I must . . . beg pardon of my reader for the frequent use of the word *idea*, which he will find in the following treatise. It being that term which I think serves best to stand for whatsoever is the *object* of understanding when a man thinks, I have used it to express whatever is meant by *phantasm, notion species* or whatever

---

[1] *Essay concerning Human Understanding*, ed. Pringle-Pattison, 1924.

it is that the mind can be employed about in thinking.' Further on he says, 'To ask at what time a man first has any ideas is to ask when he begins to perceive; *having ideas* and *perception* being the same thing.' There is no essential difference here between perceiving and thinking; all mental activity whatever, indeed all consciousness, is bundled together and referred to as 'having ideas'.

Similarly Berkeley, in 1710, opened the *Principles of Human Knowledge* with the following remark: 'It is evident to anyone who takes a survey of the objects of human knowledge, that they are either *ideas* actually imprinted on the senses or else such as are perceived by attending to the passions and operations of the mind, or lastly ideas formed by help of memory and imagination, either compounding dividing or barely representing those originally perceived in the aforesaid ways.' Once again, there is no sharp line to be drawn between perceiving apparently in the presence of an object, and thinking about it in its absence.

Hume shares this very general picture of consciousness with Locke and Berkeley. It is true that he introduces a new distinction between what we are aware of in perception and what we are aware of in thought, calling the former 'impressions' and the latter 'ideas'. This distinction, however, though it looks like an important innovation, is less radical than it seems at first sight. Indeed it does not do much to alter his inherited picture of the nature of consciousness. For the distinction between impressions and ideas turns out to be one only of degree. He says, 'All the perceptions of the human mind resolve themselves into two distinct kinds, which I shall call *impressions* and *ideas*. Those perceptions which enter with most force and violence we may name impressions; and under this name I comprehend all our sensations, passions and emotions, as they make their first appearance in the soul. By ideas I mean the faint images of these in thinking and reasoning.'[1] And he goes on, 'The common degrees of these are easily distinguished; though it is not impossible but in particular instances they may very nearly approach each other. Thus in sleep, in a fever, in madness, or in any very violent emotion of the soul, our ideas may approach to our impressions: as on the other hand it sometimes happens that our impressions are so faint and low

[1] *Treatise*, Pt. I, sec. 1. Quotations from Hume's *Treatise* are taken from the edition of L. A. Selby-Bigge (O.U.P., 1888), henceforward referred to in the notes as S-B.

that we cannot distinguish them from our ideas. But notwith-standing this near resemblance in a few instances, they are in general so different that no one can make a scruple to rank them under distinct heads.[1]

It is to be noticed that Hume actually defines ideas as images. From the outset, then, he regards imagination, the image-making faculty, as playing a crucial role in our thinking. At the very least it supplies us with ideas to think about. It is what reproduces impressions so that we can think about things in their absence. It is dubious, to be sure, how far the reproduced impressions are to be thought of as mental *pictures*. But the language of 'faint image' may be taken to suggest this. In any case, there is no doubt that sometimes, especially in Book I of the *Treatise*, Hume speaks as if ideas *were* pictures, and thus as if 'imagination' were being used by him in one of its most ordinary senses, as that which enables us to see things 'in our mind's eye'.

Let us try to see in a little more detail how Hume thinks that the imagination actually goes to work. In Book I, Part I, section 3, he distinguishes between memory and imagination as two different faculties by which we repeat our impressions, and present these impressions to ourselves as ideas. Again the distinction is in terms of force and vivacity. Ideas presented by memory are much more lively and strong than those presented by imagination. 'When we remember any past event, the idea of it flows in upon the mind in a forcible manner; whereas, in the imagination, the per-ception is faint and languid, and cannot without difficulty be preserv'd by the mind steddy and uniform for any considerable time.'[2] There is a further difference, that the memory is 'in a manner ty'd down' to produce its ideas in the same order as the original impressions were received, whereas the imagination has liberty 'to transpose and change its ideas'.

This last mentioned difference turns out to be extremely im-portant for Hume. On it turns the distinction between simple and complex ideas. Hume, like his predecessors, tends to assume that impressions come into our minds through the senses as single, simple items. These philosophers do not, on the whole, raise difficulties about what counts as a single impression, how long a single impression is supposed to last, how to count impressions at any moment of consciousness, or anything of the kind. Perhaps,

[1] S-B, p. 1.   [2] S-B, p. 9.

in Hume's case, the word 'impression' itself, with its metaphorical sense of pressing one seal onto one piece of wax, made it easier to overlook all such possible ambiguities. Where Hume talks about 'complex impressions' he means impressions which come through more than one of the senses at the same time: we receive a complex impression of the apple before us in that the impressions of colour, taste and smell, which we may receive all at once, are distinguishable from each other. Now the imagination may, in forming an idea, join different parts of such a complex impression with parts of other complexes, or with simple impressions which came originally at a different time. So I may form the imaginary idea of a fruit which is dark purple and soft but which smells and tastes like an apple. Each of the ideas I have here (of purple, softness, apple-taste and smell) must have been derived from some simple impression, but the impressions need not have come to me joined as I have joined them in my imagination. Though no idea can exist even in the imagination which was not caused to exist by a previous impression, yet there is a sense in which the imagination is creative, in that it can construct what it likes out of the elements at its disposal.

However, although to a certain extent the imagination is free, there are limitations on its freedom. It is in the exploration of these limits that Hume begins to elaborate the special role of imagination in our understanding of the world. He argues that, although the imagination is free to join ideas together in any way that it pleases, and although this freedom is in fact one of the distinguishing characteristics which mark off imagination from memory, yet it does not always join ideas at random. There is a kind of bond between different separable ideas, by which one idea 'naturally introduces' another. Hume says 'This uniting principle among ideas is not to be consider'd as an inseparable connexion; . . . nor yet are we to conclude that without it the mind cannot join two ideas; for nothing is more free than that faculty: but we are only to regard it as a gentle force which commonly prevails, and is the cause why, among other things, languages so nearly correspond to each other; nature in a manner pointing out to everyone those simple ideas which are most proper to be united into a complex one.'[1] There are, it turns out, three uniting principles, three features, that is to say, which our

[1] Pt. I, sec. 4; S-B, p. 10.

ideas actually possess, in virtue of which the mind is conveyed from one to the other and unites them. These three features are resemblance, contiguity in time or space, and causal connexion. (The last of the three, when Hume comes to analyse it, turns out itself to be complex and at least in part the product of imagination, but in the present context he treats it as if it were a simple observable *fact* that two ideas may be so related.) In memory, then, our ideas are bound to occur to us in the temporal and spatial order in which their originating impressions occurred. In imagination, on the other hand, the three principles of union supply the place of the inseparable connexion by which they are bound to each other in memory. Hume is not prepared to carry his analysis further. He speaks of a kind of attraction between ideas. 'Its effects are everywhere conspicuous; but as to its causes, they are mostly unknown, and must be resolved into original qualities of human nature which I pretend not to explain.'[1]

Let us now see how these principles are supposed to work in our forming complex ideas of substances, and in our understanding and use of general terms. The ideas we have of substances (gold, silver, and so on, and also cats, dogs, and other material objects) are, like all ideas, derived from impressions. We learn about substances through the senses. But the impressions we get of these things are, like all impressions, divisible into simple, single impressions, impressions of a particular colour, texture, smell and so on. These particular impressions go together in groups so often that we come to call each group by a name, 'gold' or 'cat'. So an idea of a substance is a complex idea, derived from a group of impressions and attached to a name. So much Hume tells us in section 6 of Part I. But we know that we can think in abstract and general as well as in concrete and particular terms. If our ideas are all derived from impressions, and if our impressions are all particular and concrete, how can ideas be abstract? It is at this stage that Hume introduces the faculty of imagination. In Part I, section 7 he argues that all ideas are particular and are ideas of specific things with specific properties. But a particular idea may be used, as abstract ideas are supposed to be used, to 'go beyond its nature', and it may refer not only to the particular thing it represents but generally to things of that sort. He says, 'When we have found a resemblance among several objects, that often occur

[1] Pt. I, sec. 4; S-B, p. 13.

to us, we apply the same name to all of them. . . . After we have acquired a custom of this kind, the hearing of that name revives the idea of one of these objects, and makes the imagination conceive it with all its particular circumstances and proportions. But as the same word is suppos'd to have been frequently applied to other individuals, that are different in many respects from that idea which is immediately present to the mind; the word not being able to revive the idea of all these individuals only touches the soul . . . and revives that custom which we have acquir'd in surveying them. They are not really and in fact present to the mind, but only in power.'[1] Imagination has a part to play here in that it forms further images for us, related to the image we *first* thought of in relation to the word which we are using or seeking to understand. But it seems that Hume places imagination under the control of custom. We must have the custom first, and then the image-forming faculty can get to work. Thus, let us suppose that I read the word 'cat'. Immediately, because of a previously formed habit, the image of a particular cat, my own cat, Simpkin, comes into my mind. I know, however, that what I am reading is not about Simpkin but about 'the cat' in general. And I can understand that the properties of the cat referred to, perhaps that it can see in the dark, belong not only to Simpkin of whom I have an image, but also to other cats. So my imagination *can*, though it need not, form images of numbers of other cats. It may even be so good as to produce images of counter-examples, if necessary. 'For this is one of the most extraordinary circumstances in the present affair, that after the mind has produc'd an individual idea, upon which we reason, the attendant custom, reviv'd by the general or abstract term, readily suggests any other individual, if by chance we form any reasoning that agrees not with it. Thus, should we mention the word "triangle", and form the idea of a particular equilateral one to correspond with it, and should we afterwards assert *that the three angles of a triangle are equal to each other*, the other individuals of a scalenum and isoceles which we overlook'd at first immediately crowd in upon us, and make us perceive the falsehood of this proposition, tho' it be true with relation to that idea which we had form'd.'[2]

Once again, Hume refuses to try to account for the custom which underlies the imaginative function here. He says, 'To

explain the ultimate causes of our mental actions is impossible.'
But one thing should perhaps be noted. He thinks that, in this
respect, everyone's mental action is the same, or at least is based
upon the same principles. The most general account he can give
is in terms of resemblance. 'As the individuals are collected
together, and plac'd under a general term, with a view to that
resemblance which they bear to each other, this relation must
facilitate their entrance in the imagination, and make them be
suggested more readily upon occasion.'

It seems that Hume is here talking about our thinking of
objects, cats or dogs, in their absence. The medium of the *word* is
essential for his account of abstract ideas, and therefore it is
essential to the function of imagination in this respect. Imagination operates according to its three principles, and particularly
according to the principle of resemblance, to enable us to think
not of one thing at a time, but of things in general. What Hume
does not say is that we need imagination in order to apply the
general word 'cat' to the animal before us. We are not, apparently,
required to exercise imagination in order to identify Simpkin as a
cat, nor to recognize another cat as a cat, though not Simpkin.
But the question may be raised why we should not need imagination here too. For to recognize Simpkin as a cat is to apply the
general word 'cat' to him. And how are we to understand this
word both as general and as applicable to the particular thing
before us, if all we have is the particular collection of impressions
of Simpkin which happen to be under our hand or before our
eyes? How can we be expected to know that he is like other
creatures, except by carrying in our minds a set of images with
which to compare him? However, Hume does not say that we
do this. He seems to think that blind habit is enough to get us to
say 'cat' if asked 'what is Simpkin?' or to think 'cat' if we see
him in the chair. Imagination has so far been assigned a role
only in our thought about objects in their absence, not in the
application of descriptive terms to them when they are before our
eyes.

However, there is another, more fundamental, role which
Hume does ascribe to the imagination when objects are actually
before us, and are being perceived. Since he believes that our
knowledge of the world is derived from impressions, which are
separate, short-lived and constantly succeeding one another in our

experience, and since impressions are necessarily what are impressed on each one of us individually, he is faced with the problem of accounting for the obvious fact that we think of the world as containing objects which are *not* of this kind, but which are on the contrary permanent, lasting and independent, in some sense, of ourselves. We distinguish, indeed, within our own experience, between our sensations, momentary twinges, itches or feelings that are fleeting, and we believe could not exist if we were not there to feel them, and on the other hand our impressions of external objects, which seem essentially to be impressions of objects *waiting* to be observed by us or another, and existing continuously in such a way that we and other people can come back to the same object and observe it again and again. The problem of accounting for our unthinking belief in such objects arose for Hume entirely because he insisted that all our experience of the world must ultimately, and on analysis, be described in terms of our impressions, and an impression is something which we each of us receive at a particular time, *in* ourselves. He thought, as we have seen, that there is no intrinsic difference between my experience of an 'internal' sensation such as a twinge of pain, and my experience of something 'external', the sound of a flute for instance. If, from within, there is no real difference between my impression of pain and my impression of the note played on the flute, why is it that in the first case I do not believe that my pain could outlive my feeling it, whereas in the second case I do believe that the sound could go on even though I ceased to hear it? The continuity of the object which I believe in, in the case of the flute but not in the case of the pain, is connected with its independence of me. What makes me distinguish in this way?

Hume's answer to these questions, which are fundamental to post-Cartesian western philosophy as a whole, is to be found in the section of the *Treatise* entitled 'Of Scepticism with regard to the Senses' (Book I, Part IV, section 2).[1] He is here concerned not with the question how we come to form general ideas, say of cats, but of how we come to form the idea that a particular cat, Simpkin, is seen and heard by me again and again; why we believe that the same cat enters and re-enters our lives, having a continuous existence which is independent of our own.

He divides the question into two parts. First he asks why we

[1] S-B, p. 187.

attribute continued existence to objects even when we are not experiencing them, and secondly why we suppose them to have an existence distinct from our mind and senses. But he regards these two questions as in a way the same, since 'if the objects of our sense continue to exist even when they are not perceiv'd, their existence is of course independent of, and distinct from, the perception: and *vice versa*, if their existence be independent of the perception and distinct from it, they must continue to exist even though they be not perceiv'd.'[1] I propose, in the remarks that follow, to accept Hume's assumption that if one can describe the way in which we come to believe in the *continuous* existence of objects, then one has accounted also for our belief in their independence and distinctness, and that one then will have accounted, in general, for their 'externality' and 'publicity'. The fact is that Hume has various different senses which he ascribes to the word 'distinct', some of which seem to be logically connected with continuity and some of which do not. But his point about the imagination can quite properly be made with respect to continuity only. For it is perfectly certain that one of the essential beliefs that we hold with regard to objects in the world is that they have a continuous existence which is not interrupted each time that we blink, or turn away. If we can see that Hume regards the imagination as having an essential role in forming *this* belief, then we shall certainly have to say that, for him, imagination enters into our most ordinary perception of the world. And this is what I want to suggest.

Hume has three candidates for that element in us which produces our belief in the continued existence of objects. The candidates are our senses, our reason and our imagination. He regards it as absolutely obvious that the senses cannot give rise to this belief, since the impressions we get through our senses are discrete and discontinuous. We are perpetually blinking, or moving or going to sleep, and this in itself breaks up our perceptions into short bits. If we had nothing but the senses to rely on, then we would believe that the world was made up of nothing but discontinuous things. Impressions, according to Hume's original definition, come to us without any strings attaching them to external objects. We must consider them simply as bits of sense experience. He reiterates this basic assumption in the present

[1] S-B, p. 188.

context: 'Every impression . . . , passions, affections, sensations, pains and pleasures are originally on the same footing; and . . . whatever other differences we may observe among them, they appear, all of them, in their true colours as impressions or perceptions.'[1] The senses themselves, therefore, cannot supply us with any material for our belief in the continued existence of things in the world.

He deals more briefly with the possible claim that reason may do so. He notices that people are inclined to believe in continued objects as the causes of *some* perceptions but not others. We are not inclined to attribute continued existence to pain or pleasure, but we are inclined to do so when our impression is of colour or sound, as well as of bulk and solidity. Philosophers, Hume says, are prepared to argue that bulk and solidity are really in the bodies we perceive, and have a separate existence, while they argue that colours and sounds have no such separate existence. (He is here referring to the distinction between primary and secondary qualities, drawn by Locke.) But he says that these philosophical arguments are known to few and it is not by them that children, peasants and the greater part of mankind are induced to attribute objects to some impressions and deny them to others. Hume is not, unfortunately, very clear in his statement of what it is that the greatest part of mankind, or the vulgar, do actually believe. He allows that people unreflectingly distinguish between those perceptions or experiences which are, and those which are not, *of* something continuously existing. He also asserts that the vulgar 'confound perceptions and objects and attribute a distinct and continued existence to the very things they feel or see.'[2] Elsewhere he speaks of the unphilosophical part of mankind (that is all of us at one time or another) as 'such as suppose their perceptions to be their only objects and never think of a double existence, internal and external, representing and represented.'[3] The 'double existence' which, according to Hume, the philosophers believe in is the existence at one and the same time of my perception (or idea, in Locke's sense of the word) and the cause of it, the primary qualities in the body which cause me to have the ideas which I have, and of which my ideas are copies. The vulgar do not believe this story. But of course, as Hume himself allows, they do distinguish those cases where there is continuous existence and

---

[1] S-B, p. 190.   [2] S-B, p. 193.   [3] S-B, p. 205.

those cases, such as pain, where there is not. And, more important, they do in fact distinguish between their own perceiving and what it is that they perceive. This is not to say that they believe in a *double* existence in the philosophers' sense, but rather that they believe in two sorts of existences, or two sorts of objects; appearances or aspects of a thing, and the thing itself. They are quite happy to talk about a fleeting glimpse they may have had *of* a person, what they actually heard *of* a conversation which was going on in the next room. The whole of language (an expression, after all, of what the vulgar think) is full of ways of distinguishing appearances from reality. This is why Hume has such difficulty in trying to make intelligible, and ascribe to the vulgar, a view which their language is not naturally designed to convey, namely that there is no distinction to be made at all between continuing objects and fleeting objects, and that all are alike 'objects'. But in spite of these confusions, it is possible for us to understand Hume's problem. How is it that when perception itself is all fragmentary and broken up, and when we learn all there is to be learned about the world through perception, we yet would claim to know, or would assume without question, that the world contains objects which are *not* fragmentary, but which have a continuous existence of their own? Neither for the philosophers nor for the vulgar can reason or sense provide the basis for this assumption. There is therefore nothing left which can provide it except imagination.

Hume argues that the notion of continuous existence arises from the concurrence of some qualities of our impressions with some qualities of the imagination. In itself this is not a wholly intelligible remark, but it becomes a little clearer as we go on. The qualities of impressions in question are constancy and coherence. These, like resemblance and contiguity, are features which some of our impressions as a matter of fact do display. We ascribe continuous existence to things where we have collections of impressions either virtually unchanging (as is the case with the groups of impressions we call 'mountains' or 'houses') or whose changes are regular (as are the seasonal changes of trees or the changes in a fire as it gradually dies over a period of time). Now the imagination, Hume says, 'when set into any train of thinking, is apt to continue even when its object fails it, and, like a galley put in motion by the oars, carries on its course without any new impulse.'[1] So the imagination completes the uniformity which is indeed to a limited extent actually to be found in our impressions, by supposing continued existence of objects, to make the uniformity greater still. It is the same with the constancy of our impressions as with their coherence. When we have constantly similar impressions of, let us say, the sun or the sea, the imagination is apt to disregard the gaps in our perception, and regard our successive perceptions not merely as similar to each other, but as strictly identical. If our different impressions are very like one another, then the imagination passes very easily from one to another as we have seen above. But it passes so easily that it may feel as though there were only *one identical* object present to the mind. The imagination, that is, confuses similarity with identity, and thus the fiction arises that there *is* an identical object, the sun, when all we actually have is a number of very similar perceptions of light, heat and so on. 'The smooth passage of the imagination along the ideas of the resembling perceptions makes us ascribe to them a perfect identity.'[2] 'When the exact resemblance of our perceptions makes us ascribe to them an identity, we may remove the seeming interruption by feigning a continued being which may fill those intervals and preserve a perfect and entire identity to our perceptions.'[3] And we not only feign the idea, but we believe in it. We do this because we have, besides a present impression of the heat and light of the sun, a further present *memory idea* of the sun as we have experienced it before. Thus the imagination which fills in the gaps in our experience is supported by the memory, which brings a very lively and vivid idea to mind of what we have experienced before. And so the fiction of the imagination acquires that liveliness and force which according to Hume is what constitutes a belief.

Thus, in Hume's system, the imagination has the function of compelling us to believe that there are objects in the world which exist continuously. And so it is by means of the imagination that we can recognize the sun when we see it again as *the sun we saw yesterday*, or identify Simpkin, our cat, as the cat who has been out all night, but has come in to be fed in the morning. It is remarkable that in describing this function of imagination Hume constantly uses such words as 'feigned' or 'fictitious'. Notoriously, at the end of the chapter on scepticism he says of himself, 'I feel myself at

[1] S-B, p. 198. [2] S-B, p. 205. [3] S-B, p. 208.

present . . . inclined to repose no faith at all in my senses, or rather imagination . . . I cannot conceive how such trivial qualities of the fancy, conducted by such false suppositions, can ever lead to any solid and rational system.'[1] And he goes on to spell out once more how the imagination works by confusing similarity of perceptions with identity, and simply gets us into the habit of assuming the continuous and separate existence of objects. He concludes that 'carelessness and inattention alone can afford us any remedy.' If we are sufficiently careless and inattentive we shall succumb to the seduction of the imagination, and go happily on in the world surrounded by comfortingly constant, solid separate objects. It is imagination alone which creates for us the world we like to have, in which we can not only confidently understand the word 'cat', but securely identify our old friends, the very same cats we saw yesterday. Imagination is not only the helpful assistant; in this chapter, it has turned out to be the deceiver, who gives us an altogether unwarranted sense of security in the world. It is like a drug, without which we could not bear to inhabit the world.

Nevertheless, in spite of the low view of imagination expressed at the end of Part II, Hume does, somewhat surprisingly, later distinguish between good and bad, serious and frivolous work which the imagination has to do. In Part IV, section 4, he writes as follows: 'I must distinguish in the imagination betwixt the principles which are permanent, irresistible, and universal; such as the customary transition from causes to effects, and from effects to causes: And the principles, which are changeable, weak, and irregular. . . . The former are the foundation of all our thought and actions, so that upon their removal human nature must immediately perish and go to ruin. The latter are neither unavoidable to mankind, nor necessary, or so much as useful in the conduct of life. . . . One who concludes somebody to be near him, when he hears an articulate voice in the dark, reasons justly and naturally; though that conclusion be deriv'd from nothing but custom, which fixes and enlivens the idea of a human creature, on account of his usual conjunction with the present impression. But one who is tormented he knows not why with the apprehension of spectres in the dark, may perhaps be said to reason, and to reason naturally too: but then it must be in the same sense, that a malady

[1] S-B, p. 211.

is said to be natural; as arising from natural causes, tho' it be contrary to health, the most agreeable and natural situation of man.'[1] There is a difference, in fact, between the 'just' and the 'unjust' exercise of imagination. The former is not only founded upon a well-established custom, and produces ideas which are genuinely related to an appropriate present impression, but moreover its use is absolutely essential to our proper understanding. For only with its help can we interpret our experience in order to make rational use of it.

This distinction becomes, in the hands of Kant, the all-important distinction between the transcendental and the empirical imagination. Kant has several words which may be translated by the word 'imagination', but the most important of these is the word '*Einbildungskraft*', which suggests a power of making images, pictures or representations of things. This word is sometimes used in the ordinary everyday sense in which we may distinguish the real from the imaginary, the waking from the dream or daydream experience. In this sense of the word what a man has the power to imagine or represent is a matter of his own particular psychological character, and of what has happened to impress, amuse or frighten him in his life. Kant uses the same word for this fiction-making power, which varies widely from one man to another, and for the power which is fundamental to our perceptual understanding of the world, which is universal and the same for everyone. This is the *a priori* or transcendental imagination.

Hume, as we have seen, like his predecessors, had conceived of human beings receiving into themselves a series of impressions of the world, through their senses. If someone wanted to, he could report these impressions one after the other as a series. But because the impressions actually exhibit a certain regularity and similarity, we become accustomed to lumping sets of them together and giving the recurring set a name, such as 'dog' or 'cat'. We use the imagination in two ways. First, on hearing the name 'cat' we can produce an image of a set of impressions which is suitable to be the bearer of the name. But secondly when we receive a set of cat impressions and then another set, after a gap, we are led by the imagination to group these sets together and think of them as constituting one particular continuously existing *object*. It is imagination which makes us think of the cat, the

[1] S-B, p. 225.

individual cat, as an object to be seen again and again, existing when we do not see him.

Now Kant accepted as a given fact that we move in the world, talk of it, indeed perceive it as a world full of independent objects, many of which behave in a regular and predictable way, and which we place firmly and all the time outside ourselves in space, and separate from ourselves in time. This just is the nature of our experience. His question is 'How is such experience possible?' He takes it to be self-evident that we can be aware of things only as they appear to us, so how is it that we assume that these appearances will present themselves as they do, as solid separate objects, related to each other by causal laws and connected with each other in an orderly and relatively predictable manner? The aim of his whole critical philosophy is to lay bare the features which our experience must have, if it is to be experience of the world as we know it. It is on the basis of the necessity of these features that we are entitled to claim, as he thinks we can, that some things about the world are known to be true for ever, for the future as well as the past. We are not here concerned, however, with Kant's arguments relating to such knowledge as we can claim, or rather this is only indirectly our concern. We are concerned with an earlier stage of experience. For the function of the imagination, as he conceives it, is prior to knowledge. It operates in the presentation to us of objects in the world; and without objects knowledge would have no subject-matter.

But there is also a second function, related to the first, and that is to enable us to apply general words to *sorts* of objects in the world. Hume had thought that it was simply by custom or habit that we came to apply the word 'cat' to groups of impressions. In the presence of a group of impressions we, as it were automatically, say to ourselves the word 'cat'. In the absence of the impressions, but on hearing the word, we can, by means of imagination, produce a suitable image; but if the impression is actually with us, the imagination has no work to do. If we have the impression itself we do not need the reflection of it. Custom alone is enough to enable us to identify the experience. But Kant saw a connexion between the need for imagination to play what we have referred to as its first role, namely to give us the concept of a continuously existing independent object-in-the-world, and the need for it also to enable us to recognize an object as an object of a certain kind. For if we had a set of impressions, however frequently they came to us together, it would still be possible for us to think of them as mere impressions. In order for it to be right to apply a general term, say 'cat', we need, here as well, to conceive of the set as repeatedly forming an object, not a mere sequence of sensations. So Kant completed the account which Hume had begun of the part the imagination plays. Not only does it make objects out of some of the immediate but intermittent sensations which we experience, and induce us to say 'same cat' of these, but it also induces us to apply object-words (that is, type-of-object-words) to our experiences, so that we can recognize a kind of experience, and identify what we see as a cat.

There is a further difference between Kant and Hume. Hume seems to think that our experience can be seen to be serial and partial in the way he describes. If we open our eyes and ears, if we stretch our hands to feel, what we actually *get* is a series of impressions, which we *could* so describe, though as it happens we generally organize them to some extent before talking about them. Kant, as I understand him, does not think that we can ever actually have an experience of the world which is so serial and chaotic. He takes it for granted, indeed regards it as self-evident, that our senses alone *would* give us such an experience if we ever, as we do not, had to rely on them alone. But that we cannot find or describe such experience is precisely the proof that something besides the senses is at work in all our experience. In the *Transcendental Deduction*[1] he says, 'What is first given to us is appearance. When combined with consciousness it is called perception. Now since every appearance contains a manifold, and since different perceptions therefore occur in the mind separately and singly, a combination of them *such as they cannot have in sense* is demanded. There must therefore exist in us an active faculty for the synthesis of this manifold. To this faculty I give the name Imagination.'

Let us return for a moment to the distinction, to which attention was called just now, between the transcendental and the empirical imagination, and see if we can become clearer about what the function of each of these kinds is, in Kant's theory. The empirical function of the imagination is whatever it happens to be able to do in a particular case. In order to find out how it works for each of

[1] A 120. Quotations from Kant are taken from Norman Kemp-Smith's translation (Macmillan, 1929) and the reference numbers are those used by him.

us, we have to report on our own particular experience. For example, a man need not ever have come across a rhododendron in his life. But if a particular man happens always to have lived in Surrey then he will have learned to identify a rhododendron bush and he will be entirely familiar with the concept of a rhododendron as it occurs in his experience. He will differ from a man who might have some concept of a rhododendron, but would not know how to apply it—that is, would not recognize a rhododendron bush if he saw it. Our Surrey man will both understand the word, and thus be able to describe a rhododendron bush when there is none present, and also be able to apply the word to a bush in front of him. Now he can apply the concept either to a *kind* of bush (that is to a particular bush of the kind in question) or to an individual bush in his own drive. And both these things he can do by means of his imagination, which has unified parts of the manifold of his sensory experience, visual appearances of flowers of a certain colour and shape, of shiny green leaves and so on. These have been unified into a familiar set or group in such a way that an image of such a set can be constructed in his mind at any time. He is enabled to recognize a new bush, which he has not seen before, as a rhododendron by the imaginative grasp he has of the features of rhododendrons, that is, by having a possible image of other rhododendrons he has known. Thus Kant holds that at the empirical level a man identifies objects as being of a certain type by means of the image-making faculty. This identification, in Hume's view, was made simply by habit and custom. Kant also thinks, and here he and Hume agree, that a man is enabled to refer unhesitatingly to 'my rhododendron' day after day, because he has the possibility of an image of a rhododendron bush as the sort of thing which not only presents certain visual appearances each time it is seen, but which continues to exist through time; which persists and shows systematically different appearances, according to the different seasons. He can identify and refer to his own bush, in that it is both exhibiting rhododendron characteristics, and exhibiting the general features of an object which exists independently in space and time. Both these aids to identification are supplied by the image-forming faculty which he possesses in his imagination. When a man sees his own bush, he applies to it the concept 'my rhododendron bush', and when he sees a new bush, he applies to it the concept 'rhododendron bush'; but he could not apply either of these concepts unless he had in his mind the image of other rhododendron bushes or of his own bush on another day, images, both of them, of objects not immediately before him when he applies the concept.

Now this is so far the empirical function of the imagination. For none of us need have, as a condition of our perceiving the world at all, the ability to recognize things as rhododendron bushes, still less to recognize one of them as our bush. The empirical imagination depends for its working on the association of ideas which we just happen to have, but need not have. This kind of imagination is sometimes referred to by Kant as the 'reproductive imagination', and he says of it[1] that its working is 'entirely subject to empirical laws, the laws, namely, of association'. 'The reproductive synthesis', he says, 'falls within the domain not of transcendental philosophy, but of psychology.' What distinguishes the transcendental from the empirical imagination is that the transcendental imagination is said to have a *constructive* function. It is called by Kant the 'productive' imagination, and it is an active or spontaneous power. It is, he says, 'determinative and not, like sense, determinable merely'. It 'determines sense *a priori* in respect of its form'.

What does this mean? It seems that in Kant's system the imagination, whether empirical or transcendental, lies half-way between the purely intellectual part of our knowledge of the world, the part, that is, which consists of our having abstract concepts or thoughts about things, and the purely sensory part, which, as we have seen, he regards as totally chaotic and unorganized, if considered on its own. Without imagination, we could never apply concepts to sense experience. Whereas a wholly sensory life would be without any regularity or organization, a purely intellectual life would be without any real content. And this amounts to saying that with either the senses or the intellect we could not experience the world as we do. The two elements are not automatically joined to each other in their functions. They need a further element to join them. The joining element is the imagination; and its mediating power consists in its power to bring the chaos of sense experience to order according to certain rules, or in certain unchanging forms. The imagination obliges us to see the world as bearing these forms whenever we see it at all.

[1] B 152.

It must construct our world into objects which exist independently of ourselves, which persist through change and which manifest some regularly associated features. It is a matter of indifference what *particular* features these are. I may, by chance, have in my mind an available set of images of palm trees or of rhododendrons or of neither of these. What I must have is a collection of images with the general form of *objects*. Without this I could not perceive the world as I do. Kant held that to determine these general forms is the task of transcendental philosophy, while to determine what reminds me of a palm tree on one occasion and a rhododendron on another is the task of psychology. It is not entirely obvious that this is a proper distinction. But we can at least distinguish between particular psychological truths about individual people, which are part of the history of those people, and general psychological truths about people at large. What Kant is offering us is *a general psychological truth* about the function of imagination, but a truth which he claims is not only universally applicable, but can be shown to be *necessarily* true.

Neither understanding alone nor sensation alone can do the work of imagination, nor can they be conceived to come together without imagination. For neither can construct creatively, nor reproduce images to be brought out and applied to present experience. Only imagination is in this sense creative; only it makes pictures of things. It forms these pictures by taking sense impressions and working on them. Kant calls this activity 'apprehension'.[1] Later he speaks of the activity of the pure, or transcendental, imagination as being an activity according to rules or schemata.[2] The schema, like a particular image, is something which the imagination makes for itself, and which it then applies to experience in order to render it intelligible to the understanding. It is, it seems, a kind of readiness on the part of the imagination to produce an image where necessary. 'If five points be set alongside each other thus (. . . . .) I have an image of the number five. But if, on the other hand, I think only of a number in general, whether it be five or a hundred, this thought is rather the representation of a method whereby a multiplicity, for instance a thousand, *may* be represented in an image in conformity with a certain concept, than the image itself. This representation of a universal procedure

[1] A 120.   [2] A 140.

of imagination in providing an image for a concept I entitle the schema of this concept.'[1]

Kant does not pretend to be able to explain exactly how the formation of such rules or methods is possible for the imagination. He says, 'The concept "dog" signifies a rule according to which my imagination can delineate the figure of a four-footed animal in a general manner, without limitation to any single determinate figure such as experience or any possible image that I can represent *in concreto* actually presents.' And he goes on, 'This schematism of our understanding (which is the same as imagination) in its application to appearances and their form is an art concealed in the depth of the human soul whose real modes of activity nature is hardly likely ever to allow us to discover, and to have open to our gaze.'[2] He tries over and over again to make this mystery plainer. In the *Critique of Judgment*, where he is discussing how we come by the idea of what is normal for any given type or species, he makes another attempt.[3] The aesthetic normal idea represents the standard by which we recognize a man as a member of a particular animal species. The question is, how is this done? 'In order', he says, 'to render the process to some extent intelligible (for who can wrest Nature's whole secret from her?) let us attempt a psychological explanation. It is of note that the imagination in a manner quite incomprehensible to us is able on occasion to reproduce the image and shape of an object out of countless numbers of others of a different or the same kind. And further, if the mind is engaged on comparisons we may well suppose that it can in actual fact, though the process is unconscious, superimpose as it were one image upon another, and from the coincidence of a number of the same kind, arrive at a mean contour which serves as the common standard for all.' If we were deliberately seeking for the definition of the normal man we could reach the concept mechanically by actually measuring a thousand men and finding the mean. 'But the power of the imagination does all this by means of a dynamical effect upon the organ of internal sense, arising from the frequent apprehension of such forms.' The imagination, in doing this, does not operate in accordance with rules. On the contrary, it seems somehow to generate its own

---

[1] *Loc. cit.*   [2] B 181.
[3] *Critique of Judgment*, Book I, para 234.

rule, 'it is an intermediate between all singular intuitions of individuals, with their manifold variations, and the generic idea . . .
a floating image for the whole genus, which nature has set as an
archetype underlying those of her products that belong to the
same species but which in no single case she seems completely to
have attained.' Thus again, this time from an explicitly psychological standpoint, Kant describes the imagination as a mysterious
faculty which enables us to go beyond the immediate object of
sense, and recognize it as a member of a kind of objects, and as a
faculty which does this by means of actual images or representations which we can form for ourselves in our minds.

We are now in a position to see that (both for Hume and Kant)
it is the *representational* power of the imagination, its power, that
is, actually to form images, ideas or likenesses in the mind which
is supposed to contribute to our awareness of the world. In
Hume's theory, though this power was manifested in enabling us
to understand words uttered in the *absence* of objects as having
general application, it did not function in the *presence* of objects,
except to enable us to treat them as continuously existing, even
when we were not experiencing them. And even this power
Hume was inclined to regard as a cheat. But, in Kant's theory, the
imagination had a double role. Without it not only could we not
regard objects as properly objective, distinct from ourselves and
with a continuous existence, but we could not recognize things
we experience in the world as objects of a certain kind. And both
these functions, crucial to our actual understanding and manipula-
tion of the world, were carried out, albeit mysteriously, by the
image-forming power, whether the power merely to represent
things previously experienced, or the creative power to construct
images of a certain form, blueprints, as it were, for all future and
possible reproductive images. In Hume, the use of the word
'impression' for what we receive through the senses brings out
the fact that he regards sense experience as wholly passive.
Thought *about* the world, on the other hand, is active. Similarly,
in Kant, we are supposed merely to *receive* the manifold variety of
sensations: concepts, on the other hand, are wholly created by us,
and need have no application to the world at all. But our actual
experience of the world is neither wholly creative nor wholly a
matter of passively receiving what we are given. It is a mixture of
both elements. The question is, how such a mixture can come

about. In Hume, and still more clearly in Kant, it is the imagination which has emerged as that which enables us to go beyond the bare data of sensation, and to bridge the gap between mere sensation and intelligible thought.

PART II

Imagination and Creative Art

Hume, Kant and Schelling

It is now time to consider a further context in which the imagination is generally agreed to have a crucial part to play, and that is the context of creative art, of the production and the appreciation of works of art. It has often been maintained, particularly perhaps by commentators on Kant, that the sense of 'imagination' in which philosophers are interested when they are analysing perception or the understanding of general terms is entirely distinct from the sense of the word in which critics or aestheticians are interested; and it is further held that both these senses are different from that in which, in ordinary life, we may speak of an object as imaginary, or say that someone is a prey to imaginary illness, or can 'see' his friend in his imagination. It is obviously true that there are many different contexts in which the concept of the imagination has a function; and it would be futile to insist on a common identical meaning of the word in every instance of its use. But we should not be so much beguiled by the 'family resemblance' theory of meaning where words have a wide and varied use, that we neglect what common elements there may be. And in the case of imagination, my contention is that there is far more that is common to the concept in its various different contexts of use than has sometimes been allowed.

Hume stated that the very same faculty which we all of us must use in our interpretation of immediate experience and in our understanding of general terms is, if used more than ordinarily freely and widely, 'what constitutes genius'. It is this identification which I want to examine further. Once again, from Hume we shall be led to Kant. This time, the aim will be to see how the productive and reproductive imagination of the *Critique of Pure Reason* is related to the aesthetic function of imagination which he elaborates in the *Critique of Judgment*.

'The fancy', Hume says, 'runs from one end of the universe to the other collecting those ideas which belong to any subject.'[1] 'The ideas', he says, 'are thus collected by a kind of magical faculty of the soul, which, though it be always most perfect in the greatest geniuses, and is properly what we call a genius, is however inexplicable by the utmost efforts of human understanding.' As far as the first book of the *Treatise* goes, this is about all Hume tells us of the connexion between the everyday use of imagination and its use by the highest genius. Although by the end of the book he has told us about its everyday use in feigning for us a world of independent objects, he leaves on one side the question of its use to perfection by the specially gifted. However, in the second book of the *Treatise*, which is concerned with the Passions, he gives us more clues as to the nature of the connexion.

One must first note that, like all eighteenth-century writers who concern themselves with questions of aesthetics, he is not primarily interested in what makes a man a poet or a painter, nor in how works of art are actually produced, but in the question of taste. What is it, psychologically speaking, which makes us judge something to be beautiful or ugly? However, we shall find that this question is not altogether remote from the kinds of aesthetic question which Hume does not consider. For if a man has sufficient power of imagination to engender in himself a sense of beauty, or a love for an object of sight or sound where a man of lesser imagination might be insensible and find nothing in the object to admire or love, then he may perhaps also be able, by poetry, rhetoric or music, to arouse the imagination of his less gifted fellows and create something which they in turn will judge beautiful. This seems to be Hume's assumption, and it is this which links his discussion of taste (and those of his contemporaries also) to the question of the creative imagination properly so called.

In Hume's view, there is a close connexion between our imagination and our feelings. This connexion will turn out to be of the greatest importance in all that follows. Passions, that is desires, aversions and other emotional states, are impressions, according to Hume's terminology. They are things that we feel,

[1] S-B, p. 24.

but they are different from the impressions we get from the senses. They are called impressions of reflexion, or secondary impressions. They are, that is, items of original experience, not necessarily dependent on any preceding sense impression, and thus distinct from ideas, but closely connected with ideas. Among secondary impressions a further distinction is drawn between direct and indirect passions. Direct passions include desire or aversion, love or hatred—what may be crudely described as pro or con feelings towards an object. Indirect passions are such feelings as pride, shame, ambition, which essentially entail some thought of their object in relation to oneself or one's associates. This distinction is necessary in order to understand Hume's language from time to time, but it is not otherwise relevant to our purposes.

Impressions of sensation are, as we have seen, copied or reflected by ideas. The relation between secondary impression and ideas is different and more obscure. In the first book of the *Treatise*[1] he writes as follows: 'An impression first strikes upon the senses, and makes us perceive heat or cold, thirst or hunger, pleasure or pain of some kind or other. Of this impression there is a copy taken by the mind, which remains after the impression ceases; and this we call an idea. This idea of pleasure or pain, when it returns upon the soul, produces the new impression of desire and aversion, hope and fear, which may properly be called impressions of reflexion, because derived from it.' Later in the same section he speaks of these secondary impressions as arising 'mostly from ideas'. At the beginning of Book Two of the *Treatise* (Of the Passions) he speaks[2] of sensations of reflexion as proceeding from primary or sense impressions 'either immediately or by the interposition of its idea'. What is clear from this is that at any rate very often, according to Hume, it is an idea, whether of memory or imagination, which gives rise to a passion or emotion. In Part III, section 6 of the second book[3] he says, 'It is remarkable that the imagination and affections have a close union together, and that nothing which affects the former can be entirely indifferent to the latter. Wherever our ideas of good or evil acquire a new vivacity, the passions become more violent; and keep pace with the imagination in all its variations.' In the absence of an object, that is to say, one may form an image of it

[1] Pt. I, sec. 2; S-B, p. 7.   [2] S-B, p. 275.   [3] S-B, p. 424.

and feel desire or aversion or fear or hope with regard to it. And the more powerful the imagination to form the image, the more powerful the feelings. 'It is remarkable that lively passions commonly attend a lively imagination.'[1] One may be reminded here of Aristotle's contention[2] that it is impossible to separate desire from imagination as elements in human and animal motivation. What gets people, and other animals, actually to move is the appearance to them of something as good or desirable, and the consequent desire. For Aristotle, the word translated as 'imagination' means 'how the object appears', whether the object be present and sensed, or absent and only thought about. There is a similar thought in Hume. We may desire something (or hate it or love it) when it is before us, or when it is absent. Very often we shall desire it in its absence, and in this case its *idea* must intervene, and be that with which the passion is associated. In a quite different context, talking about politics, he writes: 'It has been observed . . . that men are mightily governed by the imagination, and proportion their affections more to the light under which any object appears to them, than to its real and intrinsic value. What strikes upon them with a strong and lively idea commonly prevails above what lies in a more obscure light.'[3]

So a lively image is intrinsically more likely to be associated with a passion than a faint image. The more lively and detailed the picture in the mind, the more intense the feeling. Indeed this may be part of the meaning contained in the word 'lively'. Now an idea is, he says, more vivid and lively when it is particular than when it is, though still in its nature particular, being used as a general idea to stand for a number of different things of the same kind. 'A general idea, though it be nothing but a particular one considered in a certain view, is commonly more obscure; and that because no particular idea by which we represent a general one, is ever fix'd or determinate, but may easily be chang'd for other particular ones which will serve equally on the representation.'[4] So it follows that if someone wants to rouse our emotions, he must try to get us to form and to concentrate upon a single particular image, and must try to prevent us from passing rapidly from one image to another.

There are other principles which Hume lays down, which

[1] S-B, p. 427. [2] *de Anima* III, ch. 9.
[3] S-B, p. 534. [4] S-B, p. 425.

determine the degree of feeling associated with our ideas. In the first place, it is obvious, he says, that we can form more vivid ideas of things which are close to us, either in space or time, or both, than of things which are distant. We can remember clearly, and therefore call up vivid images of recent pleasurable or painful sensations, and we can easily envisage pains or pleasures that are certain to come to us in a short time. Similarly, if we think that there is something agreeable or horrible in the next room, we can easily imagine it. In such cases the imagination produces relevant images, and these in turn produce related secondary impressions very readily. The ideas are, Hume says, *converted into impressions*. It is when our ideas are vivid because of contiguity in space and time that this conversion is most obvious. The same thing happens when we observe the joys and sufferings of someone else who is near to us. ' 'Tis indeed evident that when we sympathize with the passions and sentiments of others these movements appear first in our mind as mere ideas, and are conceiv'd to belong to another person as we conceive any other matter of fact. 'Tis also evident that the ideas of the affections of others are converted into the very impressions they represent, and that the passions arise in conformity with the images we form of them.'[1]

But, paradoxically, the imagination can also produce vivid images, and the related passions can be aroused, where the images are drawn from remote areas of space and time. For the mind is excited by the necessity to overcome obstacles in thinking. Thus Hume says, 'It is certain nothing more powerfully animates any affection, than to conceal some part of its object by throwing it into a kind of shade, which at the same time it shews enough to pre-possess us in favour of the object, still leaves some work for the imagination. Besides that obscurity is always attend'd with a kind of uncertainty; the effort which the fancy makes to compleat the idea rouzes the spirits and gives an additional force to the passion.'[2] The imagination is always aware of the present. It is grounded in the place and time where we are. Thus, in imagining something we are always aware, however faintly, of who and where we are. But this being so, the more remote the object of thought, the further and more adventurously the imagination has to go, to relate its ideas to the present situation. It is, in such a case, the very distance itself which is operative in making us feel

[1] S-B, p. 319.   [2] S-B, p. 422.

strongly when we are presented with the images. Hume writes: ' 'Tis evident that the mere view and contemplation of any greatness, whether successive or extended, enlarges the soul and gives it a sensible delight and pleasure. A wide plain, the ocean, eternity, a succession of several ages; all these are entertaining objects, and excel everything however beautiful which accompanies not its beauty with a suitable greatness. Now when any very distant object is present'd to the imagination, we naturally reflect upon the interpos'd distance, and by that means conceiving something great and magnificent receive the usual satisfaction. But as the fancy passes easily from one idea to another relat'd to it, and transports to the second all the passions excit'd by the first, the admiration which is direct'd to the distance naturally diffuses itself over the distant object.'[1] He goes on to argue that distance in time from ourselves excites greater admiration than distance in space, and this because of the principle of inspiration by obstacles mentioned just now. It is more difficult to imagine how the ancient Greeks lived than it is to imagine how the present-day inhabitants of Japan live; indeed we *could* go to see the latter but not the former. It is for this reason that, as he says, 'Ancient busts and inscriptions are more valu'd than Japan tables.' And, 'In collecting our force to overcome the opposition, we invigorate the soul and give it an elevation with which it would not otherwise have been acquaint'd.' And so, finally, because of the peculiar pleasures of such elevation, we come to seek out obstacles, and go out of our way to support and strengthen the feelings by such means. It is clear that this deliberate seeking of elevation, the pursuit of excitement of the feelings through the production of related images, is central to an account of how the imagination of creative artists would be supposed by Hume to operate.

In general we may say that in Book Two of the *Treatise*, Hume has introduced a new dimension to the function of imagination, which must be considered as closely connected with, if not inseparable from, the function he described in the first book. It would be inadequate to describe imagination merely as that which produces images or representations of objects; one must add that these representations will almost always be accompanied by emotions. Great men of genius not only imagine more readily,

[1] S-B, p. 433.

and draw their images from wider sources, and succeed in 'producing images which illuminate the matter in hand; besides all this, they will also, in proportion to the excellence of their images, be affected by deeper and more powerful feelings'. To say that their imagination is superior carries this other superiority with it.

If we turn now to Kant, we shall be able to trace a similar thought but, as we should expect in his philosophical system, the connexions between the use of imagination in perception and its use in creative thought are more complex and elaborate. Like Hume, in the end he regards the activity of imagination as inexplicable and unanalysable; but characteristically he makes a systematic attempt to expound it. In considering his exposition, it is to the points of identity between perceptual and creative imagination that I want to call attention.

It is in the *Critique of Judgment* that Kant explores the nature of creative thought as such. His subject matter is in fact the nature of aesthetic judgment (or this is what it amounts to). But the mode of thought involved in passing an aesthetic judgment on something is not held to be essentially different from that involved in creating or expressing something upon which an aesthetic judgment is to be passed by another. As in Hume, so in Kant, all aesthetic questions arise out of questions about taste or *the sense of the beautiful*. But it does not greatly matter, for either of them, whether we consider the kind of thinking involved in seeing a landscape, a picture, or a poem as an aesthetic object upon which we can pass the judgment that it is beautiful (or ugly), or whether on the other hand we concentrate on the activity of painting a representation of the landscape, or expressing our vision of it in a poem. It is important to grasp this limitation at the outset. Kant is not interested, any more than Hume was, in the question what makes one man a painter or poet and another merely a lover of beautiful scenery. He is interested in what makes *either* of them think of the object before him in a particular way, that is as an object of aesthetic interest.

There is a considerable difficulty in presenting a clear statement of Kant's theory of the creative imagination, or his view of the aesthetic function of the imagination in judgments, because of his own diversity of purpose in the third *Critique*. In one sense, in this *Critique*, he was attempting to make a link between the world of understanding and the world of reason. Whereas Hume spoke indifferently of reason and understanding, and opposed either of them to imagination and to sense, Kant had sharply distinguished them in the *Critique of Pure Reason*. Moreover, though, in Hume's view, reason was an active faculty which we *used*, and in this respect was different from sense in regard to which we were wholly passive, Kant's theory of our active part in constructing the world went much further. What we experience is *nature subject to laws*. But it is we ourselves, through the activity of the pure understanding, who create the laws and apply them to nature. The *a priori* laws of the understanding are called the categories, and are the laws which, of necessity, we impose upon our experience of phenomena. All our scientific knowledge of the world, as well as all our ordinary perception of it, is determined by the concepts we form by means of the understanding. These concepts, as we have seen, are *applicable to* the world of sense only through the image-forming power of the imagination. Reason, as distinct from understanding, is, on the other hand, the source not of concepts but of ideas. Of all the words in the vocabulary of philosophers, the word 'idea' is perhaps the most exasperating to the non-philosopher. For in the case of every philosopher who uses it, one has to acquaint oneself with the particular sense in which he, and perhaps he alone, is understanding it. Thus, for Hume an idea was a pale reflection of an impression. It was an image formed either by imagination or by memory. In extreme contrast to this, in Kant's vocabulary an idea in the technical sense was the product of the highest faculty of the mind, but something so far removed from sense-perception that it could never find exemplification in the world of sense. In the *Critique of Pure Reason* the ideas of reason are introduced in an almost entirely negative way. They stand for what we *cannot* conceptualize, and thus for what we *cannot* in any way experience in the world. Their function is said to be regulative. They act as a kind of limit or ideal towards which we may direct our thoughts, or rather which give direction to them. Unlike the concepts of the understanding, they can in general have no application whatever to the world of phenomena.

In the *Critique of Practical Reason*, however, Kant attempts to show that there is at least one idea of reason, that of freedom, of which we do have a direct experience in practice, though we can still form no *concept* of freedom. We experience it through the exercise of our own free will in moral choice. Moral choice leads to action which is action according to a law, freely imposed by us on ourselves. In acting morally we cannot but be aware of ourselves as free to do or not to do the act under consideration, though we are also aware that in another sense we are *bound* to do it, by a commanding law. But this law is a law of our own reason. It is a command which comes, not from some outside authority, but from within ourselves. Acting in accordance with it is thus an assertion of our freedom, for the opposite of freedom is not *being bound*, but *being bound by an outside force*. It is in such a way that we can be said to experience the idea of reason, as having application. But since we experience it thus, and not through a concept, the idea of freedom, like the ideas of God and immortality, still functions as a kind of limit to our conceptual or scientific thinking. If we think of ourselves from the standpoint of understanding, we think of ourselves as parts of nature, functioning according to scientific laws. Our awareness of ourselves as free gives us no scientific knowledge, but a grasp of a different kind. Such a general outline of reason is necessary before we can consider what Kant means by judgment.

In the introduction to the *Critique of Judgment*, Kant divides the human faculties of the mind into three, the understanding, the reason and the judgment. The faculty by which we apply scientific concepts to nature is, he says, the understanding; that by which we apply laws to our own experience of freedom is reason; and between these two lies the faculty of judgment. Now judgment in general is said to consist in the application of a concept or general rule to a particular instance, and in this wide sense of 'judgment' the faculty of understanding is also a faculty of judging. For it was precisely to the forming of general concepts and the application of them, with the help of imagination, to experience that the understanding was said to be devoted. But besides this wide sense, there is a different and special sense of the word 'judgment' which is introduced for the first time in the Third *Critique*. This is the 'reflective judgment'. The use of judgment in this narrow sense is 'where only a particular is given, and the universal has to be found for it.' Kant, that is to say, now presents us with a case where instead of applying a pre-formed concept to a given particular situation of experience, and thus by the help of imagination recognizing the particular as one of a certain kind, we may, from the contemplation of a particular situation, derive, or in some cases invent, a rule which it exemplifies.

Kant has two kinds of examples by which he illustrates the reflective judgment, the first derived from natural science, the second, analogically, from aesthetics. In the case of the natural sciences, he realizes that a scientist will generally be attempting, not to fit a given particular instance under an established principle, but rather, in observing an event or change, will be trying to frame a principle to account for it, which can be seen to be instantiated in it. In order to find such a principle in any particular case, and thus exercise the reflective judgment, Kant says that the scientist must assume the *finality of nature*. We must try to understand what he means by this somewhat mysterious notion.

Kant insists that he does not mean that nature has a purpose or aim, as a man might be said to have one. He seems to be saying something like this: one could not ever discern a principle or system to account for a given particular set of facts unless one assumed to start off with that *some* system or other existed, that the facts before one would fall in to some pattern rather than none. When a principle has been found it seems that one has found what one was looking for, and has found something which was there all along, to be discovered. In seeking for a pattern in which to arrange the facts, one is seeking something one expects to find. So the scientist must believe before he even starts that nature is such as to contain patterns or systems. To believe this is to believe in the finality of nature. Kant says, 'This transcendental concept of a finality of nature ... attributes nothing at all to the Object, i.e. to nature itself, but only represents the unique mode in which we must proceed in our reflection upon the objects of nature with a view to getting a thoroughly interconnected whole of experience, and so it is a Subjective principle or maxim of judgment.' He gives as examples of the kind of assumption which the scientist must make the assumption that there is in nature a subordination of genera and species comprehensible by us; that various kinds of causality may be reduced to a small number of principles. And he refers collectively to such assumptions as 'the adaptation of nature to our cognitive faculties'.[1]

It must be emphasized that the principle of finality does not commit us to believing in any particular pattern, but only to the existence of some pattern or other. Moreover, to hold the principle, and conduct our investigations on its basis, does not commit us to believing that nature has a statable aim, nor to believing that it was created with a statable end in view.

Having introduced the principle, Kant proceeds to add an important consideration to his account. If we succeed in finding a pattern into which to fit a series of observed facts or events, this discovery affords us a peculiar *pleasure*. Thus the concept of pleasure is linked with that of finality, albeit in a rather round-about way. Kant now leaves the discovery of laws in natural science and goes on to his other examples, the aesthetic. After this, the main part of the *Critique of Judgment* is devoted to the analysis of aesthetic judgment. It thus happens, in fact, that one tends to forget the general archetechtonic function of the work, which was to link understanding to reason by way of judgment, and to think of it rather as an essay in aesthetics. We should, however, try to bear in mind the role of the reflective judgment in general, since it is from this beginning that we shall find ourselves following a somewhat tortuous path through post-Kantian philosophy, in which the connexions between works of the creative imagination and ideas of reason are once again emphasized.

How does the principle of finality have application in the field of aesthetics? Once again, the reflective judgment cannot be brought to work without employing this principle. Kant holds that it is the perception of finality or pattern in an object, and the resulting pleasure, which is expressed when we say of the object that it is beautiful. It will be plainly seen that Kant is here primarily concerned not so much with the creative as with the appreciative imagination, as expressed in aesthetic judgments, or judgments of taste. But it can also be seen, as has been suggested already, that this is not particularly significant. What is required in us if we are to judge a work of art or a natural object beautiful is the very same as is required of us if we are to create an aesthetic

---

[1] *Critique of Judgment*, Introduction V. Quotations from the *Critique of Judgment* are from the translation by J. C. Meredith (O.U.P., 1952) and the paragraph numbers are those used by him.

object for someone else to contemplate and judge beautiful (though doubtless something more is required as well in the second case). Whether we are reading a poem or writing one, whether we are looking at a painting or painting it, our concept of the work as an aesthetic object, completed or in the process of completion, demands that we see it as possessed of a *finality of form*. When we are creating the aesthetic object it is this form which we seek to impose on our own experience. When we are contemplating the completed work we judge it to be a success if and only if this inner finality is manifest in the words we read or the sounds or shapes and colours we experience through the senses. I shall return to this later.

Meanwhile, it is still necessary to take care not to be misled by the word 'finality'. Kant speaks somewhat mysteriously of 'finality without an end'.[1] There is no suggestion that in order to find a work of art or natural object aesthetically satisfactory we have to know the *purpose* of its maker or the end he had in mind, nor that in creating a work of art, the artist has to have a specific purpose in mind. On the contrary: in so far as an object is seen to have a *specifiable purpose outside itself*, as a tool has a specific purpose or function which is made in order to fulfil that function, the judgment of that object cannot be a purely aesthetic judgment, nor the power employed in making it a purely artistically creative power. In an aesthetic judgment either we may not know the external end or purpose for which the object was made, or there may be no answer to the question 'what was it made *for*?' Yet we pass judgment on the beauty of the object. Its purpose must, if it is considered as an aesthetic object, be *internal* to itself. The end must be to display a particular form. One can perhaps see how this 'inner finality' goes with, or necessarily gives rise to, a feeling of satisfaction and pleasure. Kant refers to inner finality as the hanging together or slotting together of the multiplicity of sense. He is suggesting, then, that our pleasure in beauty is a pleasure in

[1] There is a difficulty in translation here. The words used by Kant are *Zweckmässigkeit* (finality) and *Zweck* (end). In bringing them together, then, as 'finality without an end' there is a suggestion of verbal paradox or contradiction which may be lost in the translation I have adopted. Sometimes Kant's words are translated 'purposiveness without purpose', which preserves this paradox. But the disadvantage of this translation is that 'purpose' sounds more definitely human (or anthropomorphic) than 'finality'. I have therefore, on the whole, preferred the less pointed English pair.

order, a satisfaction in our power to regulate chaos, and this may justify his use of the notion of finality. One could say 'the whole *point* of this object is that it is thus orderly.'

At this stage in Kant's argument, he introduces another essential feature of the aesthetic judgment. Although such judgments arise out of, and express, a particular kind of pleasure, yet they are not mere reports that we are pleased. For we expect, and to some extent demand, that if we judge an object to be beautiful (as opposed to attractive, agreeable or pleasant), other people shall agree with us. There is a kind of universalization, or objectivity, implied in our use of what Kant regards as the central aesthetic word 'beautiful', which, while it entails the existence of pleasure in ourselves, entails much more besides. Equally, when a creative artist knowingly produces a work of art, he does so on the assumption that other people *ought* to judge it as he judges it; or perhaps on the weaker assumption that objective judgments of value *could* be made with regard to his work. This quasi-objectivity which characterizes the truly aesthetic judgment is derived by Kant from the fact that the discovery of finality in an object is accompanied by a *particular kind* of pleasure, as much for the aesthetician as for the natural scientist who discovers finality in natural phenomena. This particular kind of pleasure he further analyses as 'the harmonious interplay of understanding and imagination'. Now these faculties of imagination and understanding are, according to Kant, the same in everyone. Therefore when I feel the pleasure of this harmony, I must expect that other people can see the object as I do, and will, if they do so, experience the same pleasure. It is the unique combination of imagination with understanding that enables us to perceive finality in the object. This finality or design is, as we have seen, internal to the object. The judgment of it is aesthetic in a literal sense, that is it is a judgment of how the thing *looks* or *sounds*. It is not intellectual. We do not identify the object as a member of a certain class of objects when we judge it aesthetically. We do not classify it as having certain characteristics or falling under certain scientific laws. Our perception, as it were, stops at the appearance of the thing, and it is within that limit that we discover its finality.

We must now try to understand more precisely how Kant thinks the imagination actually works, in revealing the finality or order in the form of an aesthetic object. When, near the beginning of the *Critique of Judgment*, he speaks in general of the aesthetic judgment, he refers to the imagination as 'the power of representation'. In the case of ordinary perception of objects in the world, there is necessarily, as we have seen, activity both of the understanding and of the imagination as a representational power. We have interpreted Kant (see page 33) as saying that we could not apply conceptual knowledge to the world unless we had the power of forming images of the objects of sense, objects *like* those to which here and now we are applying the relevant concept. We could not recognize an object as a horse unless we *could* form images of other horses. What has to be explained now is why in ordinarily recognizing a horse in a field as a horse we get no special pleasure, though imagination and understanding must be working together in harmony for such recognition to be possible, while in looking at a painting of a horse in a field, say a Stubbs, we *do* get pleasure, and thus can make an aesthetic judgment. The explanation, for Kant, seems to lie in this: in the aesthetic judgment, we are not concentrating on the concept 'horse', but on the visible form of the horse in the picture—how it *looks*. It is this particular figure in the picture upon which we have our attention fixed. We are neither concerned to make general statements about the horse and its characteristics, nor to make statements about *this* horse in comparison with other horses. We are looking, in so far as we can do so, at the forms (shapes, appearances) 'independently of concepts'. (We shall need to qualify this somewhat, later. See page 53.) Our appreciation of the forms, therefore, cannot be intellectual as it would be if we were, we might say, thinking about horses. Our appreciation of the forms must be through sensation and not intellect. What we feel is the very same working together of imagination and understanding which in ordinary perception we realize intellectually in our identification of the object before us as a horse, with the attendant ability to proceed, if we wish, to scientific statements about the horse. 'The quickening of both faculties [imagination and understanding] to an indefinite, but yet, thanks to the given representation, harmonious activity, *is* the sensation whose universal communicability is postulated by the judgment of taste.'[1] Both imagination and understanding are brought to

[1] *Critique of Judgment*, 89.

life, and made to work together at the moment when we regard a single object and concentrate on its form. In so far as we find in the form what we are looking for, a design or purpose, we find that our faculties are stimulated. This is the pleasure we get. And we assume that others can get it, both because they have the same faculties that we have, and because we think of the form we are contemplating as objectively there before our eyes (or ears).

But this is still an incomplete solution. So far, the imagination, as employed in aesthetic judgments, has been thought of as the representational faculty, that is, the faculty of making pictures for ourselves, just as it was in our ordinary, non-aesthetic perception of the world. But Kant is fully aware that in aesthetic judgments there is a further role for the imagination. In perception, the image-making faculty is bound by the laws of association, by what the world actually contains and what we have experienced. For it is only what we have experienced that we can reproduce by connecting together images from our memory. The concept of the thing before us gives a law to the imagination. We have the concept first, and fit the particular object before us into the concept by calling up images of things (or being able to do so) which accord with the conceptual law. But, as we saw at the beginning of this section, in the case of reflective judgment in general, and aesthetic judgment in particular, we have before us one singular object and there is no *prior* concept to give laws to the imagination. Therefore the imagination freely produces its own law. It invents a concept, or calls one up, to fit the visible or audible form before it. This is the concept which Kant calls finality without end. When we look at the pictured horse and judge what we see to be beautiful (a beautiful picture) we are not, obviously, judging what is before us to be a perfect horse. We are not judging that something which we see conforms perfectly to the concept 'horse'. On the contrary, we are judging that it displays perfectly a satisfying pattern, that it manifests a certain completeness in itself. In so far as we do compare the pictured horse with the real horse and think whether it is like it, and, if it *is* like, whether the original was a good specimen of a horse, then our judgment is not purely aesthetic. In the pure aesthetic judgment, we see the point of the object, as a particular object of our attention. It is this point which is the non-scientific concept produced by the imagination in its free play with the object before it. In order for the imagination to work aesthetically, it has to concentrate on *one* object. If that object were not such as to be capable of being produced before the mind's eye as an image, and reproduced again and again, we could not concentrate on it; there would be nothing except a random jumble of sensations. Imagination in aesthetic judgment, as in ordinary perception, has the function of reducing the chaos of sensation to order. But in the aesthetic contemplation of an object the order is, as it were, internal to the image. It does not consist in the image's likeness to other images which fall under the same concept. If the image can be produced, and reproduced another time, it can be so because of its internal orderliness, but there is no previously learned external rule for producing it.

One may perhaps see what Kant means, by using the example of a melody. If we recognize it as a melody, not just a jumble of sounds, we thereby perceive it as having a certain shape or form. This entails presenting it to ourselves as shaped in the way it is. This is the function of imagination. But imagination is free here from any particular concept: we could not have grasped the melody by learning first that it conformed to a rule. We had to hear the pattern *in* the sound. Without imagination, there would have been just sound; imagination makes the sound, as it were, 'presentable', and in so doing experiences the feeling of satisfaction in the discovery of order in chaos.

So imagination in its aesthetic role is still representational: it is, that is to say, still the very faculty which can create images. But it is free, and therefore, Kant says, is thought of as 'productive, and exerting an activity of its own'.[1] It is when the imagination is exercised in this new creative way that we get full aesthetic pleasure from its harmony with understanding. We cannot conceptualize this harmony, but only feel it.

It may be, of course, that in some cases of perception which is not aesthetic there is a certain pleasure to be found, as when we perceive something which will be an addition to our knowledge or will solve for us an intellectual or practical problem. But Kant says, 'here we have merely the value set upon the solution that satisfies the problem, and not a free and indeterminately final entertainment of the mental powers with what is called beautiful. In the latter case, the understanding is at the service of

[1] *Critique of Judgment*, 240.

the imagination, in the former this relation is reversed.'[1] It is the freedom of the imagination which is crucial—its freedom from the slavery to concepts of the understanding.

Kant now proceeds to an example of some significance. 'Marsden in his description of Sumatra observes that the free beauties of nature so surround the beholder on all sides that they cease to have much attraction for him. On the other hand he found a pepper-garden full of charm, on coming across it in mid-forest, with its rows of parallel stakes on which the plant twines itself. From all this he infers that wild and in its appearance quite irregular beauty is pleasing only as a change to one whose eyes have become surfeited with regular beauty. But he need only have made the experiment of passing one day in his pepper-garden to realize that once the regularity has enabled the understanding to put itself in accord with the order that is its constant requirement, instead of the object diverting him any longer, it imposes an irksome restraint upon the imagination: whereas nature, subject to no restraint of artificial rules, and lavish, as it were, in its luxuriant variety can supply constant food for his taste.'[2] Now Kant suggests, in this passage, that the free play of the imagination is something which is in itself desirable, which in itself gives pleasure, even where it does not give rise to the judgment that the object upon which the imagination is exercised is beautiful. We may get this kind of pleasure from the free exercise of the faculties upon things which in themselves could not be judged beautiful, or even interesting, by any standard of taste. He says, 'beautiful objects have to be distinguished from beautiful views of objects (or aspects of them). . . . In the latter case taste seems to fasten not so much on what the imagination grasps in this field as on the incentive it receives to indulge in poetic fiction. . . . It is just as when we watch the changing shapes of fire or a rippling brook: neither of which are things of beauty, but they convey a charm to the imagination because they sustain its free play.'[3] But Kant ought to have drawn from the pepper-garden example the further lesson that his own concept of beauty was somewhat limited; and certainly that aesthetic pleasure, that is pleasure in the exercise of the imagination, may arise from instances very different from those at first proposed. The

[1] *Critique of Judgment*, 242. [2] *Critique of Judgment*, 243.
[3] *Critique of Judgment*, 244.

pepper-garden fails as an object because the rule which we see instantiated in the form of the rows is too easily and too completely grasped by the understanding. Once we realize that the rows are strictly parallel and of such and such a length, we have a rule which could enable us to go on repeating the pattern mechanically, as a pure exercise of understanding. Certainly in such a case we can envisage more rows of the same kind; we could frame an image of such a garden in absence from it. Thus it is *amenable to* the imagination. But the imagination would here be enslaved. Yet the pepper-garden is contrasted with nature 'subject to no restraint of *artificial* rules'. The rules necessary for nature to be judged beautiful are rules of the imagination itself, rules found in the concept of form or design itself. The difficulty is that if the imagination loves to range absolutely freely and to invent its own rules or restraints, why may it not take pleasure in ranging without rule or restraints at all? Why does the qualification have to be added that only where there *is* a rule to be found will the pleasure we take in an object be pleasure in its beauty? Either Kant ought greatly to widen the concept of beauty so as to accommodate wide-ranging imaginative pleasures without rule, or he ought to allow that beauty is a limited and particular concept which by no means exhausts our aesthetic vocabulary, and that there are other aesthetic pleasures which derive from something else. In effect it is the latter course which he takes. Besides the trivial examples of our pleasure in the flickering fire or the flowing brook, Kant holds that there are other aesthetic judgments, or judgments of taste, in the making of which the imagination *is* free even from a self-imposed rule, and where its pleasures are of a high and serious kind, but where we cannot speak of its object as beautiful. These are of course the cases in which Kant speaks of the imagination as 'not estimating the beautiful, but estimating the sublime'. We must pursue this notion a bit further.

But first let us sum up: in the whole of his treatment of the subject, Kant is trying to clarify the way in which the reflective judgment operates, the way, that is, in which we formulate a general rule from a given particular instance. The general rule, in the case of aesthetic judgments, is said to be that 'an object such as this before me is beautiful because of its form', and the nature of this form has to be *perceived in* the object rather than understood intellectually *before* the object possessed of it is contemplated. But in fact, in exploring this kind of judgment, he has been led into a paradox (and here we must refer back to the picture of the horse which was discussed on page 48). For Kant's theory of beauty is that we judge a thing beautiful when we detect in it the possibility of a rule in which understanding and imagination will agree; and that this possibility will be detected in so far as we can find finality without an end in the object. Nothing else gives rise to a judgment of beauty. But this leads him to the conclusion that the only object which can display this kind of finality in a pure and unadulterated manner is a pure form, such as a spiral or a curve. These pure forms have exactly the completeness, the 'rightness', the pattern, we are looking for. It is only in relation to such objects that we can be quite certain of the purity of our judgments. Pictures and statues must count as dependent or somewhat degenerate kinds of aesthetic objects, because they are imitative, and therefore we cannot wholly detach our judgment of them from the judgment that they look *as they ought*. We judge, that is, partly whether they well or badly represent what a man or a horse does look like, and partly whether the man or horse represented by them is a good or bad specimen of its kind. The pleasure we may get from finding the rule of design or form in the particular cannot in this case arise solely from the harmonious functioning of our faculties, as it does in the judgment of pure form. A different kind of pleasure will enter into it, namely the pleasure arising from the thought that the painted horse is like a real horse, and perhaps that this horse is a good specimen, or, again, that the landscape in the painting represents a place where we would like to be. Kant is, it is true, prepared to speak of the judgment of pictures and statues as aesthetic judgments, but they cannot be the central case of such judgments. They are degenerate kinds. Thus true judgments of beauty are, according to Kant's theory, extremely limited in scope.

He tries to get out of the difficulty in two ways. First he divides beauty into two different kinds, *pulchritudo vaga* and *pulchritudo adhaerens*. And under the first heading (of free beauties which presuppose no concept of what the thing should be) he allows, besides pure geometrical forms, some flowers, birds, crustaceans, some Greek-style designs which have no intrinsic meaning, and all of music which is not either set to words or 'programme music'. Under the second heading come impure or degenerate judgments. But this solution does not wholly satisfy him. And so, more radically, he introduces a new concept altogether, not beauty but sublimity, under which category recalcitrant activities of the imagination are now to be subsumed.

It hardly needs saying, but perhaps is significant for the purpose of tracing our thread, that Kant did not invent the distinction between the beautiful and the sublime, though he used it for his own purposes. English critical theory of the immediately preceding and contemporary period was full of the discussion of this distinction and of the notion of beauty itself, and much of the contemporary debate is reflected in Kant's own distinctions. We can find such shared ideas in Addison, Home, Hutcheson, Burke and doubtless elsewhere. Something like the concept of beauty as finality without an end, and its peculiar appeal to the imagination is to be found, for example, in Addison.[1] Beauty is there ascribed to anything which 'has such a variety or regularity as may seem the effect of design in what we call works of chance' and this quasi-design is said to give pleasure to our imagination 'not so gross as that of sense, nor so refined as that of understanding'. Again in Home's *Elements of Criticism* which was translated into German, and reviewed, possibly by Kant himself, in 1760, we find that 'there is a rule for taste, though a subjective rule; so, though there is no disputing, yet there is good and bad taste.' In the same work one may find the distinction between pure beauty of form, and relative beauty which presupposes an end; and in Hutcheson there occurs the distinction between pure beauty, and that relative beauty which is a matter of good imitation. So we could show in detail that the theory of beauty of the *Critique of Judgment* is a theory very much in the current vogue, and presumably found by Kant in the new translation from English to German. As to sublimity itself, which had been debated by Addison and was discussed by Burke and many others, it had to be distinguished, according to current orthodoxy, from beauty, because the very means by which it seems to produce a pleasurable reaction, its vastness, wildness and lack of order, are the exact opposites of that limited and comprehensible orderliness

[1] *Spectator*, Essay 411.

of form which was currently supposed to be the mark of beauty, and the secret of its appeal.

But what is not part of this orthodoxy is the manner in which first beauty and then sublimity are linked by Kant to the imagination. For in Kant, the imagination is the very same image-making faculty which works in the depths of our minds to enable us to recognize objects in the world, and link the concepts of them to our actual experience. The faculty which in the *Critique of Judgment* gains pleasure from the contemplation of objects both beautiful and sublime is the faculty *which frames images*. In the case of beautiful objects, the imagination takes pleasure in its free power to frame its images; in the case of the sublime, however, its pleasure, as we shall see, is different. Now the English writers who discussed the beautiful and the sublime were interested in literature and art, in framing rules of taste, and even in raising the question why we judge aesthetic objects as we do. But they were not interested in the imagination for its own sake. They were not interested in psychology, still less in laying down a framework for all our thought about, or knowledge of, the world. For them, imagination was merely that which, conventionally, poets and painters were supposed to have. The difference between them and Kant amounts to a total difference of subject matter and of aim. The exception here is, of course, Hume. He *was* interested in psychology, and, in particular, in the imagination. And his remarks about the imaginative appeal of vastness and distance point the way to a detailed examination of the workings of the imagination with regard to the sublime. But he did not use the word 'sublime' except to describe a particular kind of style, nor did he distinguish between the sublime and the beautiful. Kant however was bound by this distinction; and if he had not been he might have produced a somewhat less paradoxical theory of his own. It is to this theory that we must now return.

The notion of beauty, as we have seen, is that of a perceptible form whose pattern, or finality, is in conformity with a law or limit, albeit, in the purest cases, a limit suggested by the imagination itself, operating freely without reference to any given concept. Imagination, in presenting us with an object as beautiful, brings the object, Kant says, under an *indeterminate concept* of the understanding. Sartre at one time suggested that the function of abstract art is to make us envisage a new thing, a shape or form which we have never seen before and shall never see again in nature. Kant might agree that this is the function of a purely aesthetic object. The sense in which the concept under which the object is brought is indeterminate is simply that it is not a scientific concept, exemplified again and again in nature; but that there is *some* concept entails that the imagination can produce an image of the form in question. *Something* can be envisaged and represented by imagination as that feature of the object which makes us say it is beautiful, even though that something is not something which falls under any known scientific category, nor is it to be referred to an external end or function.

On the other hand, when the imagination presents us with an object as sublime, it invokes an indeterminate idea of *reason*. This is Kant's initial distinction and that which we must now try to understand. 'We observe', he says, 'that whereas natural beauty conveys a finality in its form, making the object appear as it were pre-adapted to our power of judgment, so that it thus forms of itself an object of delight, that which on the other hand in our apprehension of it excites the feeling of the sublime may appear in point of form to contravene the ends of our power of judgment, to be ill-adapted to our faculty of presentation, and to be, as it were, an outrage on the imagination, and yet it is judged all the more sublime on that account.'[1] Kant seems to be saying this: the creative imagination has, as one of its functions, the exciting in us a sense of the sublime precisely in that it excites in us ideas which we realize *cannot* be represented by any visible or otherwise sensible forms—ideas which cannot be restricted or brought down to size by any image-making power of the imagination. In the contemplation of beauty the imagination is free and takes pleasure in its sense of freedom, just because it can so easily form an image. The pleasure is a pleasure in doing something which one can do. It is rather as one might learn how to play a certain kind of ornamentation in a piece of keyboard music, and take pleasure in one's ability to produce the required kind of ornament. The sound would give one pleasure but so would one's own ability to produce the sound in the right way and at the right time. Similarly the imagination, in grasping a thing as beautiful, can easily grasp the rule or design *in* the thing before it, and frame pictures or

[1] *Critique of Judgment*, 245.

presentations of the form of the thing, creating its own rule as it goes along. In the contemplation of the sublime, on the other hand, the imagination is brought to a full stop, and can go no further. All it has to work on is the form of the thing before it which suggests certain *ideas*. But no further images can be produced to render these ideas concrete or familiar. We cannot, hearing a great exposition in a Beethoven sonata (to continue with the keyboard analogy), discover any rule by which we can go on in this way for ourselves. We are reminded of the peculiar pleasure in trying to overcome obstacles which Hume invoked to account for our pleasure in the vast. Kant has observed, perhaps, the same phenomenon, but is about to make infinitely more of it, both by using the distinctions current in literary criticism of the time, and by fitting these into his whole psychological, and indeed metaphysical, system.

The distinction he is here making is so important, both for his own theory and for later theories of imagination, that we must be forgiven for spelling it out at perhaps tedious length, and in doing so, we shall have to go over some ground again. We may try to put the distinction in another way, still following Kant's own exposition of it. When we apprehend the finality, the purpose or design, in an object, we can present the form which embodies this design to ourselves in an image. Understanding and imagination thus work together in our apprehension of finality, and this is the source of our pleasure in beauty. But Kant is maintaining that we also, paradoxically, get a different kind of pleasure out of that which is apprehended as inherently contra-final. When this happens the object before us 'lends itself to the presentation of a sublimity discoverable in the mind'.[1] Kant goes on to explain how this comes about. The presentation of sublimity cannot be in the form of a sensuous image, simply because there is no form or design to be grasped in the object and therefore none to be reproduced in an image of it. But it is our own very inadequacy to form an image of the *idea suggested by the object* which constitutes our sense of the sublime.

An 'idea', it will be remembered, is, in Kant's use of the term, precisely *not* an image. It is, as it were, the opposite of an image; it is what the highest power of the mind can produce, but what can never in any circumstances be exemplified in the world, nor

[1] *Critique of Judgment*, 246.

brought before the senses to be actually observed. An idea cannot be other than a goal or ideal, never to be completely realized. And so, Kant says, 'the sublime, in the strict sense of the word, cannot be contained in any sensuous form, but rather concerns ideas of reason, which, although no adequate presentation of them is possible, may be excited and called into the mind by that very inadequacy itself which does admit of sensuous presentation.'[1] Kant argues that it is more proper to describe the sense of the sublime as producing not pleasure so much as awe or respect. For what we respect is the idea of reason itself. What we stand in awe of is the fact that we are such as to be able to frame such ideas. He says, 'Who would apply the term "sublime" even to shapeless mountain masses towering one above the other in wild disorder, with their pyramids of ice, or to the dark tempestuous ocean or such like things? But in the contemplation of them without any regard to their form, the mind abandons itself to the imagination and to a reason placed, though quite apart from any definite end, in conjunction therewith, and it feels itself elevated in its own estimation in finding all the might of imagination still unequal to its ideas.' We are in awe precisely of the human power to frame ideas which cannot be intuited. Imaginatively we stretch out towards what imagination cannot comprehend. We realize that there is more in what we see than meets or can ever meet even the inner eye.

Kant distinguishes between two kinds of sublimity, here again making use of a current distinction. There is one sublimity, the feeling of which arises from the contemplation of vast numbers, and another the feeling of which arises from the contemplation of vast power. Infinitely large numbers give us a sense of the sublime because in contemplating them the imagination calls to our mind the powers of reason, in contrast with its own feebleness. By reason we are not incapable of calculating with large numbers, but we can never make these calculations concrete by actually envisaging the numbers. The spectacle of infinite power likewise causes a feeling of the sublime because the imagination calls to our mind the idea of our own power, our rational power, contrasted with our imaginative weakness. For though our imagination is limited, our power to act freely is unlimited. We have the power freely to stand out against the

[1] *Critique of Judgment*, 245.

pressures of the world, and to obey the rational call of duty, though the heavens fall. Nature, Kant says, shows us that our senses and our ability to frame sensible images of things will fail when we contemplate some of her phenomena. 'Therefore the inner perception of the inadequacy of every standard of sense to serve for the rational estimation of magnitude is a coming into accord with Reason's laws.' And our displeasure in our inadequate senses and imagination 'makes us alive to the feeling of the supersensible side of our being, according to which it is final, and consequently a pleasure, to find every standard of sensibility falling short of the Ideas of Reason'. (It is worth noticing here, as in the discussion of beauty, that the 'final' is connected immediately with the 'pleasurable'.)

The English writers on the sublime, and especially Burke, had called attention to the need, if we are to think of the grander aspects of nature as sublime rather than simply as horrifying, to contemplate them with a lively sense of our own security. Kant, in a famous passage in the *Critique of Judgment*[1] uses this familiar thought in his own way and to make his own point. 'Bold overhanging and threatening rocks, thunder clouds piled up the vault of heaven, borne along with flashes and peals, volcanoes in all their violence of destruction, hurricanes leaving desolation in their track, the boundless ocean rising in rebellious force, the high waterfall of some mighty river, make our power of resistance of trifling moment in comparison to their might. But, provided our position is secure, their aspect is all the more attractive for its fearfulness: and we readily call these objects sublime because they raise the forces of the soul above the height of vulgar commonplace, and discover within us a power of resistance of quite another kind, which gives us courage to be able to measure ourselves against the seeming omnipotence of nature. In the immeasurableness of nature and the incompetence of our faculty for adopting a standard proportionate to the aesthetic estimation of the magnitude of its realm we find our own limitation. But with this we also find in our rational faculty another, non-sensuous standard, one which has that infinity itself under it as a unit, and in comparison with which everything in nature is small: and so we find in our minds a pre-eminence over nature, even in its immeasurability. Now in just the same way the irresistibility

[1] 261.

of the might of nature forces upon us the recognition of our physical helplessness as beings of nature, but at the same time reveals a faculty of estimating ourselves as independent of nature, and discovers a pre-eminence over nature that is the foundation of a self-preservation of quite another kind from that which may be assailed and brought into danger by external nature. This saves humanity in our own person from humiliation, even though as mortal men we have to submit to external violence.' Thus, in these two aspects of nature, its infinite size and its infinite power, we are called upon to remember the fact, demonstrated by Kant in his moral philosophy, that we may regard ourselves either as parts of that natural order, and in that aspect we are determined by laws of nature as much as every part of nature is; or we may, through our own experience of morality, regard ourselves as rational, and in this aspect we are free: we are above nature in that we can generate our own laws.

British critical theory was concerned with this very division of the sublime into two kinds, the mathematically and the dynamically sublime, in the period just before the writing of the *Critique of Judgment*. In particular, the distinction is made in highly Kantian terms in Hugh Blair's *Lectures on Rhetoric* in 1783. Blair wrote, 'All vastness produces the impression of sublimity. Hence infinite space, endless numbers and eternal duration fill the mind with great ideas. But many objects appear sublime which have no relation to space at all. Great power and strength exerted always raise sublime ideas.'[1] This passage brings out the difference between Kant and his British contemporaries. For the important thing in the *Critique of Judgment* was not the distinction between beauty and sublimity, nor the distinction between different *kinds* of beauty, nor different *kinds* of sublimity. Kant's interest was rather in founding the distinctions upon his own psychology of understanding, reason and imagination. His concern was after all not with rhetoric or style, but with the psychological and philosophical basis of our understanding of the world.

We shall see, as we attempt to follow the subsequent history of the theory of imagination, how important a step it was for Kant to connect our sense of the sublime with *ideas of reason*. Although we cannot by any stretch of the imagination represent

[1] Third lecture.

ideas of reason to ourselves by images or potential images, as we can represent concepts of the understanding, yet the recognition of something as sublime does entail the attempt, albeit doomed to failure, to experience ideas of reason directly. In making this effort, 'the feeling of the unattainability of the idea by means of the imagination' shows us that we are using imagination 'in the service of the mind's supersensible province'. Briefly, we may say that the role of the imagination here is to lead us beyond what is present to our senses towards the realization that there is something *signified by* the things before us, something which we can grasp in a way, but cannot express.

In our judgments of beauty, we feel the harmony of the imagination with the understanding: in seizing on the aspect of design or pattern *in* a particular object we are allowing imagination to create a concept or rule. At least once Kant speaks of this 'finality without ends' as if it had a specific end, namely to allow free scope to the human faculties, but I do not think that one can press this very hard. In general, finality means intelligibility; it means an object's seeming significant, but not of anything outside itself. There would be no pleasure in the beautiful form of objects if there were not the sense of bringing the freedom of the imagination to order, by a rule of understanding. But the rule has been discovered in the very appearance of the object by the imagination itself. In the case of sublimity, on the other hand, the imagination in trying to encompass the vastness of the power before it is led to the awareness of something mysteriously great in the human mind itself. We can think, but not imagine, such vastness, or such power. The idea somehow embodied in the sublime object is beyond representation or explanation, but *yet* can be apprehended by the human mind. *We* are grand, in that we can touch such grandeur and be touched by it, though we shall always struggle and fail to say what it means.

Now the difference between the active production of works of art and the appreciation of them, or of nature, is the difference, in Kant's vocabulary, between genius and taste. Genius is defined by Kant[1] as the 'faculty of presenting *aesthetic ideas*'. An aesthetic idea is defined in the same paragraph. It is a 'representation of the imagination which induces much thought; yet without the possibility of any definite thought whatever, *i.e. concept*, being

[1] *Critique of Judgment*, 314.

adequate to it, and which language consequently can never get quite on level terms with or render it completely intelligible.' An aesthetic idea is a counterpart of an idea of reason. That is to say, if in the contemplation of nature we have come upon the sublime, our struggle to represent in imagination the idea of reason we have apprehended dimly will issue, if we have genius, in the artistic representation of an aesthetic idea. The greater the genius, the more akin will be the aesthetic idea to the idea of reason—the more nearly will those who contemplate the work of art approach the apprehension of the idea of reason itself. 'The imagination', Kant says in the same place, 'is a powerful agent for creating as it were a second nature out of the material supplied to it by actual nature.' This second nature, in a way, surpasses the original nature, since the representations or images in terms of which it is presented to us are all of them attempts to reach beyond the mere appearances of things, to the ideas of reason which lie beyond them. The representations 'strain after something lying out beyond the confines of experience'. The man of genius attempts, Kant says, 'to body forth the Idea of Reason to Sense with a completeness of which nature affords no parallel'. Creative genius, then, consists in the ability to find expression, although inevitably not complete expression, for the ideas which are to be apprehended in, or glimpsed beyond, objects in the world. It is the imaginative power which finds ways of representing things to an audience who will then, themselves, be induced to think, and to go beyond immediate appearances to the significance of the appearance.

Kant's entire philosophical system is based upon the thought that there could be no scientific laws, valid for all experience, unless we ourselves, by our own understanding and imagination imposed these laws on the appearances of things. So, in the area of taste, he argues that there could be no universal judgments of beauty (and we find that there are) if it were not that we imposed on the appearance of things our own concept of finality, or design. It is true that we seem to find the design in the object; but we do this because of the constitution of our own minds: and from the same psychological source comes the pleasure we derive from the discovery of design. The finality or point of the object must not, however, be thought of as an external end. For if it were, the imagination, in contemplating the object, would be bound by the notion of this end and the judgment of the object would become scientific or mechanical. We would have to ask, does it work? Does it achieve what it is supposed to be meant to achieve? The purity and the freedom of aesthetic judgments are one and the same. But, as we have seen, Kant's insistence on purity and internal finality laid very narrow limits on what could be counted as beautiful, whether in nature or in art. The analysis of the sublime opened up far wider possibilities. *Objects* in nature or art are only in a loose sense called sublime. What is sublime is our own minds in contemplating them. For they themselves are such as to suggest to us ideas which the human mind is grand enough to be able to form, though not wholly to express. So the objects which we call sublime now take on a new role. They become symbols, standing for something different from and beyond themselves.

In ordinary life Kant thinks that the imagination has to form images in which scientific concepts may be embodied. These images are, as we have seen, are known as schemata. He says, 'Schemata contain direct presentation of a concept.'[1] Symbols are analogous to schemata; they are intended to present ideas, as schemata present concepts. But they cannot wholly succeed in presenting them, since ideas cannot be embodied for sense. Symbols, therefore, do the best they can by means of analogy and suggestion. What we perceive as sublime in nature, or what we appreciate or create in the highest art, is a symbol of something which is forever beyond it. The man of artistic genius is the man who can find new ways of *nearly* embodying ideas; and in his attempts imagination has a creative role.

Fortunately, it is no part of the purpose of this book to follow all the elements of Kant's account of creative imagination into the tangled mesh of German, or indeed of English, criticism. It is now above all that we must cling to our thread of common meaning in order to save ourselves from drowning. It is clear that all the features of creative imagination which were to be found in the *Critique of Judgment* are to be found again in different guises in post-Kantian philosophy. However, the moment we plunge into the post-Kantians, starting with Fichte and Schelling, we are aware of a change of tone. Instead of arguments, we are presented with repeated statements, obscure, dark and perhaps profound.

[1] *Critique of Judgment*, 351.

The reason for this change, this tremendous deterioration in the rational climate, is that the sharp distinction which Kant had drawn between what could and could not be known, between legitimate thought, and impossible, empty metaphysical speculation, had been done away with. Now we can to some extent blame this on to Kant himself, if indeed it is a matter for blame. And the trouble seems to lie in the *Critique of Judgment*. For in the *Critique of Pure Reason*, he had been absolutely explicit and definite on the point that ideas, ideas of reason, could not be grasped or discussed, because they could not be framed within concepts such as those of time, space or causality. The categories of the understanding could not be made to apply to anything of which we had an *idea*. These categories were devised by the mind to apply to the appearances of things. What things were *in themselves* was forever beyond our understanding to find out. And as understanding could not grasp laws which govern things in themselves but only those which govern appearances, and as ideas of reason lay beyond the world of appearance, so Imagination could not frame images of such ideas either. Ideas of reason were ideas for us only in the sense that they stood as limits to our thoughts, or as ideals to which we could move in our thoughts. In this sense they were said to be regulative. On the other hand the concepts of the understanding, as distinct from ideas of reason, had application to the world, but they gave us information not about the ultimate nature of things in themselves, but only about things as they appeared to us, about the phenomena in our world. We were for ever and inevitably confined, as far as knowledge went, to the world of what appeared to us to exist. Any attempt to go beyond the world of appearances was idle and meaningless.

In the *Critique of Practical Reason*, it is true, Kant had argued that at least the idea of freedom, which was an idea of reason, could be known to have application, through the actual operating of our own free will. We could become aware of the *reality* of freedom, in our practical ability to choose to act in accordance with the moral law imposed upon us by ourselves from within. But this knowledge, though it amounted to an experience of freedom itself, and not a mere appearance, was not, still, an imaginative grasp of an idea of reason. But in the *Critique of Judgment*, there seem to be two directions in which Kant allows that our understanding, aided by imagination, may come nearer to a comprehension of an idea of reason. First, in our experience of the sublime, we are explicitly said to try to image for ourselves ideas of reason; and even though we are doomed to failure, there is the suggestion that at least the imagination must, as it were, know how to go about the attempt, and thus make some sort of approach to the goal. Secondly, and this is more important, in creative art the man of genius expresses for us an aesthetic idea. Now that is said by Kant to be analogous to an idea of reason. Language is inadequate to such an idea, and our understanding cannot grasp it. But the imagination, in its specifically aesthetic function, can present it to us, not directly, but in symbolic form. The poet, Kant says, 'transgressing the limits of experience, attempts with the aid of imagination to body forth the rational ideas to sense, with a completeness of which nature affords no parallel.'[1] It is through such symbolism that we seem to be able to breach the otherwise impenetrable wall between ourselves and the world of ideas. And this amounts to a kind of hint that we can after all penetrate the appearance and reach the reality behind it. Thus both in art and in morality we seem, after all, to be able to approach the ultimate ideas and thus the ultimate reality that lies behind appearances, despite the warnings against any such attempt which are contained in the first *Critique*. It is noticeable that a tremendous weight is here laid on the word 'idea' as the name of that which as it were bridges the gap between reality and our thought of it; and as ideas are at least most nearly to be approached by imagination, a weight is also laid upon the word 'imagination'. It is of course a fact of history that it has often been the fate of the word 'idea' to stand for something which hovers uneasily between the mental and the physical, between thoughts and those things about which thoughts are concerned. Sometimes the ideas are conceived as actual physical objects or objects of perception somehow lying behind physical objects, as the circle itself, the real circle, is thought to lie behind the chalk circle on the blackboard. It may be that we are all of us in such a state of confusion, ontologically speaking, that we could hardly get on without some such gravely ambiguous expression. I believe, indeed, that this is probably the case. At any rate Fichte and other post-Kantian philosophers were prone, as Kant himself

[1] *Critique of Judgment*, 314.

was not, to slide between 'ideas' as something *in* the mind, what the mind creates, and as something already existing, to be *discovered by* the mind in its gradual effort to understand the nature of things.

Among the post-Kantians, it is the work of Schelling which is particularly relevant to the view of imagination with which we are concerned. If we consider his philosophy we find it dominated by the conception of Nature animated by a Rational Idea. This is particularly true of his aesthetic philosophy. In this, the imagination is presented as the truly creative faculty of man, creating, in a sense, both nature and art. For in Schelling's system what we discern in nature is an idea. There are not two kinds of stuff in the world, mind-stuff and matter-stuff: there is only one. The Kantian mystery of the thing-in-itself, lying behind the phenomena which we perceive and reduce to law-abiding order in the world, has been removed by the simple expedient of denying that there is any such mystery. What we order by means of the categories of our understanding is not mere appearances, it *is* the things themselves. For the things are also our own ideas. And therefore it can be said that the categories or rules of the mind do more than order; they create. But, very important for Schelling, the creation of the world lies below the level of consciousness. When we try to find out what this unconscious creation is, and how it works; and when we begin to do consciously what we have, all of us, always done unconsciously, then what we have is art. In the *System of Transcendental Idealism*, Schelling says, 'The objective world is only the original, still unconscious, poetry of the spirit.' The human imagination is at work in this poetry, as in what is usually called poetry. The conscious and unconscious workings of the imagination are a unity.

Schelling held that even the creative artist, deliberately and of choice painting a picture or writing a poem, works to some extent unconsciously; and in so far as he does so, it is the same unconscious spirit, that which creates the world of objects, of actual mountains and trees, which is now working in him to create the poem or the painting. But in the latter case his conscious spirit is working as well, in harmony. It is because of this harmony between the conscious and the unconscious spirit in the creation of a work of art that, Schelling says, both the artist and the person who contemplates the finished work feel satisfaction in the created object. For it is assumed by Schelling, just as it was by Kant, that if one can speak of two faculties working in harmony, then one is necessarily entitled to speak of a resultant pleasure. In the *Critique of Judgment*, after all, pleasure in the beautiful was said to arise not, it is true, from a harmony between conscious and unconscious mind, but between imagination and understanding when together they identified finality in an object.

But one should also remember that Kant was not very far from the notion of the working together of conscious and unconscious. For he held that the work of the imagination, not only in revealing to us the beautiful in the forms of nature or art, but also in enabling us to perceive and identify objects in the world, was carried on below the level of consciousness. He speaks, it will be remembered, of 'the art concealed in the depths of the human soul whose real modes of activity nature is hardly likely ever to allow us to discover.'[1] The imagination is inevitably mysterious to us because it operates below the level of which we can easily become conscious.

Although Schelling allowed some part to the unconscious in creative art, Schiller criticized him for not realizing the true importance of the unconscious element in the act of artistic creation. In a letter to Goethe of 27th March, 1801,[2] he said, 'Experience teaches us that the poet's unique point of departure is the unconscious . . . and poetry, if I am not mistaken, consists precisely in knowing how to express and communicate this unconscious . . . in other words in knowing how to embody it in an objective work of art.' Whether Schelling made enough of the unconscious or not, he certainly drew a distinction between the conscious and the unconscious working of the spirit, a distinction which, as we have seen, was already implicit in Kant. But he characterized the difference as a difference in freedom. Conscious thought is free thought. An artist, in so far as he is working at the level of consciousness, is free to present the ideas of the spirit to himself and others in any manner he pleases. And because it is the ideas of the spirit that he is presenting, he is the supreme interpreter of the nature of things, far superior in this respect to the philosopher. As a development of his theory, Schelling at

[1] B 138.
[2] Quoted by Herbert Read in his essay, 'Coleridge as Critic' in *The True Voice of Feeling* (Faber, 1968), p. 168n.

some stage introduced the notion of Divine Ideas, as those ideas which are manifested in works of art; and in his later philosophy he seemed to refer indifferently to divine or absolute ideas, to ideas of reason or of the Spirit, or infinite ideas. Ideas of any of these sorts are the object of the artist. They are what the imagination of the artist reveals to his public, and what he finds in nature itself.

We need not follow Schelling into his gradual advance towards a concept of a personal god. But it is perhaps instructive to notice that there is a sense in which it seems not to matter very much exactly *what* it is which is said to be expressed in the work of art, or discovered in the phenomena of nature by the eye of the imagination. It does not matter, that is to say, whether the ideas revealed or glimpsed are such as would be called specifically religious or not. It is the sense of infinity, of depth, of significance *beyond what words can completely convey* that it is the function of imagination in its creative role to give us; and this sense can be conveyed by the contemplation of a particular object, Schelling says, in so far as it participates in an idea. This vaguely Platonic way of talking of ideas can be seen to arise, albeit indirectly, out of the Kantian theory first of ideas of reason and then of aesthetic ideas, which we are allowed, as it were, to glimpse through the concrete and particular objects presented to us by the creative imagination, or genius.

Schelling refers to those concrete objects which do participate in the infinite ideas as symbols, and here again he is reverting to Kant. Such objects cannot be thought of as wholly particular nor yet as wholly universal, but as both. He holds that a symbol thus reaffirms the identity of the finite with the infinite, the conscious with the unconscious idea. All the different levels of creativity are encapsulated in an object which is conceived symbolically. He distinguishes between an image and a symbol. An image is a concrete particular thing or picture used deliberately as an illustration of something other than itself. A symbol, on the other hand, is not deliberately chosen to be such. It is *naturally* symbolic. It simply does manifest an infinite idea, in itself. Works of art which are properly created by an artistic genius, operating both at the conscious and the unconscious level, can come to have the very same force as do true symbols in nature. They can, that is to say, embody the universal idea in the particular, and thus be, in themselves, both universal and particular. To perceive that this is so, one needs to exercise aesthetic judgment and regard works of art with what Schelling calls 'the spiritual eye that penetrates their husk, and feels the force at work within them'.[1] In the same lecture Schelling says that we can simply see that intelligence or idea is at work in nature, as in art, because we can see design in both. It would be impossible for us to detect any *design*, whether in objects of scientific study or in works of art, if the objects were not themselves full of intelligent design. 'For that which contained no intelligence could not serve as an object for intelligence either. What was without knowledge could not itself be known.' In these somewhat mysterious words we can perhaps see what the *Critique of Judgment* has led to.

Kant had held that both in science and in aesthetics the judgment sought out a finality or inner design in particular objects; and that when such finality was discovered, a pleasure was experienced which arose from the working together of imagination and understanding. According to Schelling, we do indeed seek out such design; and that we sometimes find it is proof that there really is design or intelligence in the world. This is then taken by him to show that the world is made up of intelligence, that mind or intelligence is all that exists. He says, 'The science by which nature operates is not, of course, one which, like the human, is linked to itself by reflection; in it the idea does not differ from the deed, nor the design from its execution. Hence raw matter tends ... blindly towards regular shape, and unwittingly assumes ... forms which certainly appertain to the realm of ideas and which are something spiritual within the material.' Both the artist and the scientist discover design in nature. But the artist does more. He himself becomes, like nature itself, a creator of objects which manifest design. In speaking of the extent to which an artist ought to be bound by the forms which he finds in nature, Schelling says, 'In all natural beings the living Idea is manifested in blind operation only; if it were the same in the artist, he would differ in no way from nature. If however he were to subordinate himself entirely to nature and reproduce the existent with servile fidelity, he would produce masks, but no works of art. Thus he must withdraw from the product or

---

[1] *Concerning the Relation of the Plastic Arts and Nature*, translated by Michael Bullock. Herbert Read, *loc. cit.*

created thing, but only in order to raise himself to the level of creative energy and apprehend it in his spirit. This bears him aloft to the realm of pure ideas; he loses the created thing, to regain it with thousandfold interest, and so return, in this sense at least, to nature. The artist ought indeed to emulate this spirit of nature which is at work in the core of things, and in whose speech form and shape are mere symbols; and only in so far as he has apprehended it in living imitation has he created something true. That which ... constitutes the beauty of a work of art ... is essence, the universal, the vision and expression of the indwelling nature.' The creative imagination, then, is the faculty of seeing, and expressing again, the absolute ideas which are perceived as the pattern, design or essence of things. Imagination is the power of seeing things as they are, namely as symbolic, and of creating new symbols (and to a less extent new images) to express the ultimate nature of the world. And this creative imagination operates both at the conscious and the unconscious level.

It is all too easy to lapse with Schelling into a gasping sentiment of the profound which for many people is still what they believe philosophy ought to bring them. But though it is, to my mind, extremely desirable to avoid such floundering, yet there is a real point in being aware of it as a possibility. For in fact we shall not even partially understand the nature of imagination unless we are capable of feeling at least some sympathy with that sense of vastness and of limitless freedom which characterizes the creative imagination in Schelling's theory. It is of no use to turn away in disgust from the turgid, breathless language, nor from the wanton confounding of Kantian distinctions. We must recognize that what Kant spoke of relatively dispassionately as aesthetic ideas which could not be adequately envisaged, nor wholly expressed in language, have become the objects of a deep nostalgia. They have become that which, if we could only grasp them, would transform us. These ideas which live in nature and in ourselves have become the source of the whole significance of our life. When Schelling says, 'We do not ask for the individual. We ask to see more, namely its living idea,' he is making a demand of imagination which we can all to some extent understand, and with which we must sympathize if we are to have any grasp of the development of philosophy or any understanding of what the imagination is. We have, it is true, come a long way from Hume. But even in Hume the imagination of the artist was linked with, was indeed identical with, the imagination we all exercise perforce in ordinary perception. Without the fictions of the imagination, much as Hume deplored the fact, we would not perceive our familiar world, and this means that we would not perceive the universal element in the world. We would be lost in an ocean of particular impressions. In Schelling the same imagination which creates the poem or the statue also creates the world, which is both universal and particular. Thus, in very different ways, neither Hume nor Schelling could hold the understanding to be wholly independent of imagination. There would be no world to be understood without a prior imaginative construction.

PART III

Coleridge and Wordsworth, Theory and Practice

Imagination and the Mental Image

We have seen in Part II how imagination came to be thought of as the faculty concerned with ideas. Ideas reside both in nature and in ourselves, all one. It is because we can frame ideas that things in nature and art are significant for us. Ideas are expressed symbolically in art, but they are also expressed in nature, which has its own symbolism. So the imagination is that which allows us both to express and to understand ideas. Such theories as these, essentially German in their development, were first introduced into England by Coleridge. We must therefore pursue our thread into the tangled confusion of his theory of imagination. But at the same time the connexions between perception and art, between imagination in seeing and imagination in creating, are also to be found in the writings of Wordsworth, and are in some ways much more clearly discernible there. I do not want to argue the question of priority as between Wordsworth and Coleridge. It seems to be enough, for my purposes, to say that their thoughts were obviously not independent of each other's in the crucial period when Coleridge became interested in German philosophy and Wordsworth became interested in autobiographical writing and in the nature of his own experiences. Both must therefore be considered. But we shall start with Coleridge, since the line from Kant to Coleridge is at any rate relatively straight.

Mill, in his still rightly famous essay on Coleridge,[1] said of him that he was 'anticipated in all the essentials of his doctrine by the great Germans of the latter half of the last century'; and that he was 'the creator rather of the shape in which it has appeared

[1] J. S. Mill, *Dissertations and Discussions*, reprinted by Chatto and Windus as *Mill on Bentham and Coleridge*, edited by F. R. Leavis (1950).

among us than of the doctrine itself'. I shall take it for granted in
the following pages that there is no need to dispute Mill's words,
and hardly any need to amplify them. We know that Coleridge
was a voracious, though a careless and inaccurate, reader. We
know that he copied out great passages of German philosophy
without stating his sources, and indeed, more positively, that he
pretended to have thought of things for himself which he had
obviously borrowed, and to have been the first to think of things
which he plainly recognized, when he read them, as somehow
speaking directly to him, but which he had never actually formu-
lated himself. But none of this need concern us in detail.

However, it is impossible altogether to avoid the charges of
plagiarism brought against Coleridge, since so much that is
scholarly and fascinating in the literature is concerned with this
issue. But 'plagiarism' is, after all, a moral term; and luckily it is
not our concern to award moral marks for conduct, nor indeed
literary marks for originality or creativity. The fact which concerns us is the undisputed fact, to which Mill called attention,
that Coleridge was the vehicle for the introduction of German
philosophy into England and (more specifically related to our
purpose) that the theory of imagination to be found in his work
contains features which, wherever they recur, seem to contribute
to a true view of the imaginative function.

In any case, one must not be trapped, by the intrinsic interest of
tracing Coleridge's theory to its sources, into thinking of him as a
theorist only, still less as a pure philosopher. He was equally
interested in the question of what imagination did, how it worked
in practice. It is in this area that the influence of Wordsworth on
him and of him on Wordsworth is most difficult to sort out. I
shall not try to sort these things out in detail, nor to arrange
Wordsworth and Coleridge in order of merit, even if an order of
merit may seem to emerge. Coleridge was concerned *both* to
analyse a way of thinking *and* to find a theory, what might be
called a higher-order language, in which to state his practical
analysis of imagination, and by means of which to fit it into a
much wider theory of human nature and of nature as a whole. He
had a very strong urge to establish a metaphysical foundation for
his beliefs about imagination, beliefs which, in the first instance,
he held to be psychologically correct. It was this urge which
drove him to try first this, then that philosophical framework, to

borrow here, there and everywhere among the Germans, in the hope of fitting his thoughts into some slot or other in a system.

We shall, then, distinguish between first-order, or psychological, theory, and second-order theory. Yet even this distinction may seem artificial, and may indeed be positively misleading, if it suggests that the first was his own and the second borrowed. For there are borrowings equally in both. We must remember that Coleridge always read, and doubtless often talked, in *search* of something. He seems to have been like an adolescent whose head is full of vague, half-formed thoughts and hopes, and who reads everything in the expectation of finding his thoughts confirmed; or who marks in the margin, like Bernard in *The Waves*, those passages in a book which seem to describe his own character. Thus when he went to Germany in 1798, after he had first met Wordsworth, and when his head was full of thoughts of poetic genius and the functions of imagination, Coleridge heard and read much that was relevant to his thoughts, though his knowledge of German was still sketchy. Notebook entries, both of this time and later, which look at first like immediate expressions of his own self-analysis may yet turn out to be echoes of what he had heard, first or second hand, from others.

It may be worth quoting one example, to illustrate the kind of complication I have in mind, though to do so will anticipate a theme which will be discussed again later. In a Notebook entry made early in 1801[1] Coleridge quotes from 'Tintern Abbey', ' . . . And the deep power of joy we see into the life of things', and he adds as a gloss, 'i.e. by deep feeling we make our *ideas dim* and this is what we mean by our life . . . ourselves. I think of the Wall—it is before me, a distinct image—*here*. I necessarily think of the *idea* and the thinking I as two distinct and opposite things. Now let me think of *myself*—of the thinking being. The idea becomes dim, whatever it may be—so dim that I know not what it is. But the feeling is deep and steady, and this I call "*I*", identifying the percipient and the perceived.' On the face of it, this seems a very eccentric explanation of what Wordsworth meant. How did Coleridge come to think of it at this particular time? Kathleen Coburn comments on the passage that although the substance of the entry, as far as concerns the identification of the

---

[1] No. 921. All quotations from the Notebooks are taken from Kathleen Coburn's edition (New York, 1957) and the numbers are those used by her.

object with the subject, is exactly like the seventh and eighth Kantian theses in *Biographia Literaria* (184–5), and although *that* has been ascribed, ever since Sarah Coleridge's commentary, to Schelling, yet since Coleridge could not have read Schelling as early as 1801, this passage must be independent. She goes on, 'The entry here has all the earmarks of personal observation and ... we must take this as substantiating his often scoffed-at claim to have arrived at some of his ideas by "genial coincidence".' However, in his excellent book, *Coleridge and German Idealism*,[1] G. N. G. Orsini records in detail how he identified a source for this Notebook entry. It would unfortunately take too long to trace all the steps he took, but, briefly, the story seems to be that Fichte used the example of the wall in some lectures delivered in 1799. This was recorded in the autobiography of one Steffens, and though the autobiography was not written until 1840, he had remembered this particular example as the most notorious feature of Fichte's 1799 lectures. Apparently Fichte had insisted that all his students should actually *look* at the wall, and go through the thought-processes he described. More important, Fichte himself wrote out the example in a work published in 1797, entitled *Attempt at a new Exposition of the Doctrine of Science*. The relevant passage is this: 'When you thought of your table or your wall, you, my intelligent reader, *you* who are conscious to yourself of the activity of your thought, you were yourself the thinker in your thinking; but the thing-thought-of was for you not yourself, but something different from yourself. In short the thinker and the thing-thought-of must be two. But when you think *yourself*, you are not only the thinker but also at the same time the thought-of; thinker and thought-of must therefore be one.' This example is of no great interest in itself. But it seems to me to be sufficient to show that even in the case of Notebook entries which *look* spontaneous, and as though they were being thought out as they were made, there may nevertheless be a source, possibly not fully or rightly understood, from which the entry in some sense arose. For it is surely beyond the bounds of belief that Coleridge should have used the precise example of the wall by coincidence, when absolutely any other material object would have done equally well. Moreover, we know that Coleridge was reading some Fichte in 1801, because he

[1] S. Illinois Univ. Press, 1969.

quoted some in a letter to Dorothy Wordsworth in that year. The passage he quoted to her came, it is true, from a different work, not that which contained the 'wall' example. But the subject matter of the quotation was the same, namely self-consciousness. There can be little doubt, therefore, that he read the 'wall' example in the same year, and very likely heard about the famous lectures at the same time.

Fichte had taken over the distinction between Ego and Non-Ego from Kant. For Kant, the distinction between self, the observer, the concept-former and the observed world was the prerequisite of all experience. We carry with us in our actual awareness of the world an awareness of the self *for* whom the world is presented and by whom it is organized. This self is 'the vehicle of all concepts',[1] and therefore is presupposed in all knowledge we may have of the world. In Hume there is no hint of such an awareness. Indeed Hume denied that we could be aware of anything except impressions (or derived ideas) and he said there could be no impression of the self. Awareness of the self in the Kantian sense was non-empirical. It was universal, the same for everyone, *transcendental*, in that it was necessarily presupposed by experience. It is virtually certain that Coleridge learned of this sense of 'self' from German philosophy derived from Kant, or from an actual reading of Kant.

We should not risk, therefore, claiming any of Coleridge's views as his own original thought, even those which look most as if they were derived from his own introspection. What we can do, as Mill suggested, is simply to note the form and shape that his philosophical speculations took.

With this in mind, we may yet find the distinction between his psychological observations about the workings of imagination and his second-order speculations about this working a useful guideline. I shall accordingly start from the consideration of what Coleridge believed the creative imagination was; the account, that is, which he held to be psychologically correct, and subject to confirmation in experience.

I shall start with Coleridge's sense of loss, the loss of his own imaginative power, as a way of showing what he thought this imaginative power consisted in. I shall start, that is, with introspection and try to show how Coleridge moved from the findings

[1] *Critique of Pure Reason*, B 132 and B 400.

of introspection to the more theoretical 'I'; how he moved from what Kant might call the empirical to the transcendental Ego. What exactly he felt himself to have lost in losing his imaginative powers is most completely expressed in 'Dejection: an Ode', written in 1802. We must therefore turn to this ode, and read it, not in an attempt to answer any questions about its origins (what made him feel as he did), nor its sources in a more strictly literary sense, but simply to see what it tells us about Coleridge's beliefs—what he thought the imagination was. I quote the relevant passage:

Having described the stars behind the clouds, and the crescent moon, Coleridge says:

> 'I see them all so excellently fair
> I see, not feel, how beautiful they are.
>
> My genial spirits fail;
> And what can these avail
> To lift the smothering weight from off my breast?
> It were a vain endeavour
> Though I should gaze for ever
> On that green light that lingers in the west:
> I may not hope from outward forms to win
>
> The passion and the life, whose fountains are within.
>
> O Lady we receive but what we give
> And in our life alone does nature live . . .
>
> Ah, from the soul itself must issue forth
> A light, a glory, a fair luminous cloud
> Enveloping the earth . . .
> And from the soul itself must there be sent
> A sweet and potent voice, of its own birth,
> Of all sweet sounds the life and element.'

Coleridge then identifies the strong music of the soul with joy, 'joy is the sweet voice, joy the luminous cloud . . . We in ourselves rejoice.' And then, in the sixth stanza:

'There was a time when though my path was rough
This joy within me dallied with distress,
And all misfortunes were but as the stuff
Whence fancy made me dreams of happiness:

For hope grew round me, like the twining vine,
And fruits and foliage, not my own, seemed mine.
But now afflictions bow me down to earth
Nor care I that they rob me of my mirth;
But oh each visitation
Suspends what nature gave me at my birth
My shaping spirit of imagination.'

Imagination then, which is characterized as 'shaping', is essentially connected with joy. And joy is something that comes from within, 'we in ourselves rejoice'. Without this joy we merely see; and we may even see that things are beautiful, but we cannot feel that they are so. It is joy which converts a perception to a feeling, and it is this that is lost in the loss of the shaping power of imagination. We cannot help being reminded, though the words and the context are so different, of Hume's statement that it is the imagination which converts an idea to an impression.

Imagination, then, has two functions which go together; to shape by means of an *inner* power, and to allow us to feel. A similar distinction between what is merely seen and what is felt may be found in Coleridge's Notebook entry for 10th May, 1804[1] when he was on the way to Malta. Once again the fact that one may see things without feeling is connected by him with the lack of the shaping power to transform what is seen into something else. 'Whither have my animal spirits departed? My hopes—O me that they which once I had to check should now be an effort, Royals and Studding sails and the whole canvas stretched to catch the feeble breeze. I have many thoughts, many images; large stores of the unwrought materials; scarcely a day passes but something new in fact or in illustration, rises up in me like Herbs and Flowers in a garden in early Spring. But the combining power, the power to do, the manly effective Will, that is dead or slumbers most diseasedly.' The entry ends with some obscure words on the unconscious workings of the imagination—the kind of entry so common in the Notebooks (of which the 'wall'

[1] No. 2086.

example was another), part description of experience, or derived from experience, part remembered philosophical doctrine. He writes, 'Poetry is a rationalised dream, dealing to manifold forms our own feelings that never perhaps were attached consciously to our own personal selves. What is the Lear, the Othello, a divine dream all Shakespeare and nothing Shakespeare. O there are truths below the surface in the subject of sympathy, and how we become that which we understandingly behold and hear, having, how much God only knows, created part even of the form.' There are hints here of the generalizing and symbol-constructing functions of imagination which were crucial to Coleridge's analysis. A poet of genius, a Shakespeare, invests certain ideas or forms, such as the idea of Lear or Othello, with his own feelings which are yet universal, not personal or unique to himself. It so happens that though not consciously chosen, the chosen form is of universal significance, and therefore the emotions annexed to it become universal and shared as well. Moreover in contemplating these forms, we ourselves are to some extent creating them. To have an idea and to understand someone else's idea cannot be wholly separated. All these universalizing functions, both of Shakespeare's imagination and, on a lesser scale, of his readers', are the *combining* power. It is this power whose loss Coleridge is bewailing in the first part of the entry.

Norman Fruman in his study of Coleridge[1] suggests that where Coleridge speaks of 'hope' and 'manly effectiveness', he is in fact speaking of his fears that he is becoming impotent. The accumulation of evidence is such as to make this highly probable. But this provides no reason to doubt that Coleridge was *also* here quite sincerely regretting his failing imaginative powers, and in identically the same words. I am not suggesting that sexual impotence and imaginative impotence are the same, but only that thinking about the one may be indistinguishable from thinking about the other; the same images, the same feelings (of power, of possession, of successful *activity*) may spontaneously arise in either case. That Coleridge was becoming impotent may well be true; but that does not make his diagnosis of the nature of the imagination he has also lost any less valid. We need not think that he was *really* talking about his sexual powers, and therefore *not really* talking about his imaginative powers.

[1] *Coleridge: The Damaged Archangel* (George Allen and Unwin, 1971).

There are many other clues to the way in which the combining power of the imagination was thought to operate. In a Notebook entry for December 1804[1] when he was working in Malta, there is a rare example of Coleridge being quite funny, or at least quite sardonic, about himself. He writes, 'There are two sorts of talkative fellows whom it would be injurious to confound, and I, S. T. Coleridge, am the latter. The first sort is those who use five hundred words more than needs to express an idea . . . The second sort is of those who use five hundred more ideas, images etc than there is any need of to arrive at their object . . . Now this is my case—and a grievous fault it is. My illustrations swallow up my thesis. I feel too intensely the omnipresence of all in each, platonically speaking, or psychologically my brain-fibres or the spiritual light which abides in the brain marrow, as visible light appears to do in sundry rotten mackerel and other smashy matters is of too general an affinity with all things. And though it perceives the difference of things, yet is eternally pursuing the likeness, or rather that which is common. Bring me two things that seem the very same, and then I am quick enough to shew the difference, even to hair-splitting; but to go on from circle to circle till I break against the shore of my hearer's patience or have my Concentricals dashed to nothing by a Snore, this is my ordinary mishap.' Obviously it would be a mistake, in considering such a passage as this, to press the meaning too hard; but at the same time it is helpful to consider at least one instance where Coleridge is writing spontaneously—a thought struck him, and he wrote it down (or so it seems), and the thought was about the way his own mind worked. He *felt* intensely 'the omnipresence of all in each', and the 'all' is the universal or common idea platonically speaking, in which the particular participates, or which it can be seen to instantiate. Coleridge is saying of himself that he treats any particular, though it is an individual thing, different from other things, as an instance of something else, as signifying a universal. His 'concentrics' are the different ideas at the centre of which the individual thing stands—the thing which tends to get lost in his kind of conversation.

But he is also capable of seeing at other times that this very universality may be expressed merely by concentration on the individual itself. In writing of a man's changing taste in poetry,

[1] No. 2372.

for example (March 1805)[1] he says, 'Becoming more intimately acquainted with Nature in her detail, we are delighted with distinct vivid ideas and with vivid ideas most when made distinct, and can most often forgive—even a low image—when it *gives you the very thing* through illustration.' Admittedly in this passage Coleridge is talking about taste and style, about simile, and the way in which a poet may make something live for us. But, again remembering Hume, and his remarks on the orator who has the imaginative power to turn our ideas into impressions, we are justified in seeing here a suggestion that in the consideration of the *particular*, the general significance can be found and contemplated, and that in such contemplation a *feeling* for the thing presented is an essential part.

Coleridge connects the awareness of the universal in the particular quite specifically with emotion in a Notebook entry in February 1805,[2] an entry which is important for our purposes. 'On Friday night 8th February 1805 my feeling, in sleep, of exceeding great love for my infant seen by me in the dream, yet so that it might be Sara, Derwent or Berkeley, and still *it was an individual babe and mine*. Of love in sleep—a sort of *universal-in-particularness* of Form seems necessary—*vide* the note preceding, and my lines "All look or Likeness caught from Earth, All accident of Kind or Birth, Had passed away: there seemed no trace of Aught upon the brighten'd face Upraised beneath the rifted stone, Save of one Spirit, all her own. She, she herself and only She, shone in her body visibly." This abstract self is indeed in its nature a Universal personified ... will not this prove it (sc. Love) to be a deeper feeling, and with such intimate affinity with ideas, so to modify them and become one with them, whereas the appetites and the feelings of revenge and anger coexist with the ideas, not combine with them; and alter the apparent effect of the forms, not the forms themselves. Certain modifications of fear seem to approach nearest to this love-sense in its manner of acting.' Here Coleridge seems to me to be saying two things. First, that if, in the absence of a real object, one has a very vivid image of it (a Form) then there is a necessary connexion between feeling love for it (or fear of it) and seeing the form as somehow standing for a universal or general thing, as well as the particular thing of which it is the form or image. Secondly, he suggests that love and some sorts of

---

[1] No. 2484.   [2] No. 2441.

fear are the *only* emotions which have this universalizing power, which make us feel, that is, that the image before us has a general significance beyond itself, though still retaining its particular character. (It will become obvious, I hope, that these thoughts are so Wordsworthian that it would be idle here to try to sort out priorities.) We see here connected three things: the power of the imagination to conjure up an image; its power to make us see the image as universally significant; and its power to induce in us deep feelings in the presence of the image. We could not feel the love or the fear in question unless we had before us the representation of the object of love or fear. Neither emotion could have its effect without the presence of at least a substitute object. But the representation could not be formed as *generally* significant unless the emotion existed. These three things together make up the *combining power* of the imagination.

The above example was concerned first of all with an image presented in a dream. And obviously dream-images can have a peculiar vividness, and can therefore well be used to illustrate the imaginative power. But this power could be displayed in deliberately-formed images of waking life, and *may* also be displayed when there is an actual real object of contemplation before one. This is of crucial importance. The form in the dream or in our inner eye which is created by imagination arises along with powerful feelings. The representation and the feelings are inextricably mixed. But the same feelings and therefore the same conviction of the existence of the universal in the particular *may* arise when we contemplate an actual scene; and when this is so, we must equally recognize that it is imagination at work. One may compare the dream passage above with another Notebook entry written the previous December, of an actual observed object.[1] ' "O" said I, as I looked on the blue, yellow, green and purple-green Sea with all its hollows and swells and cut-glass surfaces—"O what an ocean of lovely forms"—and I was vexed, teazed, that the sentence sounded like a play of words. But it was not; the mind within me was struggling to express the marvellous distinctness and unconfounded personality of each of the million million of forms, and yet the undivided Unity in which they subsisted.' And in almost the next entry:[2] 'O that sky, that soft blue mighty arch resting on the mountains of solid sea-like plain, what *an aweful*

[1] No. 2344.   [2] No. 2346.

adorable omneity in unity.' To enable us to see images or individual forms of things as universally significant; to enable us in the same way to see objects in the world before us as of more than particular significance, and at the same time, and by the same process, to cause us to feel both love and fear, this seems to be the function of imagination.

We catch glimpses of truth by means of imagination. But the truths which we glimpse are not truths *about* the world; if they can be said to be about anything, it must be about ourselves. In observing the world we are necessarily aware of ourselves the observers. Here, once again, we enter the area where it is impossible to pick out what Coleridge finds in himself and what he has learned by reading Kant and Fichte and Schelling, or by talking to Wordsworth.

There is a famous passage in the Notebooks dated 14th April, 1805,[1] where he expresses what seems almost to sum up his thoughts. 'In looking at the objects of Nature while I am thinking, as at yonder moon dim-glimmering through the dewy window-pane, I seem rather to be seeking, as it were *asking*, a symbolic language for something within me that already and forever exists, than observing anything new. Even when that latter is the case, yet I still have always an obscure feeling as if that new phaenomenon were the dim Awaking of a forgotten or hidden Truth of my inner Nature. It is still interesting as a Word a Symbol.' If this passage seems to sum up his thought, it also seems typical of the origin of his thought. For he goes straight on, with no apparent break, to raise the following question 'What is the right, the virtuous feeling, and consequent action, when a man having long meditated and perceived a certain Truth finds another and a foreign Writer who has handled the same with an approximation to the Truth as he had previously conceived it?' It seems a fair inference that the second passage was suggested to him by the content of the first, and that in the first, as in the 'wall' passage quoted earlier, Coleridge was quite knowingly writing something which came more or less from the German, though attached in this case to his own situation as he looked out of the window. We could want no clearer example of the genesis of his ideas.

What has emerged so far is a concept of imagination as some-

[1] No. 2546.

thing working actively from within to enable us to perceive the general in the particular, to make us treat the particular, whether something we see or something we call up as an image, as symbolic, as meaning something beyond itself. Ideas of imagination cannot be called up by *mere* association, nor by mere likeness to one another or to what is seen. The imagination is not merely passive; it is an active combining power which *brings* ideas together, and which is at work to create the forms of things which seem to speak to us of the universal, and which at the same time necessarily cause in us feelings of love and awe.

So far I have tried to confine myself to what is relatively empirical, to that which Coleridge relates, at least in some way, to his own experience. But the move from observation and self-observation to the more grandiose theories which concern The Self rather than his own self, and The Imagination rather than his own imaginings must now be followed. To some extent this transition from empirical observation to theory, or theory-laden observation, can be traced through the Notebooks and letters. It is certainly harder as the years go by (if one studies them chronologically) to find any 'pure' descriptions, whether of nature or of psychological occurrences.

But, as I have suggested, even in using this evidence we must be careful. For it may be that in the period from 1797 until 1802, in which Coleridge recorded most of his direct and ostensibly spontaneous observations, he was nevertheless partly working on the theory which would finally seem to make such observations worth recording. He may, in part at least, have been developing a set of beliefs learned both from Wordsworth and from Dorothy Wordsworth, and, in characteristic style, have taken over from them something which he perhaps dimly thought that he could use. This is the period of his closest contact with the Wordsworths. And I sometimes get the feeling (but it is hard to substantiate this) that he himself very seldom experienced any close connexion between particular images and general insights, but believed that such connexions *ought* to exist. It is even possible to interpret the sense of loss which, as we have seen, he recorded most movingly in the 'Dejection' Ode, not as the sense of a *real* loss of something he once had, but rather as envy, as nostalgia for someone else's past, the longing for someone else's insights.

In July 1802 he wrote to Sotheby, in a letter suggesting some disagreements between himself and Wordsworth on the nature of poetry, 'A great poet must be, implicitè if not explicitè, a profound metaphysician. He may not have it in logical coherence, in his Brain and Tongue . . . but he must have the ear of a wild Arab listening in the silent desert, the eye of a North American Indian tracing the footsteps of an Enemy upon the Leaves that Strew the Forest.'[1] Here he certainly subscribed to the view that the imagination works *in* perception, and that the greater the genius, the keener the perception itself will be. In this spirit, we can read some of the Notebook entries for the years immediately before. For instance, in a famous entry dated October 1799[2] he wrote (at Barnard Castle): 'River Greta near its fall into the Tees . . . Shootings of water threads down the slope of the huge green stone—The white eddy-rose that blossom'd up against the stream in the scollop, by fits and starts, obstinate in resurrection—It *is the life* that we live.' In this passage we feel that the eye sees *in* the whirlpool the life that we live. There is a natural symbolism in the water which nevertheless could not be grasped unless the eye itself were peculiarly observant. But by 1803 we see from the Notebooks that Coleridge himself was collecting up such observations, and, as it were, *trying them out* as images. There is an entry dated October 1803[3] and headed 'Images' in which he went back over the earlier notebooks and recorded again not only the white rose of eddy foam at Barnard Castle, but several other observations from his Scottish tour, ending with 'A Host of little winged flies on the snow mangled by the Hail Storm, near the top of Helvellin.' Here his observations are being deliberately and self-consciously worked over, and selected as meaningful. In the same year there is an entry made under the influence of laudanum, which suggests his by now strong conviction that very powerful images, whether laudanum-induced or recollected from earlier concentrated looking or listening, *must* contain some meaning, *must* be capable of a general interpretation. In the entry of 23rd November 1803[4] he records 'much excitement, though very very far short of intoxication, tho' I had taken a considerable Quantity

---

[1] *Collected Letters of Samuel Taylor Coleridge*, edited by E. L. Griggs (O.U.P., 1956), vol. 2, p. 808.

[2] No. 495.   [3] No. 1589.   [4] No. 1681.

of laudanum', and he goes on, 'I put out the candles, and closed my eyes, and instantly there appeared a spectrum, of a Pheasant's tail that altered thro' various degradations into round wrinkly shapes, as of Horse excrement, or baked apples—indeed exactly like the latter—round baked apples, with exactly the same colour, the same intra-circular wrinkles, something like horse-dung, still more like flat baked or dried apples, such as they are brought in after dinner . . . *Why* those concentric wrinkles?' And then he records that he went to the window and he describes exactly what he saw: 'Over the black form-retaining Mountains the Horizon of Sky grey-white all round the whole turn of my Eye; the Sky above chiefly dark, but not nearly so black as the space between my eye and the lake, which is one formless Black, or as the black nothing-but-form-and-colour mountains beyond the grey-steely glimmery Lake and River, and this diminished Blackness mottled by the not-far-from setting half-moon . . . *O that I could but explain these concentric Wrinkles in my Spectra.*' The explanation, if he could only have found it, would presumably have been an explanation, not of their cause, but of their *sense*, and it was for this he was searching while gazing out at the dark landscape, and allowing other actual forms and images to occupy his eyes. But no interpretation came to him. It is worth remembering that all his great poetry had been written by this time. Even the 'Dejection' ode, in which his imagination is mourned for, is two years away.

From this time on, the whole question of meaning or symbolism of natural objects comes up more and more frequently and explicitly in the Notebook entries and in a more purely theoretical spirit. For instance, in November 1804[1] he wrote, 'Hard to express that sense of the analogy or likeness of a thing which enables a symbol to represent it, so that we think of the Thing itself—and yet knowing that the thing is not present to us. Surely on this universal fact of words and images depends . . . the imitation, instead of copy, which is illustrated in very nature shakespeareanised—that Proteus Essence that could assume the very form, but yet known and felt not to be the Thing by that difference of the Substance which made every atom of the Form another thing—that likeness, not identity—an exact web, every line of direction miraculously the same, but one worsted, the

[1] No. 2274.

other silk.' Again, the next month, there is the entry quoted already (see p. 82) which explicitly introduces the theoretical concepts of the sublime and the beautiful, which starts with the particulars observed: 'that Sky, that soft blue mighty Arch resting on the mountains or solid sea-like plain, what an aweful adorable omneity in unity.' Again, in the May of 1806,[1] we see him quite explicitly searching for symbols: 'The quiet circle in which Change and Permanence coexist, not by combination or juxtaposition, but by an absolute annihilation of difference—column of smoke, the fountains before St. Peter's, waterfalls, God— Change without loss—change by perpetual growth, that once constitutes and annihilates change, the past and the future included in the present—Oh it is aweful.' The identity between seeing or observing in detail, feeling, and seeing-as-symbolic comes out increasingly strongly. In the spring of 1807[2] there is a whole series of entries which link these concepts: 'the eyes quietly and steadfastly dwelling on an object, not as if looking at it or as in any way exerting an act of sight upon it, but as if the whole attention were listening to *what the heart was feeling and saying about it*.' The imagination is now thought of as actively working (even when the senses *seem* merely to be receiving impressions) to provide the insights which stem from the contemplation of images. The insights come from treating the objects of sense as symbolic; from treating them, that is, as referring to something beyond themselves. It is the function of imagination to provide this kind of seeing.

There is no doubt that by 1803, at the very latest, Coleridge had abandoned the theory of the passive nature of mind and the mechanical association of ideas to which he had previously been attached, and was substituting for it an active and creative role for the imagination, which we have seen him struggling to express.

In 1796 Coleridge had called his eldest son Hartley to show his admiration for that philosopher, who was, above all, famous for associationism. Hartley's *Observations on Man* was published in 1749, eleven years after Hume's *Treatise*, and a year after the first part of Hume's *Enquiry*. In 1794 Coleridge had written to Southey, 'I am a complete necessitarian, and understand the subject almost as well as Hartley himself, but I go further than Hartley.'[3] Being

[1] No. 2832. [2] Nos. 3027 ff.
[3] Griggs, vol.I, p. 137.

a Necessitarian meant believing that the impressions we get from the senses are necessarily and mechanically connected with other impressions or with the ideas derived from them, and originally contiguous with the first impressions. Thus, if I experience a particular sense impression, it will immediately call up ideas of other experiences which have formerly gone with it. One can therefore, entirely without fail, influence the growth of a child's mind by presenting him with experiences in series over and over again, so that he cannot help but think of the whole series if he thinks of any member of it. Like Hume, Hartley thought of experience as consisting of small discrete particles of sensation or thought, coming one after another, each as it were dragging the next with it in a chain of association. Like Hume, his language in speaking of such experience was often borrowed from Newton. The notion of one idea attracting another was central, and it was never wholly clear how literal or metaphorical such language was supposed to be. Hartley's view of the association of ideas was simpler, however, than Hume's. No other relation between ideas had to be presupposed, in his theory, except the temporal. Moreover, unlike Hume, he combined his mechanical associationist theory with extreme optimism about the human condition. Pleasures outnumber pains, and one can come, by habituation, to associate pleasure, not pain, with more and more high-minded and complex ideas. Thus human beings are infinitely capable of improving themselves or being improved. Indeed, such improvement must necessarily take place, since the process of associating pleasure gradually with higher and higher forms of experience is inevitable. A man cannot create new impressions or new ideas for himself; he can do no more than accept what comes to him through the senses. But if he is exposed to the right stimuli, he will gradually, through the habit of association, come to the highest condition of which he is capable, the framing of proper moral concepts. All this had been accepted by Coleridge, and was now rejected by him. At the same time he became critical specifically of Hume's view that our perception of the world can be thought to come in separable units or impressions. In December 1804[1] he wrote, 'how opposite to nature and to fact to talk of the *one moment* of Hume; of our whole being an aggregate of successive single sensations. Who ever felt a *single sensation*? Is not every-

[1] Notebook, No. 2370.

one at the same moment conscious that there coexist a thousand others in a darker shade or less light; even as, when I fix my attention on a white house on a grey bare hill, or rather long ridge that runs out of sight each way—the pretended single sensation, is it anything more than the light-point in every picture, either of nature or of a good painter, and again subordinately in every part of the picture? And what is a moment? It is evidently only the *licht-punct*, the Sparkle of the indivisible individed duration.' There is a unity, that is to say, in our perceptions of the world *as we have them*; and it is noticeable that in this passage Coleridge speaks of our vision of the world and of pictures as if they were practically the same. In either case the imagination as it were constructs *a scene* for us to look at, and within which we concentrate on some high-light.

By now, of course, the philosophical voice of the Germans is beginning to take over altogether. It would be impossible in a reasonable compass to expound all of Coleridge's metaphysical speculations which bear upon the imagination, even if all were available to us. Still less would it be manageable to ascribe every element in these speculations to its source in Kant or Fichte, in Schelling or Schlegel. Even where Coleridge was willing to allow that he was borrowing, he often got the ascription wrong, for there is evidence to suggest that he thought Fichte and Schelling far more original than they actually were. It is fairly clear that in general he misconceived the comparative stature of Kant and his followers.[1]

In any case, rather than undertake such a hopeless task, I shall start with some of the best-known passages in Coleridge which deal explicitly with the *theory* of imagination, and try to show how he thought that the faculty which he himself used, and which he had attempted from time to time to describe, was related to other powers of the mind, and to the universe as a whole. (For idealism, as we have seen, forces one to go as far as this in speculation. If ideas are both in the mind and in nature, one cannot stop at

[1] This may be a misleading way of putting it. Perhaps it was that Coleridge, misunderstanding Kant (see below), genuinely failed to see much difference between him and his successors in point of philosophical system. Certainly writing to Gooden in 1820 (Griggs vol. V, p. 13) he said 'I by no means recommend to you an extension of your philosophic researches beyond Kant. In him is contained everything that can be *learnt*.'

psychology, though one may start from there.) We should first
glance back at the 'wall' passage from his Notebooks (see page 74),
and notice that by 1802 Coleridge had taken over the distinction
between the Ego and the Non-Ego from Fichte. From this arose
the conclusion that a philosopher who wished to frame a theory
of knowledge, of imagination or of perception would in fact be
framing a theory of The Self. It is not that he would be intro-
specting or reminiscing about himself, but rather that in himself
he would find what was true of *the self*, universally. The transcendental, not the empirical, self would be his subject-matter. All
metaphysical theories whatever must start from this point. That
Coleridge believed this to be true accounts for a good deal of his
otherwise somewhat mysterious language, in which he claims,
for example, to be exploring 'The world without and the still
more wonderful world within'[1] or to be about to publish a book
entitled 'The Mysteries of religion grounded in or relative to the
Mysteries of Human Nature.'[2] It seems clear that Coleridge was
not particularly careful to distinguish the empirical from the
transcendental self. Introspection, or self-observation, seemed as
likely to give rise to general as to particular truths. Moreover, as
we have seen, the step taken by Fichte and Schelling to turn
Kantian theory into idealism, meant that it also became a matter
of indifference whether one spoke of the mind or of nature. The
philosophy of nature was a matter of reading off the mind's own
ideas. This is a continuous element in Coleridge's thought, from
the moment when he first encountered the work of Fichte and
Schelling. In forming a theory of mind (including a theory of
imagination) one was also, and at the same time, forming a theory
of nature.

Let us now consider the brief summary of an account of imagination which, after the elaborate preparation and preliminaries,
was all that Coleridge produced in *Biographia Literaria*. Short
though it is, it is presented as a systematic statement of conclusions systematically arrived at (though in fact it is obviously
nothing of the kind). We may reasonably take it, in any case, as a
clue to some of Coleridge's beliefs. 'The imagination then', he

---

[1] Huntington Library MS: *Coleridge Collected Letters*, vol. III, p. 279, ed. E. L.
Griggs (O.U.P., 1956).

[2] Griggs, vol. III, p. 279.

wrote, 'I consider either as primary or secondary. The primary imagination I hold to be the living power and prime agent of all human perception and as a repetition in the finite mind of the eternal act of creation in the infinite I AM. The secondary I consider as an echo of the former, coexisting with the conscious will, yet still as identical with the primary in the *kind* of its agency, and differing only in *degree* and in the *mode* of its operation. It dissolves, diffuses, dissipates, in order to recreate; or where this process is rendered impossible, yet still at all events it struggles to idealize and unify. It is essentially vital, even as all objects (*as* objects) are essentially fixed and dead.'[1]

As to the primary imagination, here we have a clear reference, first of all, to the function of imagination in all perception of and therefore all knowledge of the world. This is the role of imagination set out in the *Critique of Pure Reason*. But the creativity of this imagination is in a sense more like Schelling than like Kant. In *The System of Transcendental Idealism*[2] Schelling distinguishes between the 'productive intuition' and the 'poetic faculty'. The existence of nature is deduced from the productive faculty of the absolute I; and, as we have already seen, what was an *active* function, constituting the world-as-it-appears-to-us, in Kant becomes, in Schelling, a properly *creative* function constituting the world as it really is. All the concrete forms of nature itself are actually made by the productive intuition. How far did Coleridge go with Schelling against Kant? It may be said that he is not completely committed, at least in this passage, to idealism; for the work of actual creation is ascribed to the deity, while the human imagination is a 'repetition' in human terms of this divine activity. Perhaps we must be content to say that there is no clear answer to the question whether, in Coleridge's view, the imagination does or does not create the world. Lack of clarity on such a 'profound' question need not after all surprise us.

The poetic faculty, which is presumably the origin of Coleridge's secondary imagination, is described by Schelling thus: 'The poetic faculty is what in the first potency is original intuition, and vice versa: the productive intuition which repeats itself in the first power is what we call the poetic faculty. What is active in both is one and the same, the only faculty by which we become capable

[1] *Biographia Literaria*, Chapter XIII.
[2] *Schelling's Works*, ed. Manfred Schröter (Munich, 1927), vol. III, p. 626.

of thinking and understanding even the contradictory, the imagination.'[1]

So imagination is divided into two kinds, the productive intuition, and the poetic. Schelling, in the passage just quoted, attempts to justify speaking of the productive intuition as one kind of imagination, and it seems fairly clear that Coleridge was prepared to do this much. With regard to the secondary imagination, he seems to follow Schelling even more closely. The essential activity of the secondary imagination is *re*-creation of something out of the materials which we have first acquired from perception. It is apparent that Coleridge identifies the effort of the imagination to make something out of the materials it has acquired with its effort to idealize and to unify (to combine). Presumably the simple rehearsal of mental images, reproducing in representations what we have already acquired in perception, would not count as the work of the poetic imagination, and would be ascribed to memory alone. Imagination has to do more. It must try to create *one thing* (one thought or one form) out of the many different elements of experience; and this entails *extracting the essence* of the differing phenomena of experience.

From Schelling, then, Coleridge derived the thought that poetic imagination must be able to bring together, as Schelling says, even contradictories. He coined the word 'esemplastic' for the imagination, an epithet to which he ascribed the meaning 'shaping into one'.[2] Elsewhere he gave the word the form 'esenoplastic' and thought of it apparently as a translation of the German '*Einbildungskraft*'. In a Notebook entry which forms part of the *Ars Poetica* (compiled from the Notebooks by E. H. Coleridge) he wrote, 'How excellently the German word "Einbildungskraft" expresses this prime and loftiest faculty, the power of coadunation, the faculty that forms the many into one, In-Einsbildung. Esenoplasy or Esenoplastic power is contradistinguished from fantasy or mirrorment, repeating simply or by transposition.' It is impossible to be certain of the date of this passage, but that is not a matter of great importance. It is clear that Coleridge was impressed by the word used for imagination both by Kant and by Schelling; and he made it mean what he hoped it would mean. He assumed that the prefix '*ein* . . .' was derived from '*Ein*' meaning 'one'. In fact it is derived from '*In*'; and the whole word

---

[1] *loc. cit.*   [2] *Biographia Literaria*, chap. X.

means 'forming a picture *in* the mind'. But his false assumption at least provides evidence that Coleridge believed that the function of imagination was to bring together disparate or opposite materials.

But how did the question of opposites arise? Schelling first presented his theory of art in *The System of Transcendental Idealism*. He asserted there that it was the function of art to resolve conflicts. The aim of art was to show that, beneath apparent opposites, there is really a unity, of conscious with unconscious, of finite with infinite, of freedom with necessity. The faculty by which human beings can hope to effect this reconciliation in art is of course the imagination. There seems to be no doubt that Coleridge accepted this, lock, stock and barrel. In chapter XIV of *Biographia Literaria*, speaking of the poet, he wrote, 'He diffuses a tone and spirit of unity . . . by that synthetic and magical power to which we have exclusively appropriated the name of imagination. This power, first put into action by the will and understanding, and retained under their unremissive though gentle and unnoticed control, reveals itself in the balance or reconciliation of opposite or discordant qualities: of sameness with difference; of the general with the concrete; the idea with the image; the individual with the representative.' Here is an amazing mixture. The language of the 'synthetic and magical power' is of course Kantian. The opposites to be reconciled by poetic imagination seem to have their origin in Schelling, and the most noticeable pairs are the last two, 'the idea with the image', and 'the individual with the representative'. To avoid ambiguities, Coleridge should have put the last two items in the reverse order: 'the general', 'the representative', 'the idea'—all these must go together in contrast with 'the concrete', 'the image', 'the individual'. But this is a small point. It simply adds to the impression, which it is hard to resist, that Coleridge was here writing without thinking, just playing about with the remembered counters. And this impression is confirmed by the fact that immediately after the quoted passage, he goes on in a different manner, apparently talking not about transcendental psychology but about style. The reconciliation is now of 'the sense of novelty and freshness with old familiar objects; a more than usual state of emotion with a more than usual order; judgment ever awake and steady self-possession, with enthusiasm and feeling profound or vehement; and while the power blends and

G
93

harmonises the natural and the artificial, still subordinates art to nature; the manner to the matter; and our admiration of the poet to our sympathy with the poetry.' It would take us too far from our course to attempt to trace all these last observations to their sources. Some of them came, no doubt, from Wordsworth, or at least from reflection on Wordsworth's poetry, and the prefaces to *Lyrical Ballads*. Others came, doubtless, from the stock-in-trade of literary critics. But the beginning of the passage does not have reference only to poetry. Coleridge here lays down a role for creative imagination which could be applied to art as a whole. It was this wide concept of art that was central to Schelling's philosophy; and this part of the passage must be taken as the German or philosophical part.

The distinction between primary and secondary imagination is not maintained in the rest of Coleridge's philosophical writing. It seems in fact to have been a distinction, adopted indeed from Schelling, but used especially in the context of the focal point of *Biographia Literaria*, the *poetic* imagination. But where he is concerned not specifically with poetry, but with what we may call generalized or transcendental psychology (which in him spills over, Existentialist-fashion, into the philosophy of life), where he is, that is to say, adopting the role, not of a literary critic, but of a proper philosopher, then he is concerned no longer with primary and secondary imagination, but with imagination as a mediator between reason and understanding. For he takes over this Kantian distinction. But, whether knowingly or not, he takes it over in its transformed idealist form, as he found it in Fichte and Schelling. Let us see what he made of it.

Understanding is the faculty by which we acquire exact, scientific and factual knowledge of the world. It is, as Kant said, the faculty which deals in concepts and rules. Reason on the other hand is the faculty of ideas. But ideas are no longer, as they were in Kant, merely regulative, lying altogether outside our grasp. Already transformed by Schelling, ideas for Coleridge are what actually lie behind all the forms of nature. They are the objects of our intuition, what we glimpse behind the world. For nature itself, as we saw, is, in Schelling's theory, something which we create. It is, to put it crudely, a mental entity. So there is no harshness in saying that ideas are *in*, or are *constitutive of*, nature. In this connexion, Coleridge was fond of dividing people into Platonists and Aristotelians. In a letter to Gooden (14th January, 1820)[1] he wrote, 'There neither are, have been, nor ever will be but two essentially different schools of philosophy: the Platonic and the Aristotelian. To the latter ... Emanuel Kant belonged; to the former Bacon and Leibniz and in his riper and better years Berkeley, and to this I profess myself an adherent. He for whom ideas are constitutive will in effect be a Platonist and for those for whom they are regulative only Platonism must be a hollow affection.' As a matter of fact, for what it is worth, Kant would have denied that he was more Aristotelian than Platonic. In the *Critique of Pure Reason*[2] he says of Plato, 'He knew that our reason naturally exalts itself to forms of knowledge which so far transcend the bounds of experience that no given material object can ever coincide with them, but which must none the less be recognised as having their own reality, and which are by no means fictions of the brain.' And these are ideas. He thus presents Plato's ideas as, like his own ideas of reason, existing essentially beyond our experience. To this extent, then, he would perhaps have claimed to be a Platonist.

But all that this shows is that the dichotomy of Platonists and Aristotelians is misleading. It also, I think, shows how confused Coleridge's view of Kant's theory actually was. For Coleridge was a reader with neither historical sense nor the ability to distinguish things which are different. He was perfectly prepared to treat the ideas of reason as genuinely identical with Platonic ideas, and to hold that, in placing them beyond exemplification in any object of the senses, Kant was somehow saying that they did not exist.

Moreover, there is independent evidence that Coleridge misconceived the Kantian sense of 'Understanding' which was correlative with reason. He sometimes spoke of the categories, or pure concepts of the understanding, as conceptions *formed from materials furnished by the senses*; that is to say, he did not grasp the difference, absolutely crucial to Kant's theory, between the *a priori* and the *a posteriori*, between what we bring to the world, and what we collect from it. He thought of the understanding as forming rules *from* given sensible examples (in Kant the function of the judgment not the understanding). The whole nature of Kant's Copernican Revolution, according to which he argues that the

<hr>

[1] Griggs, vol. V, p. 13.   [2] A 314.

understanding *applies* concepts *a priori to* the materials of the senses, seems to have escaped him, and, as he misunderstood 'Understanding', so he also misunderstood 'Reason'.[1] We must not look in Coleridge, then, for any consistent or detailed understanding of Kant. Instead we must think of him as choosing, among whatever philosophers he read, what suited his own tastes. Thus, we can easily understand what it was in Schelling's philosophy that appealed to him. For we have seen how Coleridge thought his own imagination worked, how it enabled him first to separate himself from the object of his thought or his perception, and then to discover in the particular object a general form; then how deep feeling was connected with this discovery, uniting the separated self, which feels, once again with the object which the same self perceives. So it was not simply that he read first Kant and then Schelling, and regarded Schelling as an improvement on Kant. It was rather that he found in Schelling an account of the unifying function of the imagination, its ability to pierce the superficial shell of the particular and the individual and to reveal the universal idea, which he had been groping towards himself.

Both Hume and Kant had seen the connection between the imagination as it functions in our ordinary life in the world, and the imagination of the poet or the genius, which they were inclined to say was simply a special, heightened, form of the imagination we all possess. But within the framework of Schelling's philosophy the connexion between the poetic or generally artistic use of the imagination and its use in ordinary life is

[1] The confusion of Kant's philosophy, and particularly the confusion over the meaning of Reason and Understanding is exemplified again in J. S. Mill's essay on Coleridge, which nevertheless gives so excellent an account of what Coleridge believed that it is worth quoting: 'He [Coleridge] claims for the human mind a capacity of perceiving the nature and properties of Things-in-Themselves. He distinguishes in the human intellect two faculties, which, in the technical language common to him with the Germans, he calls understanding and reason. The former faculty judges of phenomena, or the appearances of things, and forms generalisations from these: to the latter it belongs, by direct intuition, to perceive things, and recognize truths, not cognizable by our senses. These perceptions are not indeed innate, nor could ever have been awakened in us without experience; but they are not copies of it: experience is not their prototype, it is only the occasion by which they are irresistably suggested.' And Mill goes on to quote the empiricist criticism of such philosophy, that it makes 'imagination, and not observation, the criterion of truth' and that such philosophers 'lay down principles under which a man may enthrone his wildest dreams in the chair of philosophy'. A few hours of reading Coleridge's philosophical writings sharpens one's sympathies with the British empiricists; but they must not be allowed to include Kant in their strictures.

different. It is no longer enough to say that some people have
more imagination than others, and these are the artists. One can
be more specific than that. The artists are now supposed to be
those who perform largely consciously what the rest of us perform unconsciously. For them, the imagination is, at least in part,
subject to the will. The 'combining power' which Coleridge felt
himself to have lost, in losing his ability to write poetry, is the
power *voluntarily* to combine, *deliberately* to seek out the universal
significance in the particular perceived object. But even without
this special power, we must all of us *involuntarily* create for ourselves a significant universe and to some limited extent grasp those
ideas of reason which inform whatever we see and hear, whether
we are poets and artists or not. For, as we have seen, Schelling
held that 'the ideal work of art and the real world of objects are
products of one and the same activity' (see page 68). It is indeed true
that he also says (and Coleridge transcribes this in 'On Poetry or
Art') that the artistic genius works partially unconsciously. The
artist's genius consists in a balance between conscious and
unconscious activities. However, the impulse to create a new
world of art is conscious, while our impulse to create our own
perceptual world is necessarily below the level of consciousness,
as much for Schelling as indeed it was for Kant.

Yet more obviously, Coleridge was drawn to the theory of the
natural symbol which he found in post-Kantian German philosophers. Here, again it seems to me that he leapt, sometimes with
more enthusiasm than understanding, on a theory which exemplified what he *wanted* the imagination to be. By means of the symbol,
he hoped to show the imagination as that which somehow joined
the reason to the understanding. Kant had argued that we must
use imagination in order to connect the chaotic deliverances of the
senses to the orderly rules of the understanding, formed *a priori*
to be applied to the world. Only by means of our power to form
images could we represent to ourselves the manner in which a
general concept could apply to what we experience. Similarly,
Coleridge believed that the imagination could make the ideas of
reason concrete, by means of actual experienced objects. For reason
had become, as Mill put it, the faculty of intuitive knowledge of
all those general truths which were not scientific.

It is not at all certain to what extent Coleridge read or understood the *Critique of Judgment*. He might have found described

97

there, as we have seen, a faculty (the judgment) which, whether in science or criticism, drew general conclusions from particular instances, and also he might have found that what the artist was expressing was called an 'aesthetic idea', akin to an idea of reason, an idea which could not be completely expressed. Moreover in the *Critique of Judgment* Kant himself had drawn a parallel between the function of the imagination in enabling us, in perception, to apply the concepts of the understanding to the world, and, in art, to intuit, or partially intuit, aesthetic ideas. He says[1] that the presentation of concepts or ideas (the work of the imagination) can be divided into two kinds: 'Either it is schematic, as where the intuition corresponding to a concept comprehended by the understanding is given *a priori*, or else it is symbolic, as where the concept is one which only reason can think and to which no sensible intuition can be adequate. In the latter case the concept is supplied with an intuition such that the procedure of judgment in dealing with it is merely analogous to that which it observes in schematism ... *Schemata contain direct, symbolism indirect presentations of a concept.*' But for the developed doctrine of the symbol Coleridge did not need to search in Kant, but rather to read Schelling and Schlegel.

Perhaps the account of the symbol which lies closest to Coleridge's other beliefs about imagination is to be found in his Appendix C to *The Statesman's Manual*. He says, 'with particular reference to that Reason which I have attempted to contradistinguish from the Understanding, I seem to myself to behold in the quiet object on which I am gazing more than an arbitrary illustration, more than a mere *simile*, the work of my own fancy. I feel an awe, as if there were before my eyes the same power as that of the reason, the same power in a lower dignity, and therefore a symbol established in the truth of things. I feel it alike whether I contemplate a single flower or tree or meditate on vegetation throughout the world, as one of the great organs of the life of nature.' In Appendix B to *The Statesman's Manual*, in a passage very clearly borrowed from Schlegel,[2] he wrote, 'Now an Allegory is nothing but a translation of abstract notions into a picture language, which is itself nothing but an abstraction from

---

[1] *Critique of Judgment*, 59.

[2] Cf. A. W. Schlegel, *Lectures on Dramatic Art and Literature*, trans. J. Black (London, 1815), p. 88.

objects of the senses. On the other hand, a symbol is characterised
by a translucence of the special in the individual, of the general in
the special, of the universal in the general: above all by the translucence of the eternal through and in the temporal. It always par-
takes of the reality which it renders intelligible; and while it
enunciates the whole, abides itself as a living part in that unity of
which it is the representative.' So the natural symbol emerges as
something which the eye of the imagination alone can interpret as
meaningful. It actually *contains* the very properties which it also
signifies in general; and the interpretation suggests itself to us
inevitably, we do not deliberately have to think it up, or see the
object before us as similar in certain respects to another object.
Neither allegory nor simile is, in this sense of the word, natural,
in the way that a symbol is. We are reminded inevitably of
Coleridge's own description of the white eddy-rose, which *was*
permanent, self-renewing, 'obstinate in resurrection' itself, and in
which we could *see* 'the life we live'. If we think of this example,
the chaotic words begin to fall into place.

The connexion between this kind of symbolic interpretation of
the world and the imagination is made a bit clearer in another
passage from Appendix B. Coleridge is reiterating his version of
the distinction between reason and understanding: 'Of the dis-
cursive understanding which forms for itself general notions and
terms of classification for the purpose of comparing and arranging
phenomena, the characteristic is clearness without depth. It
contemplates the unity of things in their limits only, and is
consequently a knowledge of superficies without substance. So
much so indeed that it tangles itself in contradiction in the very
effort of comprehending the idea of substance. The completing
power which unites clearness with depth the plenitude of the
sense with the comprehensibility of the understanding is the
imagination, impregnated with which understanding itself
becomes intuitive, and a living power. Reason, without being
sense, understanding or imagination, contains all three within
itself as the mind contains thoughts, or the expression is in the
face.' Here reason is thought of in a new way. It is presented as
categorially different from understanding or imagination. The
expression is not identical with the face, but you cannot separate
them, and examine them apart. All you can do is *refer* to them

separately. So reason, in this passage, can be conceptually, but not in fact, separated from understanding and imagination.

Finally, in the same appendix Coleridge writes, 'Imagination is that reconciling and mediating power which, incorporating the reason in the images of sense, and organising, as it were, the flux of the senses by the permanence and self-circling energies of the reason, gives birth to a system of symbols, harmonious in themselves and cosubstantial with the truths of which they are conductors.' No one can pretend that these words are clear; and it may well be true, as has sometimes been said, that where Coleridge stops quoting someone else, he becomes more than usually incoherent. But it is possible, even though the words will not bear minute examination, to extract the general sense of what he was saying. Imagination is that with which we actively bring together different perceptions, to show their essential unity. It is also that with which we both perceive individual things, and take them as significant of the universal ideas which lie behind them. We would be incapable of grasping after universal ideas if it were not for our reason. But we need to add imagination to reason. For without imagination we could never have the sense of awe which we experience in the fact of some exemplification, in real concrete fact, of a universal idea. Our feelings as well as our powers of perception are engaged.

The secondary imagination, that of the poet, although it is, in *Biographia Literaria*, relegated apparently to a lower place than the primary imagination, is in fact presumably the grander. For it is that which picks out what are natural symbols, and brings the high feeling of significance to what would otherwise be mere ordinary perception of the world. But the fact of the matter is, as we have seen, that Coleridge does not consistently distinguish between poetic imagination and the imagination used in unifying and understanding our perceptions. Nor does he want to do so. For the function of adding depth to clarity can be carried on both in the writing of poetry, and in the contemplation of the world where no artistic object, poem or picture, is created at all. The failure to make much of the distinction between the primary and the secondary imagination is not accidental. It fits with the general tenor of Coleridge's thought.

It is this depth-producing function of imagination which Coleridge above all ascribed to Wordsworth. Of his first encounter with him he wrote: 'It was not . . . the freedom from false taste . . . which made so unusual an impression on my feelings immediately, and subsequently on my judgment. It was the union of deep feeling with profound thought; the fine balance of truth in observing with the imaginative faculty of modifying the objects observed; and above all the original gift of spreading the tone, the *atmosphere*, and with it the depth and height of the ideal world around forms, incidents and situations, of which for the common view, custom had bedimmed all the lustre, had dried up the sparkle and the dew drops.' And he then goes on to quote from his own remarks about genius, which first appeared in *The Friend*, Number 5: 'To find no contradiction in the union of the old and the new; to contemplate the ANCIENT of days and all his works with feelings as fresh, as if all had then sprang forth at the first creative fiat characterizes the mind that feels the riddle of the world, and may help to unravel it.'[1]

In this passage, as it seems to me, we can find the effects of Coleridge's theorizings and borrowings and philosophical speculations, but sharpened into an analysis of his own remembered judgment of Wordsworth. We can see how, feeling as he did the sensation of depth and universality in particular experiences, he both recognized this feeling as something essential in himself, and also sought not only to analyse it, but to legitimize it, by referring it to the absolute underlying truth of the place of the human mind in nature. In his literary criticism he was concerned to distinguish true imaginative insight, that which discovers and understands natural symbols, from mere wit, or deliberate fancy, which deals in similes and allegories, in pictures and images which produce no sense of awe. This concern can of course be seen largely as a consequence of the immediate critical climate in which he wrote. Distinctions between fancy and imagination, between talent and genius, between beauty and sublimity were the common currency of English critical writing in the late eighteenth century. For our part we may be more concerned to try to distinguish true imaginative insight from sentimental feelings of significance or profundity; the language of genuine hard thought from what has become a mere habitual or routine obscurity, in which thought itself becomes buried in the turgid mud of language. But though we may often find Coleridge guilty of generating such obscurity,

[1] *Biographia Literaria*, chap. IV.

we must remember that it was, after all, new to him, and by no means routine. He found in German metaphysics just the materials he needed to justify his own belief that *in understanding one's feelings* one can understand the riddle of the world, and that it was imagination which brought together the feelings, the actual love and awe, with the understanding.

Did Wordsworth share this belief? Did he hold that, if he united deep feeling with profound thought, as Coleridge said, he did so in virtue of the power of his imagination? There is no doubt that he did, and that to this extent his theory of imagination ran parallel with Coleridge's own. But, much more than Coleridge, he was capable both of expressing his own response, his own deep feelings and profound thoughts, and of analysing what it was that he was doing. More clearly than Coleridge's, his theory of imagination can be seen to have grown out of his experience. It is in Wordsworth above all, as I shall hope to show, that we can see the connexion between the three uses of imagination: between imagination as we use it in perception, in the conjuring up of images of things once perceived, and finally in the insight which may be expressed by the artist or the man of genius. This connexion is both demonstrated in his practice and stated in his theory. Indeed in his case we can hardly separate the two.

It will be appropriate at this stage to take a brief retrospective look at how the imagination was thought to function by Hume and then by Kant, for we seem to have come a long way since then. Taking Hume and Kant together, we saw a developing account of imagination as that which functions both in the presence of an object of perception in the world, and in its absence, when we turn to it in our thoughts. Imagination both presents and re-presents things to us. Its power is the power of forming images, which may be used as the means of interpreting what is before our eyes and ears in the perceptual world, or as *constituting* our interpreted world, when we are separated from the actual objects of which our images *are* the images. We can neither recognize what is before us, nor concentrate upon the significant aspect of things, without the imaginative faculty. Thus our perception and indeed all our intelligible thought about the world is dependent on *what we contribute by this faculty*, which when it is intensified beyond the normal degree amounts to genius. Furthermore, both Hume and Kant acknowledge that imagination is closely associated with our emotions, and indeed cannot be separated from them. The free imagination in its creative role may see quite ordinary objects as significant in a new way, and may make us feel in a new way. The interpretative function of imagination, which is its normal role, may be heightened, so that what is before our eyes takes on a new meaning. This power is identical with the power of representation, of forming images of things, in order to think about them in their absence. Images, then, begin to look like our way of representing significance to ourselves. We shall come back to this in Part IV.

There is evidence that Wordsworth was aware from his childhood onwards, though we cannot say how articulately, of the attractions of idealism; and this forms a natural link between himself and Hume. For the Humean language of 'impressions' and 'ideas', or Berkeley's language, in which thoughts, images and perceptions were all of them 'ideas', would naturally make sense to him. He was capable of reflecting on the relation between himself and what he experienced through the senses, and was always liable to feel that the objects of sight and hearing were not truly external, but somehow *in* his own mind. But he was a non-philosophical idealist, for whom the thought that what we see and hear is in our minds is alarming, and reduces the world to a dream-like and insubstantial status. Moreover, he seems to have shared the non-philosophical belief that the sense of touch is somehow exempt from the arguments that apply to the senses of sight and hearing, so he was able to reassure himself that the world was not a mere dream by touching things, like Dr. Johnson, who refuted Berkeley by kicking a stone. He says of himself, 'I was often unable to think of external things as having external existence, and I communed with all I saw as something not apart from but inherent in my own immaterial nature. Many times while going to school have I grasped at a wall or tree to recall myself from this abyss of idealism.'[1] If we can believe what he says of himself (and there is no good reason not to) then it is reasonable to look even in his earliest poems for some signs of his awareness of the relation between himself as observer and what he saw and heard, even though we know that the full theory of the constructive or constitutive power of the imagination did not come until later.

---

[1] Fenwick note to the Ode, 'Intimations of Immortality'. (Notes dictated to Isabella Fenwick, 1843: known as the 'Fenwick Notes'.)

But before we can consider Wordsworth at all, there are one or two cautions which must be observed. It is necessary to try to expose some of the general assumptions current at the time when Wordsworth was growing up. In the first place we should consider some assumptions about literature. Certain views of the function of poetry had become part of an orthodoxy, which would have been, if not acceptable, at least familiar, to Wordsworth. In the middle of the eighteenth century there had appeared a translation into English of a work by du Fresnay written in 1665, called *De Arte Graphica*. There is a famous stanza in this work which reads:

> 'Ut pictura poesis erit similisque poesi
> Sit pictura . . . '[1]

This was a doctrine that was endlessly expounded and elaborated at the close of the century. It was the age of the picturesque. One does not have to infer this standard of taste from contemporary poets or painters; on the contrary. To an extent astonishing to us, every educated person seems to have had a *theory* of taste, or of the beautiful and the sublime. Everyone accepted the need for a theory of beauty, and the theories were at least as much talked about as the paintings or the poems which were supposed to exemplify them. Moreover, the theories had reference as much to landscape as to painting or poetry; indeed landscape increasingly came to be thought of as something *to be made*, all nature a vast potential garden.

Picturesque poetry, then, was largely descriptive; poetry aspired to the condition of painting. A few, including the famous Uvedale Price, whose essay in the picturesque was quoted in *Northanger Abbey*, thought that there could be picturesque music as well as poetry and painting; but for most theorists, the picturesque referred if not to the visual, then essentially to poetry which was like painting, in that it described something which was *fit to be painted*. Such theory was, in part, a theory of style. It also introduced a particular way of looking at the world. One thought of the external world in terms of *prospects*. A prospect or a view is, as it were, framed; it is something isolated, to be looked at.

---

[1] 'A poem will be like a picture, and let a picture also be similar to a poem . . . '.

Such a way of looking at the world did not carry with it any particular theory of perception or any particular epistemology. What one saw might be isolated and regarded, as we should say, from an aesthetic standpoint, and yet one might think of the actual *perception* as a matter of impressions implanted by the senses on the mind; and these might be associated with other impressions mechanically. I shall come back to this in a moment. Wordsworth, however, brought to the presumptions of this poetic theory his feeling of idealism, if we may call it that. He naturally had a sense of the world, including the world of picturesque landscape, as *his* world, in some deep way lying behind his eyes, in his own mind. The framed pictures were pictures for which he was, in a sense, responsible. What in the end was to become a belief in the creative power of the imagination began as a somewhat ambiguous sense of the importance, in what we see, of the actual images we can form in our mind's eye. To have this sense was to add a new dimension to the theory of the picturesque; but we must not forget that the theory was there.

Other presuppositions were not so much literary as philosophical. And here we shall come again upon the connexions between Wordsworth and Coleridge. We know that Wordsworth was an enthusiastic believer in the associationist doctrines of Hartley, as was Coleridge himself at one time. Associationism must, therefore, be taken into account as part of the background. Coleridge, who was still an admirer of this theory in 1796, had rejected it, or so he claimed, by 1801 (see page 88). In a letter to Thomas Poole written in March 1801[1] he said, 'The interval since my last letter has been filled up by me in the most intense study. If I do not greatly delude myself, I have not only completely extricated the notions of Time and Space; but have overthrown the doctrine of Association, as taught by Hartley.' He was at this time, as we have seen, learning about Kant for the first time. Now Kant was doubtless discussed at length by Coleridge and Wordsworth together. In 1800 Wordsworth was still writing (in his preface to the *Lyrical Ballads*) as a disciple of Hartley. Both the necessity of the laws of association of ideas, and the inevitable improvement of those men who are introduced to the right ideas, are doctrines which find expression in the preface. He speaks of the habitual connexion between certain thoughts and influxes of

[1] Griggs, vol. II, p. 708.

feeling which are 'modified and directed' by thought, and he says that if both the feelings and the thoughts are good, then 'such habits of mind will be produced that by obeying blindly and mechanically the impulses of those habits we shall utter sentiments of such a nature and such connexion with each other that the understanding of the being to whom we address ourselves, if he be in a healthful state of association, must necessarily be in some degree enlightened, his taste exalted and his affections ameliorated.'[1] This is certainly pure Hartley. And there is little substantial change in this actual passage in the 1802 edition of the preface. There is, however, a possible modification of these views elsewhere in the 1802 edition, as we shall see. By 1804 Coleridge definitely claimed to have talked Wordsworth out of his adherence to Hartley. He wrote to Poole in January 1804[2] of his own escape from the 'pernicious doctrine of Necessity' and claimed to have a 'better clue' for helping others to escape likewise. And he adds, 'I have convinced Southey, and Wordsworth, and W., you know, was even to extravagence a Necessitarian.' So we must allow that Wordsworth's gradual move away from associationism had something to do with Coleridge's similar move, and his increasing belief in the active power of imagination had some connexion with the growth of the German influence on Coleridge. By 1801 Coleridge was denying (in the March letter to Poole quoted above) that the mind was a mere spectator in the world. And in writing to Southey in August 1803 he actually expounded a different account of the association of ideas which strongly suggests their connexion by the power of imagination. For he says, 'I hold that association depends in a much greater degree on the recurrence of resembling states of feeling than on trains of ideas, and if this be true Hartley's system totters.'[3] Even earlier, in December 1800, in writing to Poole he had proposed for himself as a serious study 'a metaphysical Investigation of the Laws by which our feelings form affinities with each other, with ideas and with words.'[4] And we remember how inevitably the imagination is combined with feelings as well as with images. So Wordsworth

[1] Wordsworth and Coleridge, *Lyrical Ballads*, ed. by R. L. Brett and A. R. Jones (Methuen, 1968), p. 247.
[2] Griggs, vol. II, p. 706.
[3] Griggs, vol. II, p. 960.
[4] Griggs, vol. I, p. 651.

and Coleridge gradually turned together against Hartley and towards a view of the active imagination. But there are further complications which should be noticed. For in 1797 Coleridge wrote the poem, 'This Lime Tree Bower My Prison', in which the following lines occur:

> ' . . . so my friend
> Struck with joy's deepest calm, and gazing round
> On the wide view, may gaze till all doth seem
> Less gross than bodily, a living Thing
> That acts upon the mind, and with such hues
> As cloathe the Almighty Spirit, when he makes
> Spirits perceive his presence.'

There is a number of verbal echoes in this poem of Wordsworth's poem 'Lines Left upon a Seat in a Yew Tree'. But the lines just quoted do not seem directly derived from Wordsworth. When Coleridge sent a copy of the poem to Southey he appended the note, 'You remember, I am a Berkeleian.' The reference to Berkeley was specially intended as a gloss on the lines quoted above. For Berkeley had held that all our experiences are ideas, which are the ideas of God, the supreme spirit, who allows us to experience them. There exists nothing in the world except spirits and ideas; and when we perceive the world, we are in fact perceiving God's ideas which he has caused us to share. This poem was written very shortly after Coleridge's first lengthy meeting with Wordsworth. Did they, when they first met and talked, share that feeling for idealism, which, as we have seen, Wordsworth ascribes to himself as a spontaneous feeling of his boyhood? How did either of them reconcile enthusiasm for Berkeley with total acceptance of the theories of Hartley? For in Berkeley's system there was no such thing as necessity or causation except that causation by which a spirit could cause an idea to occur, either in himself or in another spirit (as God causes us to receive ideas of things in the world, in a certain regular order). Such questions as this cannot be answered with any certainty, and it would be a mistake to press them too far. We cannot sort out, as we have seen, in the case of Wordsworth and Coleridge, which of them thought of something first, or who persuaded the other of what. But more important, it would be futile to regard this as a matter of great consequence, since neither was a systematic thinker, and for both of them it was perfectly possible to accept a number of ideas and theories which were mutually incompatible. Accepting a theory meant nothing but finding it attractive. It meant embracing it as something already in some sense familiar, and taking what one wanted while leaving the rest alone. Coleridge, as I have already suggested, treated philosophical theories as friends. You may love many friends who do not agree among themselves, and you may get crazes for people because you see in them some qualities which may not, in truth, be their most obvious qualities. It is because of this unintellectual attitude to philosophy that Coleridge can never be taken seriously by professionals. He knows nothing about philosophy, but he knows what, for the time being, he likes. There is no doubt that Coleridge understood that this was true of himself. In a letter to Thelwall written in December 1796, before the influence of Wordsworth need be taken into account, he wrote, 'my philosophical opinions are blended with, or deduced from, my feelings, and this I think peculiarizes my style of writing.'[1] Incidentally, in the same letter he also refers to himself as 'a Berkeleian'. And this is the year in which we are sure that he still greatly admired Hartley, because he named his first son after him. His son Berkeley was born in 1798 but there is every reason to believe that Berkeley attracted him long before that.

Much of what has been said of Coleridge could be equally applied to Wordsworth. We need, it is true, to remind ourselves of the assumptions he must have made, and of the climate of thought in which he wrote. But as to the actual content of his beliefs at any given time, it would be a mistake to systematize it too much or try to state with too much precision what it was. Unacceptable as it may seem to people of a precise turn of mind, the crucial fact about Wordsworth was the existence of his imagination and his own belief that this faculty gave him insight. The *content* of the insight, *what* it was that he claimed to understand by means of imagination, is less important. Thus critics of Wordsworth often try too hard to answer such questions as whether at this time he was a pantheist, at that an orthodox Christian, whether he did or did not believe that there was one life in all nature, and so on.

To take the example of the one life: of course we know that

[1] Griggs, vol. I, p. 279.

Coleridge used this expression. In a letter to Sotheby (September 1801)[1] he wrote, 'Nature has her proper interest; and he will know what it is who believes and feels that everything has a life of its own and that we are all One Life.' But perhaps the operative phrase here is 'believes *and feels*'. We cannot pursue these questions as if to believe in the One Life on the one hand and not to believe in it on the other is a sharp and clear dichotomy. Again, there is a kind of absurdity in the questions raised by Jonathan Wordsworth[2] as to whether Wordsworth held the belief that the moral life was *in* the forms of nature or that it was not: whether the secret and mysterious soul was *in* the shapes of nature or not in them. Just as it would be ridiculous to demand of a religious person a yes or no answer to the question 'Is God Love?', so it would be absurd to hold a pistol to a poet's head and demand that he should answer the question, 'Is Nature Animate? Yes or No.' Yet Jonathan Wordsworth, normally one of the most sensitive of critics, appears to hope for just such an answer from Wordsworth, with, in addition, the hope that a scrutiny of the poems will yield an exact date on which he can be shown to have stopped believing in pantheism, and taken up with something else. The beliefs themselves, because of their intrinsic vagueness, their inevitable non-literalness, defy such treatment. And in any case, such beliefs form part of those assumptions which it has been the purpose of the last few pages to try to uncover; and where a belief is in the air, where it is part of contemporary *mythology*, it is impossible, except in rare cases, to say of anybody that he fully believes or wholly disbelieves it. The history of religious belief is enough to confirm this.

That pantheism *was* thus in the air is beyond dispute. The notion that all nature is animated, is literally inspired by some universal breath of life, was a notion with which neither Wordsworth nor Coleridge nor any of their literate contemporaries could fail to be familiar. It was all about them. Coleridge's own poem, 'The Eolian Harp', written in 1796, was a serious use of an image which was, to quote Geoffrey Grigson, 'the really prime romantic image.' The extent to which the harp was a cliché is admirably brought out in Grigson's note to Coleridge's poem.[3] 'It seems,' he

---

[1] Griggs, vol. II, p. 864.
[2] Jonathan Wordsworth, *The Music of Humanity* (New York, 1969).
[3] *The Romantics* (Routledge, 1942).

writes, 'that the Aeolian harp was invented by the Scottish com-
poser James Oswald who died in 1796. He acted on a hint in the
Greek commentary of Eustathius, which Pope found while trans-
lating Homer: the hint was that wind on strings could be made to
produce harmonious sounds. He experimented, failed, and tried
again when told that an ordinary harp on a Thames houseboat
had sounded in the wind. Finally he devised the "harp of Aeolus
... the God of the Winds" to fit into the window. This was
before 1748. The harp became popular. Thomson writes about it
in "The Castle of Indolence" (1748). Smollett's smart adventurer,
Ferdinand Fathom, uses it to seduce a country girl. (*Ferdinand
Count Fathom* came out in 1753, and Smollett says that country
people knew nothing of this new instrument.) The harp now
begins to romp through literature. Christopher Smart has a bit of
it in "Jubilate Agno". There are poems about it by Mason (who
made his own harp), Dibdin and Mrs. Opie. Gilbert White
mentions it in 1775 in a letter. Sir John Hawkins gives an account
of it in his *History of Music* (1776) and William Jones in his
Physiological Disquisitions (1781) ... William Jones says: "If we
consider the quality of its harmony, it very much resembles that of
a chorus of voices at a distance; with all the expressions of the
forte, the *piano*, and the *swell*; in a word its harmony is more like
to what we might imagine the aerial sounds of magic and en-
chantment to be, than to artificial music—we may call it without
a metaphor the music of inspiration." '

We see Coleridge himself using the image in passing as an
absolutely obvious, probably scarcely noticed, simile in a letter to
his wife in January 1803,[1] in which he complains that his son,
Derwent, had been given tea to drink, 'And this for a child whose
nerves are as wakeful as the strings of an Eolian harp.' The force
of the image in his 1796 poem is, of course, to suggest just those
pantheistic doctrines about which the critics become excited. But
how vaguely they are suggested:

> 'And what if all of animated nature
> Be but organic Harps diversely fram'd
> That tumble into thought, as o'er them sweep
> Plastic and vast, one intellectual breeze,
> At once the soul of each, and God of all?'

[1] Griggs, vol. II, p. 909.

We have entered the area where metaphor and belief cross.

Pantheism, after all, is a natural outcome of—indeed not to be wholly distinguished from—the belief that nature is the language of God. And this, as we have seen, was propounded by Berkeley and by no means only by him. One of the most explicit statements of such a view, certainly, in this case, a statement of belief, is to be found in William Law (quoted in Walton's *Notes and Materials for an adequate biography of William Law*): 'Temporal nature, opened to us by the Spirit of God, becomes a *volume* of holy instruction, and leads us into all the mysteries and secrets of eternity. For as everything in temporal nature is descended out of that which is eternal and stands as a *palpable visible outbirth* of it, so when we know how to separate the *grossness death and darkness* of time from it we find what it is in its eternal state. Fire, and light, and air in this world are not only a true resemblance of the Holy Trinity in Unity, but are the Trinity itself in its most *outward lowest* kind of existence or manifestation; for there could be no fire, fire could not generate light, air could not proceed from both, these three could not be thus united, and thus divided, but because they have their root and original in the tri-unity of the Deity.' We know how much Coleridge admired Law, and *his* master, Jacob Boehm. Perhaps to quote the words in which Coleridge describes his debt to Boehm and Law is to show what we should look for, philosophically, in both Coleridge and Wordsworth. In *Biographia Literaria*, chapter IX, he says, 'The writings of these mystics added in no slight degree to prevent my mind from being imprisoned within the outline of any single dogmatic system. They contributed to keep alive the *heart* in the *head*; gave me an indistinct, yet stirring and working presentment, that all the products of the mere reflective faculty partook of DEATH, and were as the rattling twigs and sprays in winter, into which the sap was yet to be propelled, from some root to which I had not penetrated, if they were to afford my soul either food or shelter.' And, after all, Kant, by whom both Wordsworth and Coleridge were in the end to some extent won over, had argued that aesthetic ideas, the ideas towards which the imagination reached in art and poetry, could not be *completely* expressed in words. It was the function of the imagination in its highest form to aim towards that which it could never wholly grasp. We must beware, then, of trying to be too specific about *what* the imaginative object was, and attempt to concentrate on the *manner* in which the imagination sought its object.

Let us return to this question. Between 1800 and 1802 Wordsworth altered the preface to the *Lyrical Ballads* in a suggestive way. In the passage near the beginning, where he states his principal object in writing the poems, he originally said that he would make the incidents of common life interesting by tracing in them the primary laws of our nature. In the revised version he said that he would throw over the incidents of common life 'a certain colouring of the imagination whereby ordinary things should be presented in an unusual way', and then would 'make them interesting etc.' The introduction of the imagination here is significant. For the main addition to the 1802 version is a long passage on the nature of the poet. Having said that the poet is a man of more lively sensibility than other men, who 'rejoices more than other men in the spirit of life that is in him', he goes on as follows: 'To these qualities he has added a disposition to be affected more than other men by absent things as if they were present; an ability of conjuring up in himself passions which . . . do more nearly resemble the passions produced by real events than anything which, from the motions of their own mind merely, other men are accustomed to feel in themselves; whence . . . he has acquired a greater readiness and power in expressing what he thinks and feels and especially those thoughts and feelings which, by his own choice, or from the structure of his own mind, arise in him without immediate external excitement.' And he goes on, in the next paragraph, to refer to 'those passions, certain shadows of which the Poet thus produces or feels to be produced, in himself.'

Now here we seem to have not just a vague reference to the high imaginative powers of the poet, but a pretty specific account of what the poet's imagination will actually *do*. And *what* it will do is enable its possessor to be uncommonly 'affected by absent things as if they were present'. This is, quite obviously, the imagination at work in its image-forming role. It is the original function of the imagination to reproduce things, to enable us to think them, and above all to feel them, when they are not actually before our eyes; so the poet is credited by Wordsworth with an intensified version of the very faculty which we all of us exercise at the moment when we reflect on the past, the future, or the otherwise absent. And this is precisely what both Hume and Kant suggested was the case. In particular this language goes back to Hume and to the connexion between images ('ideas' in Hume's sense) and feelings.

We may now at last return to Wordsworth's early temptations towards idealism. For him, as a boy, it was as if the world in his mind and the external world were all one stuff. To reassure himself of the externality of the world, he had to touch something in it. Sight in particular (and sound to a less extent) were in some way *in* himself, they were his own ideas. We have come once again upon the crucial ambiguity of the *idea*. Something of this ambiguity is to be found in all of Wordsworth's writings, though it is most essential to the period starting in 1798. His philosophical interest in perception and imagination and his final belief in the constitutive power of imagination may have been the result of his association with Coleridge; but there could have been no such use made of the imagination if he had not already had a strong *sense* of the way in which imagination enters into, and forms part of, perception.

Roger Sharrock, in his British Academy lecture, *The Figure in a Landscape*,[1] refers to Wordsworth's 'creative nostalgia' and he remarks that from the period of his very earliest poems two phenomena, *lapse of time* and *distance in space*, provided Wordsworth, more than anything else, with the means of focusing his imagination on an object. He could write of something with insight *only* when he was literally separated from it in space or time. In the same lecture, Sharrock emphasizes a point, perhaps first made by Dr. Johnson, that even a poet writing in the picturesque or descriptive tradition must order his description in time; he must, to put it crudely, describe *first* one thing and *then* another. He must dictate to the reader the order in which things come to his attention. He is not, to quote Sharrock, a camera, but a consciousness. This being so, the intermixture of the poet's view with the poet's thought becomes increasingly important, as he becomes increasingly aware that he is in fact exercising choice, and may, for example, be giving prominence to aspects of a scene which the laws of perspective would conceal or diminish. Thus, 'The Evening Walk', one of Wordsworth's first published poems, is an attempt at almost pure landscape painting, or at least a guided

[1] O.U P., 1972.

tour; and there is even a note to the set-piece description of Rydal Falls: 'The reader who has made the tour of this country will recognize in this description the features which characterize the lower waterfall in the gardens of Rydale', which seems to spell the thing out in the most unimaginative possible fashion. But even in the 1793 addition to the manuscript he speaks of the charm of the scene which can . . .

> 'Through the mind, by magic influence
> Rapt into worlds beyond the reign of sense
> Roll the bright train of never-ending dreams . . .'

As early as this we can perhaps see that he was becoming more interested in the *mind of the beholder* of the fall, than strictly in the fall itself. The 'view' or 'prospect' was beginning to be seen as something at least partly mind-dependent.

Five years later, in 1798, we have the most complete account of the function of the imagination in 'Tintern Abbey', and in 'The Pedlar' which was written in the same year but later incorporated, with alterations, as the first book of *The Excursion*. Much later, in 1816, Wordsworth is reported by Crabb Robinson to have spoken of the function of imagination as that by which 'the mere fact is exhibited as connected with that infinity without which there is no poetry'. It is from his own poetry of the 1798 period (the period of closest association with Coleridge) that we can learn *how* he thought the imagination brought about this connexion of the particular and finite with the infinite and universal.

We should start with the consideration of a passage from 'The Pedlar' (in its 1798 version).

> 'While yet a child, and long before his time
> He had perceived the presence and the power
> Of greatness, and deep feelings had impressed
> Great objects on his mind, with portraiture
> And colour so distinct that on his mind
> They lay like substances, and almost seemed
> To haunt the bodily sense. He had received
> A precious gift, for as he grew in years
> With these impressions would he still compare
> All his ideal stores, his shapes and forms,

> And being still unsatisfied with aught
> Of dimmer character, he thence attained
> An *active* power to fasten images
> Upon his brain, and on their pictured lines
> Intensely brooded, even till they acquired
> The liveliness of dreams. Nor did he fail
> While yet a child, with a child's eagerness
> Incessantly to turn his ear and eye
> On all things which the rolling season brought
> To feed such appetite. Nor this alone
> Appeased his yearning; in the after day
> Of boyhood, many an hour in caves forlorn
> And in the hollow depths of naked crags
> He sat, and even in their fixed lineaments,
> Or from the power of a peculiar eye,
> Or by creative feeling overborne,
> Or by predominance of thought oppressed,
> Even in their fixed and steady lineaments
> He traced an ebbing and a flowing mind
> Expression ever varying.'

In his essay, *Romantic Paradox*, Colin Clarke[1] persuasively illustrates Wordsworth's awareness of the ambiguity of sense experience, and particularly the ambiguity of the sense of sight. We have seen that he was puzzled by the fact that *what we see* is both inner and outer. Clarke speaks of his 'latent awareness of the paradox, a feeling for the ambiguity and the strangeness of perception, a largely unconscious perplexity' which was, he says, the 'cause' of some of Wordsworth's finest poetry.

This perplexity is reflected in the words used to describe perception which take on the ambiguity of perception itself. The words 'image', 'form', and even 'shape' and 'colour', as they appear in Wordsworth's poetry, all stand for the inner *and* the outer, and object *and* the idea of the object. In the passage just quoted, the forms of things seen in his youth lay, still thing-like, in the pedlar's mind, and haunted his seeing in future. Moreover, these substance-like images were in the first place impressed on his mind by deep feelings and could not later be separated from feelings, when they were recalled in the absence of their original objects. It becomes impossible, as we consider the passage, to

---

[1] *Romantic Paradox*: *An Essay on the Poetry of Wordsworth*, C. C. Clarke (Routledge and Kegan Paul, 1962).

separate the function of the eye from that of the mind in perception, nor can either be separated from the function of the reproductive imagination which forms and re-forms images of what has been perceived for the mind to brood on.

This passage from 'The Pedlar' is central to Wordsworth's thought. It is only one of innumerable passages in which he, as it were, states his thesis; that we can understand things (and incidentally write about them) only if we can form images of them in the mind. What Hume refers to as 'ideas', entities derived from sense impressions which can be 'had', thought of, inspected, what are for Kant the creations of the reproductive imagination, are called by Wordsworth 'images' or 'forms'. As we have seen, both Hume and Kant thought that this very same reproductive or idea-forming power was also at work in our perception of the world, when actual objects were present to the seeing eye; and, in the same way, in Wordsworth the visible things in the world, the very things *from* which the images are derived, are also referred to as images, or forms, shapes or colours.

Now the image, whether *in* the world or *in* the mind, is essentially something which generates feeling. The object of the feeling or emotion is the image itself. Analysing the emotion, one is also analysing or coming to understand the object, as something of more than particular significance. The emotion-laden 'seeing' of the image (whether inner or outer) is identical with 'seeing' the truth, not now only about the image itself, but about it as a representative thing. We learn the nature of things in general from the particular, significant, case. And we can see that the case *is* significant, if we can see it as a form, something which can be produced and reproduced by our imagination.

Thus the power of the imagination to produce images in the absence of the object becomes crucial to Wordsworth's own poetry, and to his theory of it. But because of the ambiguity of perception, there is for him a qualitative identity between seeing and seeing-in-the-mind's eye. The difference is only that when we see in the mind's eye we can concentrate upon those images which are meaningful, which we are enabled indeed to form *because* of the significance of that which they represent. Thus the feeling engendered by the image may be more powerful in the absence than in the presence of the object, or at least we may have more time to understand it. It is for this reason that Wordsworth held that poetry arose out of *recollected* emotion. It is for this reason that the daffodils, once seen, *thereafter* constituted the bliss of solitude.

The most explicit statement of the role of images in Wordsworth's understanding of the world comes in the famous passage of 'Tintern Abbey'.

> ' . . . Once again
> Do I behold these steep and lofty cliffs,
> Which on a wild secluded scene impress
> Thought of more deep seclusion; and connect
> The landscape with the quiet of the sky. . . .
>   Though absent long
> These forms of beauty have not been to me
> As is a landscape to a blind man's eye:
> But oft in lonely rooms, and mid the din
> Of towns and cities, I have owed to them
> In hours of weariness sensations sweet,
> Felt in the blood and felt along the heart,
> And passing even into my purer mind
> With tranquil restoration: . . .
>   Nor less, I trust
> To them I may have owed another gift
> Of aspect more sublime; that blessed mood
> In which the burthen of the mystery,
> In which the heavy and the weary weight
> Of all this unintelligible world
> Is lighten'd: that serene and blessed mood
> In which the affections lead us on,
> Until, the breath of this corporeal frame,
> And even the motion of our human blood
> Almost suspended, we are laid asleep
> In body, and become a living soul:
> While with an eye made quiet by the power
> Of harmony and the deep power of joy,
> We see into the life of things.'

We need not now follow Wordsworth into the autobiographical part of the poem but look only at the end of his prayer for Dorothy, that

> 'In after years
> When these wild ecstacies shall be matured

> Into a sober pleasure, when thy mind
> Shall be a mansion for all lovely forms
> Thy memory be as a dwelling place
> For all sweet sounds and harmonies: Oh then
> If solitude or fear or pain or grief
> Should be thy portion, with what healing thoughts
> Of tender joy wilt thou remember me,
> And these my exhortations.'

It is the images which he has been able to create for himself in the absence of the actual observed landscape which have had upon him the effect of restoration, and which have led him to an understanding of the life of things; and it is this kind of healing understanding which for the future he desires for Dorothy. Nature by itself, however ecstatically enjoyed, cannot have this effect. It is only nature mediated by the power to retain images that has it. But there is more to it than this. The very power we have to retain such images affects the manner in which we perceive things here and now. As we have seen, it is impossible wholly to separate present perception from the image-making, and hence from the creative power. 'The scene', as Colin Clarke says, 'is at once substantial and insubstantial, present and past.'[1] This carries the implication that the scene is at once presented and represented or construed by the percipient. To draw again on 'Tintern Abbey', Wordsworth there speaks in a way which demands that we mix imagination with perception.

> ' . . . of all the mighty world
> Of eye and ear, both what they half-create
> And what perceive.'

And in a fragment from the same year, 1798, he wrote:

> 'There is creation in the eye,
> Not less in all the other senses; powers
> They are that colour, model, and combine
> The things perceived with such an absolute
> Essential energy that we may say
> That these most godlike faculties of ours
> At one and the same moment are the mind

[1] *op. cit.*, p. 40.

And the mind's minister. In many a walk
At evening or by moonlight, or reclined
At midday upon beds of forest moss
Have we to Nature and her impulses
Of our whole being made free gift, and when
Our trance had left us, oft have we, by aid
Of the impressions which it left behind,
Looked inward on ourselves, and learned, perhaps,
Something of what we are. Nor in those hours
Did we destroy . . .
The original impression of delight,
But by such retrospect it was recalled
To yet a second and a second life,
While in this excitation of the mind
A vivid pulse of sentiment and thought
Beat palpably within us, and all shades
Of consciousness were ours . . . '

The creativity of the senses, the deep feeling with which sense impressions are formed, the power that we have to recreate in absence the impressions which we gained in the presence of the great objects of nature, these are together the functions of the imagination.

In 'The Prelude', the creative power of imagination is presented in more grandiose terms. Here 'imagination' is the name given to the faculty which enables us to learn in a particular way. By it we are enabled to understand the significance of the universe, to grasp its life and its depth directly, as a felt experience. What it is that is thus understood can hardly be explained except by an account of the experience itself. If one could share the experience one would share the understanding. The famous 'spots of time' can be isolated by Wordsworth just because they demonstrably carry with them this awareness of significance. There is no reason to suppose that the imagination whose role is thus described, and which is crucial to the argument of 'The Prelude', is in any way different from the power, defined in 'Tintern Abbey' and 'The Pedlar', whose function was to create and reflect upon images. Reproducing, creating, understanding, all these are thought of as functions of the same faculty, and are exercised, albeit mysteriously, in the high moments of sense perception, and afterwards in recollection. There is a relation, moreover, between these high moments of experience and the need to express the understanding which they seem to give. The experience itself carries with it a sense that it somehow *must* be perpetuated. Perhaps the clearest statement of this connexion is in 'The Recluse' (written in 1801). Wordsworth writes:

> 'Of ill-advised Ambition and of Pride
> I would stand clear, but yet to me I feel
> That an internal brightness is vouchsafed
> That must not die, that must not pass away. . . .
> Possessions have I that are solely mine,
> Something within, which yet is shared by none,
> Not even the nearest to me and most dear,
> Something which power and effort may impart:
> I would impart it, I would spread it wide.'

To return to 'The Prelude', the early books are full of explicit statements of the effect upon the poet's mind of the forms and images of nature. Such forms and images, still ambiguously poised between the outer world and the inner, were *intrinsically* feeling-laden. Hume had noticed as a bare fact that ideas or images are connected inevitably with passions, to the extent that ideas, which are copies, may be turned into impressions, impressions of *feelings*, which are originals. Hartley had used this same connexion as a basis for his optimistic mechanism, according to which we shall necessarily be led higher and higher by the association of pleasure with sense impressions of a particular kind. Now Wordsworth placed this fact at the heart of the mysterious active power of imagination. It was indeed because of its connexion with feelings that he held the exercise of the imagination to be worth cultivating for its own sake or, which came to the same thing, for the sake of the emotions which went with it. Such emotions could not be justified nor recommended for any further consequence they might bring. They were simply worth having in themselves.

In the childhood passages of 'The Prelude' the Presences of Nature are represented as exercising an influence that was partly unobserved, or at least unremarked, by the child who was given up, as far as his conscious life was concerned, to 'vulgar joys'. Yet even then, from time to time, there was an awareness of something working on and in the mind.

'... mid that giddy bliss
Which like a tempest works along the blood
And is forgotten, even then I felt
Gleams like the flashing of a shield; the earth
And common face of Nature spake to me
Rememberable things ...

'And if the vulgar joy by its own weight
Wearied itself out of the memory,
The scenes which were the witness of that joy
Remained in their substantial lineaments
Depicted on the brain, and to the eye
Were visible, a daily sight; and thus
By the impressive discipline of fear,
By pleasure and repeated happiness,
So frequently repeated, and by force
Of obscure feelings representative
Of things forgotten, these same scenes so bright,
So beautiful, so majestic in themselves,
Though yet the day was distant, did become
Habitually dear, and all their forms
And changeful colours by invisible links
Were fastened to the affections.'[1]

So far, though nature spoke rememberable things, yet the mind
of the child was represented as totally passive; the association
between impressions and feelings seem to be thought of as
necessary and automatic, in a purely Hartelian way. Moreover,
many of the conventional ingredients of the pleasurable sense of
the sublime are suggested. One may compare the passage just
quoted with Hartley, *Observations on Man*, proposition xciv: 'If
there be a precipice, a cataract, a mountain of snow etc. in one
part of the scene, the nascent ideas of fear and horror magnify and
enliven all the other ideas, and by degrees pass into pleasures
suggesting the security from pain. In like manner the grandeur of
some scenes, and the novelty of others, by exciting surprise and
wonder, i.e., by making a great difference in the preceding and
subsequent states of mind, so as to border upon or even enter the
limits of pain, may greatly enhance the pleasure.' Fear, the impressive discipline, is connected inevitably with pleasure. But

[1] 'The Prelude', Book I.

Wordsworth went on to undermine this picture. He drew a crucial distinction between the mere pleasures which could arise from the perception of beautiful objects, and the creative and formative power which such objects could call up, and by which in turn the objects could be called up. It was indeed this *creative* power which had gleamed occasionally for the child, like the flashing of a shield. The vision of natural objects, as distinct from the mere sight of them, however beautiful, required the active intervention of mind, even though the vision might not be recognized as such until afterwards.

Wordsworth distinguished three attitudes towards nature.[1] The first was that which was governed by conventional or fashionable judgments of the beautiful and the ugly.

> ' . . . Even in pleasure pleased
> Unworthily; disliking here, and there
> Liking: by rules of mimic art transferred
> To things above all art . . . '

This is clearly the attitude of those who were concerned with the picturesque. Secondly, there is an attitude which he himself at one time adopted

> '. . . giving way
> To a comparison of scene with scene,
> Bent overmuch on superficial things,
> Pampering myself with meagre novelties
> Of colour and proportion; to the moods
> Of time and season, to the moral power
> The affections and spirit of place
> Insensible . . . '

A regard for nature, this, which still has a good deal of the external, the mere observer's and the collector's spirit. Both these are contrasted with the imaginative vision:

> ' . . . I had known
> Too forcibly, too early in my life,
> Visitings of imaginative power

[1] 'The Prelude', Book XII.

> For this to last; I shook the habit off
> Entirely and for ever, and again
> In Nature's presence stood, as now I stand,
> A sensitive being, a *creative* soul.'

It is this creativity, to which Wordsworth returned after his temporary absorption in the 'aesthetic', that is analysed in the next lines:

> 'There are in our existence spots of time
> That with distinct pre-eminence retain
> A renovating virtue, whence, depressed
> By false opinion and contentious thought,
> Or aught of heavier or more deadly weight,
> In trivial occupations, and the round
> Of ordinary intercourse, our minds
> Are nourished and invisibly repaired.'

The renovating virtue is said to lurk

> 'Among those passages of life that give
> Profoundest knowledge to what point, and how
> The mind is lord and master—outward sense
> The obedient servant of her will . . . '

In experiencing one of these 'spots of time', that is to say, one is experiencing *oneself*, not as a passive recipient of sensible appearances, but as a contributor to them. The senses present to us what *we make* them present.

In the 1850 version of 'The Prelude', this passage is closely followed by an example of such heightened vision drawn from childhood. When he was very young, he became separated from the 'ancient servant' who was looking after him on his pony. While he was alone, he terrified himself by discovering the still visible carving of the name of a murderer. And at this moment his eye fell on a girl.

> 'A girl who bore a pitcher on her head,
> And seemed with difficult steps to force her way
> Against the blowing wind. It was in truth
> An ordinary sight; but I should need
> Colours and words that are unknown to man,

> To paint the visionary dreariness
> Which, while I looked around for my lost guide,
> Invested moorland waste and naked pool,
> And beacon crowning the lone eminence,
> The female and her garments vexed and tossed
> By the strong wind. When in the blessed
> Hours of early love, the loved one at my side,
> I roamed, in daily presence of this scene,
> Upon the naked pool and dreary crags
> And on the melancholy beacon fell
> A spirit of pleasure and youth's golden gleam:
> And think ye not with radiance more sublime
> For these remembrances and for the power
> They left behind? So feeling comes in aid
> Of feeling, and diversity of strength
> Attends us, if but once we have been strong.
> Oh mystery of man, from what a depth
> Proceed thy honours. I am lost, but see
> In simple childhood something of the base
> On which thy greatness stands: but this I feel,
> That from thyself it comes, that thou must give,
> Else never can receive . . . '

In this passage we can see a whole number of different thoughts, derived as it may seem from many different sources. Without attempting to enter into a detailed chronology, we can nevertheless say that Wordsworth was writing of imagination in this way between 1798 and 1805, the year that 'The Prelude' was finished. This period coincides with the period of his closest connexion with and deepest love for Coleridge. Thus it is likely that he was as much excited as Coleridge was by the German concept of the transcendental imagination. He was certainly feeling at this time towards a view of imagination working 'beneath the level of consciousness', which was to this extent *like* Kant's view, even if not derived from it. In the last book of 'The Prelude' he speaks of the imagination as a stream, flowing out from a deep cave:

> ' . . . we have traced the stream
> From darkness, and the very place of birth
> In its blind cavern, whence is faintly heard
> The sound of waters.'

Of himself at Cambridge, when he had been distracted from his course of learning from Nature, he says,

> ' . . . Hush'd meanwhile,
> Was the *under soul*, lock'd up in such a calm
> That not a leaf of the great nature stirr'd.'

Again of himself, and others, in childhood, he says,

> ' . . . we love, not knowing what we love
> And feel, not knowing whence our feeling comes.'

Not only images and perceptions, then, but their accompanying feelings were capable, he thought, of being formed below the level of consciousness. This in itself constitutes a break from the simplicities of Hume or Hartley. It connects, too, in a devious way with his long-felt attraction towards some kind of Berkeleian idealism. Both together suggest a continuous activity of the mind whether we recognize it or not. Both are together found expressed in a fragment, dated by Ernest de Selincourt between 1798 and early 1800.

> 'I seemed to learn . . .
> That what we see of forms and images
> Which float along on minds, and what we feel
> Of active or recognizable thought,
> Prospectiveness, or intellect, or will,
> Not only is not worthy to be deemed
> Our being, to be prized as what we are,
> But is the very littleness of life.
> Such consciousness I deem but accidents,
> Relapses from the one interior life
> That lives in all things, sacred from the touch
> Of that false secondary power by which
> In weakness we create distinctions, then
> Believe that all our puny boundaries are things
> Which we perceive and not which we have made:'

This fragment suggests both that Wordsworth thought of consciousness as only a part of life and thought, and that he was capable of *welcoming* idealism, not treating it as an 'abyss'. In this mood, he seems to regard the distinction between the mind and the hard, separate *objects* in the external world as false, a matter of 'puny boundaries'. Though this fragment was not included in 'The Prelude', a good deal of its spirit was left. Certainly we recognize the suggestion that conscious thought is only a part of our whole mode of thought: and we recognize the continuity of mind and its objects, the impossibility of distinguishing thought from thing, or feeling *in* nature from feeling *in* the mind. The forms of nature, he says, 'have a passion in themselves'.[1] The Kantian Copernican revolution according to which we must regulate the world by our own concepts before we can learn the regularities of the world, and according to which we could not even perceive the world of objects unless we constituted it first by our own schematism of the imagination, has become, if not a cliché, at least a leitmotif:

> ' . . . that thou must give
> Or never can receive.'

And earlier, in Coleridge's,

> ' . . . O lady, we receive but what we give.'[2]

The two-way relationship, the giving and receiving, between mind and nature, is most explicitly stated in the last book of 'The Prelude', and there is explicitly linked with the imagination. Wordsworth is describing the expedition to see the sun rise from

---

[1] 'The Prelude', Book XIII.

[2] This particular phrase, while central to Wordsworth's thought, may incidentally be taken as an example of the complex connexion between Coleridge and Wordsworth at this time. Coleridge's ode 'Dejection', from which the phrase comes, was first a letter to Sara Hutchinson, written on 4th April, 1802 (or, rather, what was later published as the ode was part of a longer verse letter). We need not strain our credulity by trying to believe Coleridge's claim to have written all three hundred and forty lines of this letter in one night; in any case, that claim is irrelevant to the chronology. In this version, the quoted phrase reads, 'Oh Sara! we receive but what we give.' The poem in this version contains very obvious borrowings from the first two stanzas of Wordsworth's 'Immortality' ode. We know from Dorothy Wordsworth's journal that these two stanzas, which contain the thought of beauty being visible but not felt as a glory, were composed at breakfast on 27th March, 1802. In May and June 1802, Wordsworth composed 'The Leech Gatherer', perhaps as a kind of answer to Coleridge on Dejection. On 19th July, 1802, Coleridge copied the less personal parts of the 'Dejection' ode again in a letter to Sotheby, and there said that he had originally written them as a letter to Wordsworth. The quoted line there reads, 'O Wordsworth! we receive but what we give.' Later still, he again quoted part of the ode in a letter to the Wedgwoods, written in August 1804, and there the

the top of Snowdon, undertaken during a vacation from Cambridge. The description in itself is as near as possible to a direct expression of heightened perception. In the visionary experience, the natural phenomena are all of them seen as significant of something beyond themselves. For when Wordsworth came to reflect on the remembered image of the sight he saw it as 'the type of majestic intellect'. He saw it, that is, as a symbol not deliberately chosen as such, but revealing its sense to him inevitably, as he thought about it in absence. The vision symbolized his own mind and the mind of others like himself,

> 'One function, above all, of such a mind
> Had Nature shadowed there, by putting forth,
> 'Mid circumstances awful and sublime,
> That mutual domination which she loves
> To exert upon the face of outward things,
> So molded, joined, abstracted, so endowed
> With interchangeable supremacy,
> That men, least sensitive, see, hear, perceive
> And cannot choose but feel the Power which all
> Acknowledge when thus moved, which Nature thus
> To bodily sense exhibits, is the express
> Resemblance of that glorious faculty
> That higher minds bear with them as their own.
> This is the very spirit in which they deal
> With the whole compass of the universe;
> They from their native selves can spread abroad
> Kindred mutations; for themselves create
> A like existence: and whene'er it dawns
> Created for them, catch it or are caught
> By its inevitable mastery,
> Like angels stopped upon the wing by sound
> Of harmony from Heaven's remotest spheres.
> Them the exalted and the transient both
> Serve to exalt; they build up greatest things
> From least suggestions . . . '

---

line reads, 'Oh William . . . ' The quoted line from 'The Prelude' was presumably written after 1802, and must be taken to be a conscious quotation, or echo. All we can say about this kind of story is that Wordsworth and Coleridge shared their thoughts. Much of their writing of this period is a kind of dialogue; not an argument, but a conversation, in which it is almost impossible to ascribe ideas to their authors.

And then the Hartleian emotions of fear and horror are introduced, transformed:

> ' . . . to fear and love
> To love as prime and chief, for there fear ends,
> Be this ascribed; to early intercourse,
> In presence of sublime or beautiful forms,
> With the adverse principles of pain and joy . . .
>
> This spiritual love acts not nor can exist
> Without imagination, which, in truth,
> Is but another name for absolute power
> And clearest insight, amplitude of mind,
> And Reason in her most exalted mood.'

Coleridge well understood this concept of the 'feeling intellect'. Once again it would be idle to try to determine how much of the impassioned language of the last book of 'The Prelude' arose directly out of things which Wordsworth and Coleridge had discussed. After all, it was written with Coleridge in mind. What we have, whoever first thought of it, is a coherent, deeply felt and convincing explanation of the intrinsic value of a certain way of looking at the world. Coleridge at any rate, as we have seen, in the somewhat cool hour in which he wrote of Wordsworth in 1817, spoke with obvious truth of what first impressed him when he got to know Wordsworth. 'It was not . . . the freedom from false taste . . . which made so unusual an impression on my feelings immediately, and subsequently on my judgement. *It was the union of deep feeling with profound thought.*' He also understood, as C. C. Clarke has pointed out, the ambiguity of 'images', objects in the mind and in the world, both what we immediately perceive and what we may think of after the perception has passed away. In one of the Notebooks written in Malta,[1] he wrote, 'Thought and Reality, two distinct corresponding sounds, of which no man can say which is the Voice and which the Echo. O the beautiful Fountain or natural well at Upper Stowey. The images of the weeds which hung down from its sides, appeared as plants growing up, straight and upright among the water weeds that really grew from the bottom, and so vivid was the image that for some

[1] April 1805, No. 2557.

moments, and not till after I had disturbed the water, did I perceive that their root were not neighbours, and they side by side companions. So—even then I said—so are the happy man's *thoughts* and *things* (in the language of the modern philosophers Ideas and Impressions).' There is no direct evidence, but also perhaps no reason to doubt, that he was thinking of Wordsworth when he spoke of the 'happy man' in this context. He was doubtless thinking of him at Upper Stowey when the reflections of the weeds first suggested their own natural symbolism to him.

This closeness of thought to things, a closeness such that there is even the possibility of their being mistaken one for the other, is to be explained in terms of the dual function of the imagination, its function both in the presence and in the absence of the object. For Wordsworth himself, both in his practice and in his reflections upon it, the two functions have come together. Moreover, this very same doubly-functioning imagination has become, for him, the essential means of understanding, and of rightly valuing the world, and human life in it. Both in Hume and in Kant, the imagination which allowed us to envisage things in absence was itself a necessary part of our interpreting things when they were before our eyes. Both Hume and Kant, moreover, thought of genius as that very same faculty raised to a higher power. In our consideration of Wordsworth it has become clearer that there is sense, and a very precise sense, in identifying the imagination of genius with the faculty of forming images of objects in the world, whether these are now perceived or have been perceived in the past. In order to pursue this identity further, it is necessary now to consider in rather more detail the image-making aspect of the imagination. Hume was, as we saw, fairly casual in his account of 'ideas'. Sometimes 'ideas' are images, sometimes they are not. Even when there is no doubt that one could substitute the word 'image' for 'idea', it is still far from clear exactly what images *are*, and how they compare with actual perceptions. Kant throws no more light on this problem. We must still raise the question what is actually meant by an image. Does the employment of imagination depend on the creation of some form of *picture* in the mind? Is not all talk of 'the mind's eye' a poor and misleading metaphor? Was not Hume wrong to hold that ideas and impressions differed in intensity only? Was not Wordsworth equally wrong to use words such as 'form' and 'image' to stand *both* for the objects of sight in the world *and* for what is 'seen' in the private and inner chamber of the mind? These are the questions to which, with the help of some later philosophers and psychologists, we must now address ourselves.

PART IV

The Nature of the Mental Image

Phenomenology, Sartre and Wittgenstein

What is the connexion between images and the imagination? This is one version of the question to which we must now turn. We have followed, albeit somewhat wanderingly, a thread which has led from the concept of imagination as both seeing in the mind's eye and part of ordinary perception, to imagination as creative. Thence we have come to a point where the image-forming, the creative and the interpretative roles of imagination seem to come together, in Wordsworth's *use* of these faculties, as well as in his theory. We must now try to discover whether this somewhat tenuous thread will survive a fuller examination of mental images, for without some understanding of the nature of these we cannot hope to understand imagination itself. In seeking such an understanding, we may in general agree with Sartre[1]: 'Any theory of imagination must satisfy two requirements. It must account for the spontaneous discrimination made by the mind between its images and its perceptions; and it must explain the role that images play in the operation of thinking.'

In order to attempt to satisfy these requirements, we must go back to a question left largely unanswered at the end of Part I. Hume acknowledges the 'spontaneous discrimination' between images and perceptions in normal cases. But we must try to find further clues, if we can, as to what he thought imagining was actually like. We must therefore go back to his first definition. Having distinguished, at the very beginning of the *Treatise*, between impressions and ideas by saying that they differ only in the degree of 'force and liveliness with which they strike upon the mind', he goes on to list as impressions all sensations, passions and emotions as they make their *first* appearance in the soul; and

---

[1] *The Psychology of Imagination* (1940); English translation (Methuen, 1972), p. 117.

as ideas the *faint images* of these in thinking and reasoning. It is clear from this definition that according to his theory, as indeed we have already seen, imagination operates in the region of ideas, and not of impressions (though, as we have also seen, powerful imagination may serve to convert an idea into an impression). Ideas are in some sense *copies* of impressions; and mental images, as we ordinarily understand them, are at least one kind of idea. It is this kind of idea which is the same sort of thing as an impression only weaker, and which may sometimes be converted into an impression in its own right. That it is supposed to be the same sort of thing as an impression is shown by the fact that Hume believes we may sometimes confuse ideas and impressions. 'In sleep, in a fever, in madness or in any very violent emotions of the soul, our ideas may approach to our impressions: as on the other hand it sometimes happens that our impressions are so faint and low that we cannot distinguish them from our ideas.'[1] Hume goes on to spell out the likeness between impressions and ideas: 'The first circumstance that strikes my eye is the very great resemblance betwixt our impressions and ideas in every other particular except their force and vivacity. The one seems to be in a manner the reflection of the other; so that all the perceptions of the mind are double, and appear both as impressions and ideas. When I shut my eyes and think of my chamber, the ideas I form are the exact representations of the impressions I felt.'[2] And though one may form a complex idea from a number of simple impressions, joining the elements together as they were never joined in actual experience, yet if one confines one's attention to the simple elements of experience, the reflection theory holds absolutely. 'That idea of red which we form in the dark and that impression which strikes our eye in sunshine differ only in degree, not in nature.' In the *Treatise*, Part I, section 3, Hume attempts to mark off more accurately those ideas which are specifically ideas of *imagination* from those of memory. Here again the difference is said to be a difference in degree of vivacity: 'We find by experience that when any impression has been present with the mind, it again makes its appearance there as an idea; and this it may do after two different ways: either when, in its new appearance, it retains a considerable degree of its first vivacity, and is somewhat intermediate betwixt

[1] S-B, p. 2.　　　　　　　　　[2] S-B, pp. 2-3.

The Nature of the Mental Image

an impression and an idea; or when it entirely loses that vivacity, and is a perfect idea. The faculty by which we repeat our impressions in the first manner is called the memory, and the other imagination.'[1] And later[2] he says, 'A man may indulge his fancy in feigning any past scene of adventures; nor would there be any possibility of this from a remembrance of a like kind were not the ideas of the imagination fainter and more obscure.' Apart from this, the distinguishing feature of imagination is that it is active. It may 'transpose and change its ideas'. Imagination is of its very nature free, whereas memory is tied to the production of ideas joined as they were, and in the order in which they originally came as impressions.

Imagination, then, consists in *having* (seeing, hearing, tasting etc.) weak experiences. It also consists in the joining of these experiences together by a principle of association which is, however, not absolutely binding. The principle of association is 'a gentle force that commonly prevails'; but it does not prevent the imagination from proceeding actively and, perhaps, consciously on its own course of joining and connecting ideas with one another. Thus if, as Hume would have us do, we accept the view that imagination almost always accompanies perception of objects, *what* accompanies perception is a number of weak or faint copies of the same kinds of thing as we are actually perceiving at a given time. I have a *strong* experience of the visual appearance of the tree before me, and a *weak* experience of the back of the tree which I cannot see. And if I assert that the tree is the one I saw yesterday, and that it continued to exist during the night when I did not see it, I have a weak experience of the-tree-yesterday, which is a copy of my strong experience of the-tree-today. Because it is of the very nature of the faculty of imagination to slide smoothly from like idea to like idea, and to continue in any course once set, producing more and more similar ideas according to the principles of association, so it comes about that we actually confuse many similar ideas with one identical idea. We believe, for instance, that the tree is *one thing which we perceive,* even the back of it which we may never have seen at all except in the pale copy produced by the imagination. And we believe that the tree is the very same tree as it was yesterday, although the image of yesterday's tree is in fact a different thing, necessarily, from the impressions of

[1] S-B, p. 8.   [2] Pt. III, sec. 5; S-B, p. 87.

133

today's tree. Likewise we believe that the tree will still exist tomorrow, and be the same tree, by a confusion between the tree we see now (our impression) and the image (idea) of the tree-tomorrow which we can form in our mind.

The confusion is between a weak and a strong version of the same thing. There is, it must be said, a good deal of muddle in Hume's use of the criterion of strength or vivacity, as against weakness or faintness, as a means of distinguishing impressions from ideas. He seems to use the same criterion as a means of making a number of different distinctions. Impressions and ideas, ideas which do, and those which do not constitute belief, ideas of memory and those of imagination, all these are supposed by him to be distinguished from each other by degrees of vivacity. Perhaps the confusion stems from a central confusion in the concept of belief itself. For it might be argued that when we distinguish 'spontaneously' between perception of the real world and our imaginings, we do so according to whether or not we *believe in* the existence of what we perceive. So Hume should have said that we believe in the existence of the external, independent world and do not believe in things which we merely imagine or even remember from the past. But what he did say was that imagination, that which produces the weak and non-believable ideas, feigns a continuity of existence which constitutes our acceptance of an independent world. How can belief be thereby generated? In distinguishing between memories and imaginary ideas he tries to say that the difference is in vivacity *and* a kind of necessity in the time-sequence of our ideas. How important is the supposed vivacity in this distinction? He was himself aware of the inconclusiveness of his account. In the appendix to Book I of the *Treatise*[1] he writes, 'I conclude ... that an opinion or belief is nothing but an idea, that is different from a fiction, not in the nature or the order of its parts but in the *manner* of its being conceived. But when I would explain this *manner*, I scarce find any word that fully answers the case. ... An idea assented to *feels* different from a fictitious idea, that the fancy alone presents to us: and this different feeling I endeavour to explain by calling it a superior force or vivacity or solidity or firmness or steadiness.' He realizes further that he has constituted a problem for himself in the very use of these terms with respect to the imagination as

[1] S-B, p. 628.

it is employed in the creative arts. For there, above all, people are said to produce lively and vivacious ideas, but it is not the case that such ideas are always, or even occasionally, such as to engender *belief*. In another part of the appendix to Book I, speaking of poetry, he says 'How greatsoever the pitch may be to which the vivacity rises, 'tis evident that in poetry it never has the same *feeling* with that which arises in the mind when we reason, though even upon the lowest species of probability. The mind can easily distinguish betwixt the one and the other; and whatever emotion the poetical enthusiasm may give to the spirits 'tis still the mere phantom of belief or persuasion.'[1] And again, 'A poetical description may have a more sensible effect on the fancy than a historical narration. . . . But still the ideas it presents are different to the *feeling* from those which arise from the memory or judgment. There is something weak and imperfect amidst all the seeming vehemence of thought and sentiment which attends the fictions of poetry.' And thus we are somehow kept from 'augmenting our belief upon every encrease of the force and vivacity of our ideas.' So force and vivacity alone cannot be the test by which we distinguish between belief and non-belief, nor therefore, perhaps, between what we take to be perception and what we take to be imagination or dream.

But despite these reservations, we have to conclude that Hume retained the definitions as he first propounded them, and that ideas were, on his view, just weaker versions of impressions. However, it may be objected that I am making Hume's theory look more extraordinary than it really is by insisting that what props up our perceptual experience—what as it were rounds it out—is a series of *images*, or actual copies of sense impressions. For, it may be argued, despite what some commentators believe, by 'idea' Hume does not always mean 'image', 'picture' or 'copy'. When he speaks, for example, of the function of reason being the comparison, the joining or disjoining of ideas, he is not necessarily to be thought to mean that reason has images as its counters to play with. Reason deals not with pictures but with concepts. May not Hume, then, be taken to mean that it is the *thought* or *concept* of dog-object or table-object which fills out the gaps in our perceptual experience? But I think that this will not do. Let us consider once more the case of my belief that the tree I can see

[1] S-B, p. 631.

has a continuous existence and that it is independent of myself. In order to understand the role which Hume assigns to the imagination in the forming of this belief, it is necessary, to think of the imagination as actually *confusing* ideas with one another, and with present perceptions, or impressions. The function of the imagination here was, as we saw, to *feign identity* when all there is, in fact, is similarity. Now this function entails the notion of comparing two or more items, and the items must be thought of as basically of the same kind, and only slightly different from each other. Thus the imagination can work in the way it does only because ideas are *like* (of the same general kind as) impressions. So I think we are bound to hold that Hume is here thinking of ideas as images—such, that is, as to be capable of being confused with impressions. In seeing the tree today, I actually believe that it (the tree that I see) is the same as the-tree-that-I-saw-yesterday, and as the-tree-that-I-will-see-tomorrow. But 'the-tree-that-I-saw' and 'the-tree-that-I-will-see' are the names not of impressions but of ideas. In this case, if I believe in identity it must be because an idea is an image, exceedingly like an impression.

It will be noticed that in expounding his theory, and especially in defining the terms in which it is set out, Hume constantly appeals for confirmation to our actual experience. He asks us to examine, as it occurs in ourselves, the difference between seeing and imagining, or between imagining and remembering. The appeal is to what we can all discover to be the case by introspection. We are reminded of Sartre's demand of a theory of imagination, that it should satisfy the spontaneous distinction we all make between perceptions and images. And there is here what may be felt to be a general difficulty in method. In talking about imagination, there seems no way to avoid a certain appeal to introspection. And yet we are often told that this is a hopelessly unreliable source of knowledge, since, by definition, it cannot be checked by different observers. It is said that, even supposing one can reach any truths by this means, they cannot be general truths, since it is impossible to distinguish facts which happen to be true of a particular individual from facts or general principles which have application to all human beings. Yet, whatever the drawbacks of the method, the fact of the matter is that we cannot abandon it altogether. It is inevitable, for example, that, in reading Hume, we should test what he says, even if he did not expressly instruct us to, against our own experience. We inevitably raise the question 'are images really just like perceptions only fainter?' And we tend to try to answer this experimentally, by first looking at the table in front of us, and then shutting our eyes and trying to imagine or visualize the table. And so we proceed through all Hume's distinctions and assimilations. In the end the implausibility of Hume's theory of imagination is borne in on us because it does not fit our own experiences of imagining. Later, we shall have to consider some more elaborate attempts to characterize the imagination by such introspective and essentially practical methods as these. Meanwhile, I would simply content myself with saying that they are unavoidable. Moreover, we can, difficult though it may be to do accurately, draw a distinction between what one might call autobiographical introspection and analytic introspection. There is a difference between saying, 'Last night I dreamed about a Mozart Symphony', and saying, 'Dreams may take this or that form', even if the *ground* for the latter statement is the actual recollection of various dreams. Thus it is justifiable to reject Hume's account of imagination, and to base one's general judgment that it will not do, not upon a rival theory, but upon the finding, in experience, that there are more radical differences between seeing things and visualizing them, between perceiving and imagining, than Hume allows. What these differences are we must consider shortly.

Meanwhile we must try to see whether Kant, whose role for the imagination in perception is, as we have seen, an extension of Hume's, gives us more adequate help in trying to answer the question what imagination *is*. Here, alas, we must briefly report that he does not. As we saw in Part I, the chief word which Kant uses for imagination is *Einbildungskraft*. This word has, as part of its meaning, the notion of forming pictures, images or representations. We know therefore that in speaking both of the empirical and of the *a priori* functions of imagination, Kant must mean us to understand that the mind forms a kind of picture, either a particular picture of a rhododendron bush, or a general picture of a bush, or a yet more highly general picture of a permanent and independent object. He must mean that it is through, or with the help of, such pictures that sense experience and our concepts of things are brought together, that sense and knowledge conform to each other. But one feels inclined to say that to speak of a picture or image in this context must be metaphorical. For one thing, we may ask, what is a *general* picture? Are particular pictures specific and detailed, while general pictures are unspecific and vague?

It is exactly at this point that we urgently need to pause and make a determined effort at clarity. If we speak of pictures in such a context are we or are we not committing ourselves to metaphor? In what sense, if any, do we wish to say that exercising imagination involves having pictures before the mind's eye? Is there any totally non-metaphorical way of describing the phenomena in question? These are the very questions, or some of them, which we must try to answer. But one clue to the answer may still perhaps be extracted from Kant's account of the role of the imagination in perception. The word *Einbildungskraft* may perhaps be taken to suggest an *ability* to form pictures. Perhaps when Kant says that in the application of a concept to the world in perception we need the faculty of imagination, he might be taken to mean that, though we need not form an actual picture or image of the kind of thing which we are perceiving, yet we must be *able* to form such a picture—there must be the possibility of our envisaging objects of a certain kind. Thus if we identify something as a rhododendron bush, we do so only in the light of being *able to* envisage other bushes of the same kind. Again, if we identify the bush as the same bush which we saw in the drive yesterday and which has had a particular history, we must do so in the light of being able to form a picture of a bush (of any kind) as a thing which persists through time, which grows and decays. So, in our immediate recognition of what is before us, there is built a possibility, which could at any time be actualized, of the framing of images of other bushes, or of other aspects of this bush. And these images or representations could be mental pictures or they could perhaps be pictures on paper. The point at issue is whether the thing we see is seen by us as something which *could* be represented.

Perhaps we tend, in thinking of images, to become unduly concerned with the problems attached to visual images (we shall find this again and again in the present part of the subject). It is perhaps more readily intelligible to suggest that in the case of

sounds, in order that we should perceive a sound as an identi-
fiable object of attention, in order that is, that we should perceive it either as a specific sound, e.g. middle c played on a flute,
or as a sound which, though we cannot specify it exactly, has
occurred before in our experience, we have to be able to conceive of it as *reproduceable*. If we had absolutely no way of 'hearing
the sound again in our head' or reproducing it in another way,
then we should not be able to recognize it *as* a sound at all.
Perceiving a sound entails picking out a part of our total experience at a given moment as having sound-characteristics; and
that we *can* do this entails that we must be able to give ourselves a
kind of run-through of sound-characteristics if we choose to. If we
could not do this at all, then from our standpoint the world
would contain no auditory features. Admittedly, the nature of
these possible representations, the potential pictures, the auditory
runs-through, is very obscure. It is to be hoped that it may become a little clearer in due course.

In the meantime it is worth looking again at what Kant says
about the empirical faculty of the imagination in the *Critique of
Pure Reason*[1] (see page 28): 'What is first given to us is appearance.
When combined with consciousness it is called perception. Now
since every appearance contains a manifold and since different
perceptions therefore occur in the mind separately and singly, a
combination of them such as they cannot have in sense is demanded. There must therefore exist in us an active faculty for the
synthesis of this manifold. To this faculty I give the title imagination.' So far, this is just a reminder of what the imagination does.
Then he goes on: 'Since it has to bring the manifold of intuition
into the form of an image it must previously have taken the
impressions up into its activity, that is have apprehended them.
But it is clear that even this apprehension of the manifold would
not by itself produce an image and a connexion of the impressions
were it not that there exists a subjective ground which leads the
mind to reinstate a preceding perception alongside the subsequent
perception to which it has passed, and so to form whole series of
perceptions. This is the reproductive faculty of imagination, which
is merely empirical.' This empirical function is itself possible,
Kant goes on to say, only because it is founded on an objective
principle, which demands that the imagination brings its

[1] A 120.

representations together in certain rule-governed ways. But this is to go over old ground.

In the quotation above it will be noticed that the imagination in its empirical function has two tasks. It has to bring the manifold of intuition into the form of an image, and it has to reinstate a preceding perception alongside a subsequent perception into which it has passed. The function of the empirical imagination is thus to *solidify* the chaos into an image, to *stop* it, by creating an orderly series which the mind can contemplate. And this it does by bringing up past experiences and laying them beside the present, to form, as Kant says, a combination. And all this is possible because *a priori* the imagination is capable, in general, of *reproducing* experience in the form of objects of attention. Kant's actual words, 'bring into the form of an image', 'reinstate a preceding perception', seem to me to be compatible with the view that although exercising imagination *may* consist in forming actual pictures or reproductions of sights or sounds, it may also consist in a kind of confidence that one could do this, that the object perceived is in some sense imaginable or reproduceable in other manifestations or at other times, or that similar objects could be imagined or reproduced. If this confidence were lost, then no recognition of dogs or bushes would be possible. On this interpretation, the imagination makes perceptual objects recognizable by its *power* to produce representations of similar things. We are not thereby committed to saying that in perceiving a dog I *actually* form an image of another dog, or of this dog yesterday, but to saying only that I could do so, and know that I could. Thus the imagination is the power to produce images, and the possibility of image-forming is, in an underlying way, a part of perception. If this is a justifiable interpretation of Kant, then apart from all other reasons which may make us regard Kant as going infinitely further in understanding what he is at than Hume, we can certainly claim that his account of the role of imagination in perception is greatly to be preferred, on the grounds that, though it makes use of the concept of the mental image, it does not demand that we think of the image as a pale or weak copy of a perceptual experience. It does not perhaps commit us to any specific view of the nature of the image itself.

Before leaving Kant, we may add this. The *a priori* function of the imagination by which it makes concepts applicable, in general, to the manifold of sensation is, as we saw in Part I, known as the Schematism. Perhaps some support for the foregoing interpretation of Kant may be drawn from the *Critique of Judgment*, where a contrast is drawn between the schematism and the empirical use of the imagination. Kant says,[1] 'Intuitions are always required to verify the reality of our concepts. If the concepts are empirical the intuitions are called examples: if they are pure concepts of the understanding, the intuitions go by the name of schemata.' These intuitions are of objects we *can* sense. They are visible, or otherwise sensible, forms. So, if I am to be able to employ a concept, whether one which I must use in order to think of the world at all (an *a priori* concept) or one which I just happen to have learned (the concept of 'dog' or of 'greyhound'), I must be able to present to myself a visible or audible form which exemplifies the concept. Either I must be able to present to my mind an example of a dog, or a greyhound, or I must show myself how such an example *could* be produced in general. This is the representational function of the imagination.

Up to now, we have been assuming, as both Hume and Kant assumed, that the exercise of the imagination, whenever it occurs, in some way or other entails the forming of mental images, or at least the possibility of their formation. We have carried this assumption into our examination of both Hume's and Kant's accounts of the role of imagination in perception. But the whole notion of the mental image has been strongly under fire in the twentieth century, and our next task must be to question our assumptions from this point of view: is it possible that there can be such a thing as an image, in the way we have taken for granted? At the same time as the mental image has become suspect, there has also arisen, and from the same source, a new theory of perception which does not involve the imagination at any stage. The common source of both these connected alternative theories is the philosophical theory or set of theories known as phenomenology. I want to postpone the discussion of the phenomenological attack on images, and first introduce phenomenology by means of one version of its theory of perception, although the consideration of this may seem to be a rather lengthy digression from our main theme. At this stage I can only

[1] *Critique of Judgment*, 59.

plead for patience in the hope that, in the end, the digression may not appear wholly irrelevant to our overall purpose.

The father of phenomenology is generally agreed to have been the German philosopher Franz Brentano, whose most famous work was completed in the nineteenth century, but who died in 1917. Brentano defined mental, as opposed to physical, activity as that which is directed towards an object. For this feature he used the scholastic word 'intentional'. All mental or psychological acts whatever, and this of course included emotions and acts of imagination, were characterized essentially by being directed upon some object. A thought was necessarily a thought *of* something, a feeling a feeling *about* something. Thus, in the case of imagination, according to his theory, if I imagine my absent friend, my consciousness has as its object my friend, but I think of him in a particular way, namely imaginatively. In perception there are only two items to be introduced into any account of the matter, the perceiving person, and the thing he perceives. So in the case of imagination there are only *two* items, I, who am imagining, and my friend, who is the object of my imagination. Into the accounts neither of perceiving nor of imagining do we need to introduce a third item, the image or mental content. I shall return to this theory later. The next great name in the phenomenological movement, and certainly the major influence upon the theories we are now about to consider, was Edmund Husserl. In Husserl's mature philosophy the notion of intentionality is rendered more complex than it was in Brentano's theory. In an intentional act we not only direct our attention towards an object, but we also essentially discover a meaning *in* that to which we turn our mind. Husserl draws a distinction, of a somewhat messy kind, between a *thing perceived* and a thing *as it is perceived*. He explains the distinction by an analogy with language. There is one object meant by a word and a multiplicity of objects as they are meant. The object as it is meant will vary from one person to another, and from one time to another, depending upon what features of the object are best known to, or most important to, the user of the word. There is one essential object meant, for instance, by the word 'Oxford'. But 'Oxford as it is meant' may be infinitely, or almost infinitely, various. For one person it may mean the second division football team, for another the place where the dictionary is published, for another a kind of shoes, and so on. This theory is full of holes as regards language, and in any case, even if it were not, it is not clear how far Husserl wishes to press the analogy between language and perception. But the force of it is fairly obvious. Groups of different perceptual experiences, objects as they are perceived by two different people or by the same person at different times, are all related to one object perceived. And this is, he says, because they are all 'animated by a certain way of comprehending, or "intending"'. The different objects as they are perceived are thought of as having a common meaning. The object perceived, which is this common meaning, is said to be transcendent to the particular acts of perception. Perception itself creates or constitutes objects perceived by endowing particular perceptual experiences with significance.

Husserl arrives at this conclusion by means of what was called the phenomenological method of reduction. The method consists in an attempt to eliminate all presuppositions about the nature of things (one is to put the world in brackets) and thus to turn experience into 'pure phenomena' which one is then to examine. Brentano had also tried to confine himself to the description of the content of consciousness, and to isolate whatever was *given*, as an object of experience. Husserl found, however, that in isolating what was given immediately to experience, one discovers that the given itself necessarily carries with it general implications; it points beyond itself to something universal and beyond the perceiving subject. This is simply what experience reveals, if it is properly examined. Though we may put on one side all our general knowledge of things, yet we shall find that there is a general significance in what we actually and immediately perceive, and that this general content cannot be removed by any exercise of reduction.

The phenomenological method is a kind of introspective method, in that we have to attempt to consider what we experience, and then to isolate within our experience a 'pure phenomenon'. Husserl is claiming that as a matter of fact we cannot discover, by any introspective effort, a pure experience which does not have some general significance beyond itself. If we pretend that we can do this, we shall radically misrepresent the nature of perception. His theory is thus opposed to both Hume's and Kant's. For, in the first place, perceptions cannot be described as mere momentary impressions about which the question must be raised how they relate to material objects as we naturally think of them. My perception of a tree, according to Husserl, is not a green item of momentary occurrence which needs to be related, by some magical or mysterious faculty, to other similar occurrences, before I can identify what I see as a tree. On the contrary, in perceiving, I perceive the essential tree. If we consider our perceptions as they actually occur, and without presuppositions, we shall find that each perception carries in it a general sense. Nothing else is needed. 'Could an infinite intellect', Husserl writes, 'have more knowledge of "red" than that he simply looks at it?' There is no gap between concept and object. In seeing, we immediately see an object as instantiating a concept. Moreover, we have no need of a magical faculty to help us to recognize a particular object as the same through a period of time. We do not have to invoke imagination to 'feign' the continuing existence of the thing. If a man hears a sustained note in music he does not hear it as a succession of momentary sounds. That is to say, if one required him at any particular moment to report what he was hearing, he would have to include in his account the sound *considered as part of a sustained note*. Each moment of the note is heard as *pointing* to the long note. So far Kant at least would agree with Husserl. But he would argue that this fact demonstrates that function of the imagination which is to create for us the very possibility of hearing a sustained note persisting through time, rather than a disordered succession of sounds, even though this function is carried out below the level of consciousness. Husserl on the other hand simply asserts that this is part of perception itself, and that it cannot be further analysed.

I want to examine the phenomenological theory of perception in a little more detail. For, paradoxically, although phenomenologists exclude imagination from our perceptive awareness of the world, yet the role of imagination in this awareness becomes clearer the more one considers the theory which attempts to do without it. It will be convenient to look at the theory as set out by Merleau-Ponty in *The Phenomenology of Perception*,[1] since this work has the relatively limited aim of expounding and elaborating Husserl's theory specifically as it concerns perception. It is therefore completely relevant to our concern in a way that Husserl

[1] 1945. English translation by Colin Smith (Routledge and Kegan Paul, 1962).

himself is not, as well as being somewhat easier to follow. In *The Phenomenology of Perception*, then, Merleau-Ponty aims to reveal how man is connected with the world through perception; and he aims to do this without employing the presuppositions of either science or common sense. What both scientists and practitioners of common sense refer to as knowledge is in any case based on perception; it is therefore, he says, the philosopher's task to lay bare the perception which lies behind knowledge.

The basic assumption which we must start by putting aside is that there is an absolute distinction between the perceiving subject and the object perceived. The whole of the efforts of both Hume and Kant can be seen as attempts, on the assumption of such a distinction, to bridge the gap again, and explain how the perceiving subject comes to have objects to think or speak about. At the very beginning of his investigation Merleau-Ponty argues that the Humean account of impressions, associated together by their actual similarity, is nonsensical. Impressions could not be associated together at all if it were not that they were already imbued with significance. (We are reminded of Coleridge's arguments against Hartley.) 'The sensations and images which should be the beginning and end of all knowledge never make their appearance anywhere other than within a horizon of meaning, and the significance of the percept, far from resulting from an association, is in fact presupposed in all association.'[1] In Hume's theory, the similarity between one impression and another was an actual relation which 'gently forced' the imagination to present us with one idea after another. The concept of similarity was never itself examined. It was taken to be a primitive, observable phenomenon, as was succession in time and contiguity in space. Merleau-Ponty argues, on the other hand, that the very notion of similarity is meaningless unless we can apply it, and we can do so only in a context in which similar things are *significantly* similar. To observe two phenomena as similar is already to interpret them in one way rather than another. 'An impression can never by itself be associated with another impression. Nor has it the power to arouse others. It does so only provided that it is already understood in the light of the past experience in which it coexisted with those which we are concerned to arouse.'[2] In actually receiving an impression, that is

[1] *Op. cit.*, p. 15.　　　　　　[2] *Op. cit.*, p. 17.

to say, we immediately understand it in a certain way, we do not *first* receive an impression and *then* understand it to be associated with other impressions.

So far, though Merleau-Ponty is plainly rejecting Hume's account of our 'objectifying' the world, he has not explicitly rejected Kant's. For Kant also held that in actual experience we could not come upon impressions of the world which were not already and necessarily cast in a certain mould, and connected with others. The *a priori* function of the imagination was precisely to present our actual sense experience in a particular form, laid down necessarily in the pure concepts of the understanding, and we could never in fact receive our experience otherwise than so presented. For the imagination, in this manifestation, worked unconsciously, and was not subject to our whim. Its work was done before we consciously perceived or described things.

It is to the denial of this account that Merleau-Ponty turns next. The dismissal of the Humean view, he argues, carries us only part of the way. 'It is true that psychologism has been left behind, that the meaning and structure of the percept are for us no longer the outcome of mere psycho-physiological events. . . . But although what we perceive may be expressible in terms of some internal law, this law must not be considered as a model on which the phenomena of structure are built up. It is not because the "form" produces a certain state of equilibrium, solving a problem of coherence, and, in the Kantian sense, making the world possible that it enjoys a privileged place in our perception; it *is* the very appearance of the world, and not the condition of its possibility. It is the identity of the external and internal, and not the projection of the internal on the external.'[1] Here, then, is the notion which he has now to try to explain, the notion, that is, of the *identity* of the external and internal. Roughly, this identity exists, he argues, because we ourselves are bodies in a world of bodies, and our perception of the world, quite literally our contact with it, is through our bodies. Therefore it follows that we necessarily perceive things as objects, as things available to our bodies, if we perceive them at all. The perception, for example, of an object as at a distance from myself is not something which can be analysed as, on the one hand, part of the manifold of sensation *plus*, on the other hand, a concept of space applied

[1] *Op. cit.*, p. 60.

to the sensation by the imagination. It is, on the contrary, an immediate perception which cannot be further analysed at all. 'Every sensation is spatial: we have adopted this thesis, not because the quality as an object of sense cannot be *thought of* otherwise than in space, but because, as the primordial contact with being, as the assumption by the sentient subject of a form of existence to which the sensible points, and as the co-existence of sentient and sensible, it itself constitutes a setting for co-existence, in other words space.'[1] 'Sensation as it is brought to use by experience is no longer some inert or abstract moment, but one of our surfaces of contact with Being, a structure of consciousness, and, in place of one single space as the universal condition of all sensible qualities, we have with each quality, a particular manner of being in space, and, in a way, of making space.'[2]

It is not only space which he holds to be thus created in perception. All the qualities of objects spring into existence in this way, though some kinds of perception, obviously, are peculiarly related to one type of quality, other kinds to others. In *Eye and Mind*, the last work of Merleau-Ponty's to be published in his life-time,[3] he quotes Valéry, 'The Painter takes his body with him', and goes on from this point. There is no distinction between the world that I see and the world that I move in, touch and manipulate. There is one world in which I move and hear and see and touch, and all sensible attributes of things arise out of this contact. 'Immersed in the visible by his body, itself visible, the see-er does not appropriate what he sees; he merely approaches it by looking, he opens himself to the world.' 'Visible and mobile, my body is a thing among things; it is caught in the fabric of the world, and its cohesion is that of a thing. But because it moves itself and sees, it holds things in a circle round itself. Things are an annex or prolongation of itself; they are incrusted into its flesh, they are parts of its full definition; the world is made of the same stuff as the body.'[4]

So we cannot separate concepts from perceptions, nor one aspect of a thing from another. Perceiving it *is* perceiving it as an object and as falling under a concept; and perceiving it in one

---

[1] *Op. cit.*, p. 221.   [2] *Loc. cit.*
[3] Reprinted in *Aesthetics*, ed. Harold Osborn (O.U.P., 1972), p. 55.
[4] *Op. cit.*, p. 59.

aspect *is* perceiving it in another. 'The denomination of objects does not follow upon recognition; it is itself recognition.'[1] 'When I fix my eyes on an object in the half-light, and say "it is a brush", there is not in my mind the concept of a brush, under which I subsume the object and which is linked by frequent association with the word "brush"; but the word bears the meaning and by imposing it on the object I am conscious of reaching that object. . . . For pre-scientific thinking, naming an object is causing it to exist.' 'The unity of the thing beyond all its properties is not a substratum, a vacant X, an inherent subject, but that unique accent which is to be found in each one of them, that unique manner of existing of which they are an expression. There is a symbolism in the thing which links each sensible quality to the rest.'[2]

The conclusion is that because I am incarnate, a body among bodies, my perception of the world needs no medium through which I can translate the evidence of sense into conceptual knowledge, neither does my knowledge that there exist independent and stable objects need to be translated into sense perception with certain additions. To pretend that I need something other than perception to assure me of the existence of bodies in the world is simply to overlook the true nature of perception. The existence of the world is something, as Hume said, which we must take for granted in all our reasonings. But whereas Hume thought it proper to raise the question how we come by this belief, 'what causes induce us to believe it,' Merleau-Ponty regards this question itself as a fake. 'The world is not what I think but what I live through. I am open to the world, I have no doubt that I am in communication with it—"there is a world", or rather, "there is this world"; I can never completely account for this ever-reiterated assertion in my life.'[3]

Here, then, is a theory of perception which has no room for imagination, because perception in its most immediate sense, already contains the elements of 'going further', of generalizing and objectifying, which Hume and Kant had, in different ways, allotted to imagination, because they could not incorporate them in bare impression-having. The manifold of sensation, which Kant himself knew that we never experienced in an unmodified

[1] *The Phenomenology of Perception*, p. 177.
[2] *Op cit.*, p. 319.　　　　　[3] *Op. cit.*, preface, p. xviii.

form, but which he yet thought somehow *would* exist if another faculty than that of sense did not go to work, has disappeared from the description of perception, even as its foundation. It is an essential part of *perception itself* to construct objects in the world. One cannot, by the utmost refinements of abstraction, consider perception apart from this constructive power. Thus we end with a picture of perception as necessarily a mixture of receiving and interpreting stimuli, of passive experiencing and active constructing. It is difficult to express this notion of essentially thought-imbued perceiving in language which differentiates the views of Husserl and Merleau-Ponty from those of Kant. For Kant himself held that we *must* perceive objects as separate from ourselves and occupying space and time. But he thought that he could by analysis discover the rules or schemata according to which our imagination necessarily created for us such objects of perception. Merleau-Ponty held, more simply perhaps, but hardly more intelligibly, that because we are ourselves bodies in the world, there could be no such thing as perception if we did not perceive other bodies, constructed into bodies by our actual perceiving them. There is no room in this account for any magical faculty or occult power to explain the fact that when we perceive, we perceive independent and external bodies. Perception comes first: imagination, whatever it is, must depend upon perception.

But, leaving on one side the somewhat obscure quasi-explanation offered by Merleau-Ponty (that because we are bodies we perceive bodies), the account of perception offered by the phenomenologists has a good deal of plausibility if it is tested, as we have seen any theory must be, against actual experience (though it must not be supposed that one can actually refute Kant by any appeal to experience). The phenomenological approach has been used to a considerable extent by psychiatrists who, as part of their attempt to understand the psychological disturbances of their patients, try to get absolutely clear, direct descriptions of what the patients actually experience, in cases of illusion, delusion, hallucination or disturbed perception. The description of such abnormal phenomena may itself throw light on the normal.

Karl Jaspers is an example of one who in the early part of his career combined a commitment to phenomenology with a practical concern with psychopathology. His *General Psychopathology* (written in 1923, but not translated into English until twenty years later[1]) is a rich source of examples and descriptions which deserve to be studied as much by philosophers as by psychologists, in that they cast light again and again on the language we use, and the assumptions we make about the perceptual world. For example, in attempting to classify delusions, Jaspers writes as follows: 'The experience in the context of which delusion takes place is that of experiencing and thinking that something is real . . . . But what the experience of reality is in itself can hardly be deduced . . . nor can we compare it as a phenomenon with other related phenomena. Our attention gets drawn to it because it can be disturbed pathologically, and so we appreciate that it exists.'[2] Jaspers argues that we all believe in the reality of what resists us. Our basic assumption is that whatever we have to *contend with*, for the achievement of goals, is what is real, whether we overcome the obstacle or are defeated by it. All our experience of reality thus has a basis in something practical, something which we could possibly have to treat either as an obstacle or a tool. 'But the reality itself which we meet in practice is always also an interpretation, a meaning, the meaning of things, events or situations. When I *grasp the meaning*, I grasp reality.'[3] Thus delusions may take the form of things which I perceive in a normal way up to a certain point, but which nevertheless take on a wholly different meaning. Jaspers reports a patient, for instance, for whom two people in raincoats walking along the street, whom he would describe exactly as anyone else would describe them, nevertheless *are* Schiller and Goethe.[4] Another patient sees a man in the street and knows immediately that he is a former lover of hers.[5] He looks entirely different from this man, it is true; he has disguised himself with a wig and there are other differences. It is all a bit odd. But 'everything is so dead certain that no amount of seeing to the contrary will make it doubtful'. Of these cases Jaspers says, 'These are not considered interpretations, but direct experiences of meaning while perception itself remains normal and unchanged.'

The cases classified by him as abnormalities of perception itself are of just as much interest in the present context. For example, there is the phenomenon which he calls 'derealization'[6]

---

[1] By Huenig and Hamilton (Manchester U.P., 1963).   [2] *Op. cit.*, p. 93.
[3] *Op. cit.*, p. 94.   [4] *Op. cit.*, p. 99.   [5] *Loc. cit.*
[6] *Op. cit.*, p. 62.

in which everything is described as 'appearing through a veil'; 'Things do not look as before . . . they are somehow two-dimensional.' 'All objects seem so new and startling that I say their names over to myself and touch them several times to convince myself that they are real.' Or perceptions may come split up and separated from each other.[1] 'A bird chirrups in the garden. I know that it is chirrupping and I hear it. But that it is a bird and that it is chirrupping are two things which are poles apart. There is a gulf between them and I am afraid I shall not be able to bring them together. It is as if the bird and the chirrupping have nothing to do with each other.' It appears from these and other examples that in our normal perception of objects there is an element that, as it were, objectifies them, makes them three-dimensional, places them in space and connects the various aspects of our perception together. If this element in our perception ceases to function or becomes disturbed, then the very nature of our perceptions change. It may well be said, and I should agree, that the psychologists' distinction between 'the perception remaining the same and the interpretation changing' on the one hand, and 'the perception itself being disturbed' on the other is arbitrary, and could not be satisfactorily drawn in detail. It may also be objected that there is nothing to be gained by speaking of different 'elements' in our perception. Nevertheless, it seems to me that from the consideration of actual examples of perception, normal and abnormal, we are entitled to conclude that all our perceptions are to some extent *thought-imbued*; that we normally assume a kind of interpretation of what we see and hear, which may be said to be our *thoughts about* our experience, and that we are most likely to become aware of this interpretation when we are presented with examples of an interpretation that is different, that is disturbed or eccentric. The question which remains is whether or not we want to call this thought-element in perception 'imagination' or not. If we do so designate it, then we shall be returning to the vocabulary of Hume and Kant in preference to that of phenomenology. But we may perhaps leave this question unanswered for the time being.

Meanwhile it is high time to return from this lengthy digression to the subject which is supposed to be the concern of this Part, namely the nature of the mental image. It will be remembered

---

[1] *Op. cit.*, p. 64.

that our digression was undertaken in the interests of expounding phenomenology which is the source of the attack on the existence of the image as a thing at all, whether in the presence or the absence of its object.

Brentano, as we saw, argued that in describing a man as imagining his absent friend, there was no need of any items in the description other than the man and his friend. There was no need to incorporate any third intermediary item, the image. It was entirely in the spirit of Brentano that Ryle conceived the nature of imagination. His discussion of the subject in chapter 8 of *The Concept of Mind*[1] is the *locus classicus* of the twentieth-century attack on the image, and it is to this that we must now proceed. Like Brentano and the other phenomenologists, his aim here is to discover how one ought properly to describe certain psychological phenomena. 'The crucial problem', he says, 'is that of describing what is "seen in the mind's eye" and what is "heard in one's head". The familiar truth that people are constantly seeing things in their minds' eyes, or hearing things in their heads is no proof that there exist things which they see and hear, or that people are seeing and hearing. Much as stage murders do not have victims and are not murders, so seeing things in one's mind's eye does not involve either the existence of things seen, or the occurrence of acts of seeing them.'[2] Ryle does not, obviously, deny that acts of imagination occur; what he does deny is that acts of imagination consist in seeing or hearing copies of visible or auditory objects. 'When I fancy I am hearing a very loud noise,' he says, 'I am not really hearing either a loud or a faint noise; I am not having a mild auditory sensation, as I am not having an auditory sensation at all, though I am fancying that I am having an intense one.'[3] Here, then we have a head-on attack on Hume. It makes us profoundly uneasy to be told by Hume that images are exactly like original objects of perception, only fainter. The reason for our uneasiness, Ryle says, is that imagining a sound (having an image of a sound) is not hearing a sound at all. Therefore there can be no sense in raising the question whether the real sound is stronger or weaker, more or less vivid, than the imagined sound. There is no such object of attention as the imagined sound with which to compare the real. Hume's notion that sometimes an imagined object might be

---

[1] Hutchinson, 1949.   [2] *Op. cit.*, p. 245.   [3] *Op. cit.*, p. 250.

taken for a real one, and the other way round, is literally non-sensical, according to this demolitionist view.

Ryle holds that we may be encouraged in our tendency to think of images as things we can look at in our heads by our proneness to take seeing as the best example of perception, and therefore to take visualizing as the best example of imagining. In the case of visual perception, we may look either at a dog or at a photograph of a dog. The photograph is of course a real physical object, but it stands in a particular relation to the dog, namely it represents him. We thus have two physical objects, but one can be said to represent the other. There is a sense in which the photograph is a copy (or at least a likeness) of the dog and is caused to exist by the existence of the dog. At least the one-time existence of the dog is a *sine qua non* of the existence of a genuine photograph of him. It is very easy to think of mental images as fulfilling the same function as photographs or portraits, bearing the same kind of relation as photographs or portraits to what they are images of. Nor, as we shall see, are we wrong to think thus. But according to Ryle we go too far in our assimilation. For since we may visualize a dog in the absence of the dog itself, and may also possess a photograph of the dog in its absence, we go on to think that there is something which we can take a look at, in both cases, to remind ourselves of the dog's appearance, and that when we see the dog in our mind's eye we are inspecting this thing.

Ryle says about memory what he would also say about imagination, that we tend to exaggerate the extent to which there is an accurate account to be given of how we envisage things. We tend to speak as though we could envisage a scene, look at it more and more closely and, as it were, read off from it what we find there. 'If a description of a face is about as good in the absence as in the presence of the face, this must be due to the presence of something like a photograph of the face.'[1] So we are prone to argue. But the fact that a man can give a description of an absent face does not in itself show that he is seeing either the face or a replica of the face. He might be able to give the description just because he knew what the face was like. In Ryle's phrase, he might have 'learned and not forgotten' the characteristics of the face. There is no need to describe him as seeing anything at all, still less to

[1] *Op. cit.*, p. 276.

say that he is looking hard at his image, and reading from it the description that he gives. Yet, though we may exaggerate the possibility of accurately describing our images, there is so far no reason to deny that we have them, neither does Ryle deny this. What he does deny is that images are *like* material objects.

One has to be very careful at this point not to become too enthusiastic about demolition. Sometimes philosophers have said 'images are not things' and by this they have meant that images are not material objects, and probably also that they are unlike material objects in certain specifiable and important respects. But if they are thereby taken to be saying that there are *no such things as images*, and if this in turn is taken to imply that we never visualize things or attempt to recall things by 'seeing' them or 'hearing' them, or even 'smelling' them, then what they are saying is manifestly absurd. So we are still left with the problem of attempting to describe more precisely what such activities amount to. But we must bear in mind that our problem is what images are, not whether they exist or not. It is certain that the word 'image' is a word we shall want to retain.

Let us go back to the case of the mental picture which I may form of an absent friend, and consider it more carefully. It is simply not true that there is a total lack of connexion between mental pictures and non-mental pictures, photographs or portraits. Even though we may agree that mental pictures are not physical objects like photographs, yet we do naturally and inevitably speak of picturing in the mind; and it is impossible completely to describe our experience, in some cases of recalling or imagining, without having recourse to the visual language of pictures or images. Ryle himself, as we have said, does not deny that we see things in the mind's eye; nor does he deny the connexion between such 'seeing' and the seeing of photographs or portraits. He says, 'When a visible likeness of a person is in front of my nose, I often seem to be seeing the person himself in front of my nose, though he is not there and may be long since dead. I should not keep the portrait, if it did not fulfil this function. Or when I hear the recording of a friend's voice, I fancy I hear him singing or speaking in the room, though he is miles away. The genus is *seeming to perceive*, and of this genus, one very familiar species is that of seeming to see something when looking at an

ordinary snapshot of it. Seeming to see when no physical likeness is before the nose is another species. Imaging is not having
shadowy pictures before some shadow-organ called "the mind's
eye"; but having paper pictures before the eyes in one's face is a
familiar stimulus to imaging.'[1]

Here Ryle is going beyond a simple denial that there are
images which are like material objects, to a positive analysis of
the nature of imagining. He says that when we look at a photograph or a portrait and see it as a representation of someone,
there is a sense in which we *see in our imagination* the man of whom
it is a representation. As soon as we see the portrait before us as a
present likeness of someone who is not present, we see the original
in the portrait. The sense in which, in this case, we can be said to
'see' the original is exactly the same, he argues, as that in which we
'see the dog in our mind's eye' when the dog itself is not present.
But in this latter case there is no portrait or photograph for us to
see the absent dog *in*. Thus, there is no essential difference, only
an accidental one, between recalling the face of our absent
friend by looking at his photograph, and on the other hand
recalling it by shutting our eyes and envisaging or 'seeing' his
face. It is only that some people may be rather bad at doing the
latter, without the benefit of material aids. Now we can see more
clearly, perhaps, how it is that, in answer to the insistent question
'what *is* a mental image?', we may fall into the trap of saying that
it is a kind of mental photograph. It is because the function of the
image and the photograph may be the same, namely, to help us to
recall the visual appearance of something which we cannot
actually see before us. The essence of visualizing seems to be here,
if we can only make it a bit clearer.

It seems that Ryle has added to the simple demolitionist theory
of Brentano a further factor. A imagining B and A perceiving B
are both relations between A and B. But there is a halfway kind of
perceiving when the relation between A and B is mediated by
another object, a portrait or representation of B. Imagining B is
now likened to this kind of perception. But there is a good sense
in which A, when he looks at the portrait of B, is not perceiving
B at all. What he is doing is thinking about B, and perceiving a
canvas. So, when he is imagining B he is thinking about B and
not perceiving a canvas, or anything else at all. But he is thinking

[1] *Op. cit.*, p. 254.

visually. This is what Ryle refers to, somewhat misleadingly, as 'fancying that he is seeing'.

The part of *The Concept of Mind* which we have just discussed has, as I have suggested, sometimes misled. Perhaps it has done so partly because of the suggestion, conveyed by the word 'fancying', that the man who is doing it is either deceived, or is deliberately playing or pretending. Neither of these suggestions is necessary for a description of the case, though Ryle himself progresses from the consideration of 'fancying' to that of 'pretending'. But there is no doubt that in this particular area, the difficulties of saying exactly what one means, or indeed of finding out what one means, seem more acute the more one thinks about it. We must be prepared therefore to spend a little longer trying to get the description right. For my part I have no doubt that what we may call the phenomenological tradition, and this includes Ryle, offers a better way of describing mental images than the empiricist, or Humean, tradition before it, but has not, even so, got it completely right.

One of the main exponents of the phenomenological view is Sartre, and it is certainly worth while picking one's way through his book on imagination for the insights as well as the confusions and ambiguities it offers. But before considering him, I would like to turn for a moment to Wittgenstein (we shall come back to him again later) who, in the course of a much wider discussion, has some valuable light to throw on the nature of the image. It is true that he never approaches our question directly. Both in the preliminary studies for the *Philosophical Investigations* (*Blue Book* and *Brown Book*[1]) and in the *Investigations* itself, he is concerned quite in general with the question of the relation between our thought (and speech) about the world, and the world it refers to. His discussion of the mental image, therefore, comes into a wider context (that of meaning as a whole) than is our concern. But all the same, as is so often true of Wittgenstein, his hints and asides may guide us more successfully than someone else's direct statements, and it is in this hope that we must approach him.

In the *Blue Book*, he argues that we cannot explain how we make a word refer to a particular object by saying that we have to have an image of that object in our mind to hang the word on to, to make it mean, or 'bring it to life'. He commands us to think what

[1] Basil Blackwell, 1958.

would happen if, every time we contemplate forming an image
to give significance to a word, we substitute an actual object for
the image. 'We could perfectly well . . . replace every process of
imagining by a process of looking at an object or by painting,
drawing or modelling; and every process of speaking to oneself
by speaking aloud or by writing.'[1] 'If the meaning of the sign . . .
is an image built up in our minds when we see or hear the sign,
then let us first adopt the method . . . of replacing this mental
image by some outward object seen. . . . Then why should the
written sign plus this painted image be alive, if the written sign
alone was dead? In fact as soon as you think of replacing the
mental image by, say, a painted one, and as soon as the image
thereby loses its occult character, it ceases to seem to impart any
life to the sentence at all.' 'As part of the system of language, one
may say, the sentence has life. But one is tempted to imagine that
which gives the sentence life as something in an occult sphere,
accompanying the sentence. But whatever accompanied it
would . . . just be another sign.' Wittgenstein is not saying that
we do not use mental images in thinking about things. We may
do so. But if we do, their whole nature is to be aids to thought;
they are our means of thinking about things. They function, just
as words themselves do, as meaningful items of our experience
through which we aim towards the object of our thought. It does
not tell us anything about images to say that they are faint copies
of things which we have encountered in the world. Even if we
say they are copies, that still leaves open the question how we are
able to interpret them *as* copies, and thus to *use* them. Wittgenstein
says, 'Our difficulty could be put in this way: we think about
things . . . but how do these things enter our thoughts? We think
about Mr. Smith, but Mr. Smith need not be present. A picture of
him won't do, for how are we to know whom it represents? In fact
no substitute for him will do. Then how can he himself be an object
for our thoughts?'[2] Because we regard our minds as a store-
house, we tend to believe that if I am thinking about Mr. Smith
there must be available to me an idea or image of Mr. Smith to
which I refer. That we do sometimes find an image in our minds
when we think of Mr. Smith does not entitle us to argue, as Hume
may be said to have argued, that therefore the only way we can
know who we are talking about, when we speak of him in his

---

[1] *Op. cit.*, p. 4.
[2] *Op. cit.*, p. 38.

absence, is to produce the Smith-picture from the store and refer to it. We really know who we are meeting when we meet him in the street, and who we are talking about when we speak of him behind his back, by the connexion between our thoughts of *this* object (Mr. Smith) and our thoughts of other objects. We can identify the Mr. Smith we mean, either for ourselves or for other people, by connecting him, for instance, with yesterday's lecture, or the counter of the National Westminster Bank. How, or whether, images of these further things present themselves is a matter of indifference. We must concentrate not on the pictures but on how we interpret them, and how they spread out beyond themselves.

Two groups of quotations from the *Philosophical Investigations*[1] will illustrate this further. First, having defined the mental picture as 'the picture which is described when someone describes what he imagines' (thus focusing our attention on imagining rather than on the nature of the images themselves), Wittgenstein says,[2] 'One ought to ask not what images are or what *happens* when one imagines something, but how the word "imagination" is used. But that does not mean that I want to talk only about words. For the question as to the nature of the imagination is as much about the word "imagination" as my question is. And I am only saying that this question is not to be decided, neither for the person who does the imagining nor for anyone else, by pointing; nor yet by a description of any process.' Wittgenstein is not saying that nothing goes on, for example before the mind's eye, when we obey the command to conjure up an image of someone; but only that describing exactly what goes on, if it were possible to do this, would not constitute an answer to the question what imagining is. The true nature of imagining must be discovered by considering the relation between what we say about our image and what we say about the object of which it is an image. A *description of the image itself*, if such could be given, would miss the essence of the matter. 'Essence is expressed in grammar', Wittgenstein says. The question what 'of' means in the expression 'image of x' could be described as a grammatical question. 'We are not analysing a phenomenon (e.g. thought) but a concept (e.g. thinking) and therefore the use of a word.'[3]

[1] Translated by G. E. M. Anscombe (Basil Blackwell, 1968).
[2] *Op. cit.*, p. 370.   [3] *Op. cit.*, p. 388.

So, though it remains true that, in order to consider critically what Hume or Ryle or Sartre says about images, we need to indulge, as we have seen, in introspection, trying to think of things by way of images in order to see whether what they say occurs really does so, yet this is not the end of the matter. For it now becomes clear (and indeed it was clear all along) that in talking about images we are talking not only about a class of *things which represent*, but about a species of thinking. And in order to explore the area where these two concepts overlap, and others as well, we must consider not only, as it were blindly, what it is like to have an image of something, but when we would comfortably and intelligibly speak of imagining, representing, thinking of, and indeed perceiving an object. The peculiar difficulty of the conceptual analysis (which it goes without saying cannot be undertaken properly in this book) is that as Wittgenstein says 'many of our concepts cross here.'

The second group of quotations[1] refers back to the thought of the *Blue Book*. ' "What makes my image of him an image of *him*?" Not its looking like him. The same question applies to "I now see him vividly before me" as to the image. What makes this utterance into an utterance about *him*? Nothing in it or simultaneous with it (behind it). If you want to know what he meant, ask him. . . . Suppose that someone were to draw while he had an image, or instead of having it, though it were only with his finger in the air. He could be asked "Whom does that represent?" And his answer would be decisive. It is quite as if he had given a verbal description: and such a description can also simply take the place of the image.' Once again, an attempt to describe the actual image that we have does not answer the question what it is to imagine someone. This has got to be answered in terms of the much more general question what it is to think of someone, whether in speaking of him, describing him, in recognizing him, or remembering him when he is not there. And to answer *this* question it is misleading to concentrate on the occurrence of an inner experience. Meaning and intending (in the phenomenologists' sense) are not inner experiences. 'The contents (images for instance) which accompany and illustrate them are not the meaning or intending.'[2] 'The language-game "I mean (or meant) this (subsequent explanation of a word)" is quite different from this

---

[1] *Op. cit.*, p. 177 sqq.   [2] *Op. cit.*, p. 217.

one: "I thought of . . . as I said it". The latter is akin to "It reminded me of . . . " ' These last two forms of expression could, I suppose, be said to be psychological and contingent, in the sense that they describe something which actually happened to *me*, the speaker, but which need not have happened. A report of what something reminded me of is like a report of a dream, or of what vague imagery I am experiencing now, while I type these words. All these are psychological reports. They may, in a sense, be reports of what I am thinking about. But we are capable of thinking of several things at once, and this is why they may contribute nothing at all to answering the question 'what did you mean when you said . . . ?'

So far, then, our findings with respect to the nature of the image are wholly negative. Let us try once again to come to an affirmative conclusion by an examination of the phenomenological account of imagining. The phenomenological concept of imagining is the subject matter of Sartre's essay *The Psychology of Imagination*. Much of what he says is derived directly from those psychologists of whom Jaspers, as we saw, was one, who worked within the phenomenological framework. But he presented their examples as philosophical examples. He was interested, that is to say, as Ryle was, in the proper description of imagination, not in the pathology of perceptual disturbances.

Rather optimistically, he divides his book into two sections, the certain and the probable. The part which is supposed to be certain is that which is purely descriptive. He proposes to apply the phenomenological method to the analysis of imagination, and this entails, as we have seen, putting on one side all theories and, as far as possible, all presuppositions, and describing what it is like to exercise the imagination. 'The method', he says, 'is simple. We shall produce images, reflect upon them, describe them. That is, we shall attempt to determine and to classify their distinctive characteristics. . . . The act of reflection has a content of absolute certainty which we shall call the essence of the image. The essence is the same for everyone.'[1] His first duty, then, is to formulate the knowledge which derives from reflection, and which is immediate, certain and general. Then he will attempt to explain the concepts which have been used in the formulation, and relate them to other

[1] *The Psychology of Imagination*, p. 2.

concepts and other theories. It is at this stage that he will move from the certain to the merely probable.

Unfortunately the distinction between the certain and the probable, as one might expect, does not really work. The technique of reflection fails to come up with any pure, theory-free descriptions of imagining. No indubitable general truths are forthcoming in the first part any more than in the second. The reason is that, right at the beginning, Sartre comes up against a conceptual difficulty. He cannot, without presuppositions, determine *what* it is that he is attempting to describe, in describing the imaginative consciousness. Like Ryle, he thinks that the imaginative consciousness is at work when we look at a portrait and see it as a portrait of a real but absent man. But in such a case we may see the portrait in two ways, either just as a painted canvas or as a portrait proper. And we may switch from one way of looking at it to the other. When we stop seeing it as a portrait of a man, we may still see the canvas before us, and this is something we can exactly describe. 'When the truly imaginative consciousness wanes, there remains a residue which is describable.'[1] But no description could tell us anything about a mental image as it could about the portrait considered merely as a canvas, because if, when we are imaginatively conscious of an absent man through an image only, our imaginative consciousness wanes, then the image fades too. There is no describable residue. This is of the greatest importance. We shall find that, though we must talk in terms of images, though we must use the noun 'image', yet we shall always go wrong if we try to separate the image, and regard it as something totally distinct from that *of* which it is the image. In other words, it is impossible to describe a mental image in itself. Introspection, however prolonged or purified, cannot help us to do this, because it is *logically* impossible. It is for this reason that Sartre has to abandon the introspective method, the proposed method of certainty, and move on in the second half of the book to non-introspective conceptual analysis, in order to try to find out what imagination is and how it works. His method of progress turns out, inevitably, to be the same as Wittgenstein's.

Sartre's inability to come up with a pure non-theory-laden description of his images in general need neither surprise nor alarm us. Despite the mainly negative conclusions of the first part,

[1] *Op. cit.*, p. 16.

he lists, at the end of it, certain features which he believes are essential to an image, or rather to imagination (features which in fact are listed in more detail by Jaspers in his *General Psychopathology*). And in the second part he considers some related questions, such as the role of imagination in dreams and hallucinations and in art, and its relation to memory. Into all these fields we shall briefly pursue him.

According to the original doctrine of phenomenology, like the rest of consciousness the imagination is essentially directed towards an object. Indeed, apart from this direction towards something else, the image itself is nothing. This is the first essential feature of the image, that it is a *kind* of consciousness, a *way of thinking* of something.

Secondly, this particular manner of thinking involves what Sartre refers to as 'quasi-observation'. He says, 'If I produce an image of a page of a book I am assuming the attitude of a reader, I look at the printed pages. But I am not reading. And actually I am not even looking, since I already know what is written there.'[1] The point about quasi-observation is just this, that the image can teach us nothing, since it contains nothing which we did not incorporate in it ourselves. 'It never reveals any aspect of an object. It delivers it *en bloc*.' And this is because we know already what object it is, we are *thinking of* it, rather than examining it or observing it. In this respect the image is always impoverished. It has no richness of its own.

The third characteristic follows from the second. When we think with images, we know that this is what we are doing. We know that the image is not the thing which it represents. The differences between it and the real object is, as it were, incorporated in it, by its very nature. There can be no external criterion by which we distinguish an image from a real object of perception. The difference is built into the image itself. 'However lively, appealing or strong the image is, it presents its object as *not being*. This does not prevent us from reacting to the image as if its object were before us. It is possible for us to react to an image as if it were a perception. . . . But the false and ambiguous position we reach thereby serves only to bring out in greater relief what we have just said: that we seek in vain to create in ourselves the belief that the object really exists. . . . We can pretend for a

[1] *Op. cit.*, p. 9.

second, but we cannot destroy the immediate awareness of its nothingness.'[1]

Fourthly and finally, the image is said by Sartre to be *spontaneous*. By this he means that we are aware, in having an image, that we are ourselves doing something. In contrast with the case of perception, in which we are passive, we are, in imagination, presenting things to ourselves. In imagining we 'produce and try to hold on to the object as an image'. 'The consciousness appears to itself as being creative, but without positing that that which it has created is a real object.'[2]

Now it appears to follow from these four criteria of imagination that one must always be aware that one is imagining something when one is doing so. Just as, when seeing my absent friend in the portrait of him, I am aware that he is not before me, but that I am using the portrait as an aid to 'seeing' him, so when I am imagining his face I must be aware that there is a mental content which I am using as an *analogue*, as something which is to help me grasp the visual appearance of my friend. We may not speak of the image as a thing, like a canvas only in our heads. But we may say that in thinking with images we are thinking analogically, or by means of representations, just as we are when we look at somebody's portrait rather than at himself. And we do this consciously, according to Sartre. The image is deliberately used just as much as the portrait is.

It must be said that there is an element of exaggeration in this account. The notion that we consciously *use* a portrait as a means of thinking of someone absent from us is not wholly plausible, though it may have a certain truth, and may indeed account for the practice of commissioning portraits of public figures whom it is felt we ought to remember, but may otherwise forget. But the suggestion that the portrait is primarily an *aide-memoire* is no more acceptable than is Ryle's view that in looking at a portrait or photograph I fancy that I see the subject of it.

Moreover in the case of the mental image there is a further difficulty, apart from the dubious assimilation to portraiture. For there are occasions, or so it is often alleged, when I do in fact mistake my mental content for reality, when I mistakenly believe that what is in fact a mental image is the real thing. And Sartre admits that the existence of hallucination may at first seem to be a

[1] *Op. cit.*, p. 13.   [2] *Op. cit.*, p. 14.

difficulty for his theory in which the image, in order to be an element in thinking of a nonexistent object, must always be recognized as such. He considers how to overcome this difficulty in part II of *The Psychology of Imagination*.

The question for him is this: 'how can we abandon our consciousness of spontaneity, and come to feel passive before an image which we have in fact created ourselves, and which is nothing in itself except what we have made?'[1] 'Is it true that we confer reality, that is *actual presence*, upon these objects, which occur to a sane consciousness as absent?' Sartre answers this question, as one would expect, in the same terms as Jaspers. The specific function of hallucination is to exclude the real world. In suffering hallucination what has gone wrong is our general sense of reality. It is not that the hallucinatory object appears in the real world among other objects, but rather that the act of forming the image of the hallucinatory object totally absorbs the attention of the patient, so that his ordinary perception vanishes. Thus, in telling the story of his hallucination afterwards, the patient places what he saw or heard in ordinary perceptual space, because this is the only space there is to talk about; but his localization may be quite random. Sartre suggests indeed that the question of *where* the patient sees the hallucinatory object (does he see the devil actually in the chair in his room, for instance?) is secondary to his belief that the devil he sees is real. If he thinks it real, then it has got to be accommodated *somewhere* in space.

But how can the patient believe in the reality of the image, if, as Sartre claims, for that image to exist at all it must as it were carry its unreality on its face? The solution is that the patient who suffers hallucination is confused, not so much about the unreal as about the real. The crucial element in hallucination, that is to say, is a weakening of the normal sense of the real. Sartre asks us to consider the case of a patient who holds a conversation with an imaginary interlocutor. In fact he himself speaks all the time, but sometimes it is he who is speaking, sometimes the imaginary person, and the patient knows which is which. In such a case, even though in his part of the dialogue he really is speaking, and therefore, in a way, his report of *that* part is correct, yet one would not wish to say that his perception even of that part was normal,

[1] *Op. cit.*, p. 4.

because he interprets the words he indeed really speaks as being addressed to someone who is not there.

Sartre who, we should remember, both at the time of writing and later had experience of hallucinations, claims that the hallucinatory image has all the features of the mental image in general. It is 'furtive'. It does not stay to be examined. If you try to concentrate on it, it dissolves. But a patient who ascribes reality to his hallucinatory experience does so for two reasons. He does so first, because, as we have seen, his sense of reality is impaired, and secondly because of the strong *feeling* which comes with the experience. It is because of the feeling, the emotional content of the experience, that he adapts his life to it, feels, for instance, that he must obey the voices, or make room, real room, for the visually imagined object. At the time, the hallucinatory experience is fascinating in that it absorbs the consciousness and excludes the normal consciousness of the world (as indeed may the experience of day-dreaming, or of following a narrative). Afterwards the patient speaks of the experience as if it were real. But to do this is to embark on a course of self-deception, or even of deliberate pretence. It does not make sense to ask whether the hallucinatory voice he 'heard' and a real voice are real in the same way. It would be more proper to say that the distinction between real and imaginary has disappeared for him because of the powerfully affective nature of the images he has. This is obviously not contradicted by the fact that the images may be of trivial or ludicrous things, like the lobster which Sartre used to experience following him in the streets. The feeling of importance or significance that comes with the image may not in the least depend upon its being an image of what we would normally think of as an important or significant thing.

This way of talking about hallucinations makes the hallucination a kind of waking dream; and this seems intelligible. For in dreams, obviously, the images take over. It is not that in a dream we confuse images with reality. We simply do not at the time have any idea that there could be two sorts of items to confuse. Our ordinary consciousness has ceased. Each image in a dream comes along as if it were connected with other images in the way in which, in the real world, things are perceived as connected with other things. But this does not entail that there is a dream world as well as a real world of things. We think in dreams by means of images, which have a 'world-like' character because they present themselves to us without our conscious effort. It is still true that we create our own images, but in a dream we are completely fascinated by them, and they have the special feature of seeming to follow one another necessarily. Because we are asleep we cannot detach ourselves from our thoughts, and, for example, wonder what may happen next or whether something is possible or not. In a dream there seems no distinction between the thought that something might happen and its 'happening'.

We can, it seems to me, trace various degrees of fascination by our own thoughts. We can chart (which comes to the same thing) a progressive failure of control over them. We may, for instance, raise a question such as 'what would happen if I said that to him?' And then we may imagine ourselves saying it and imagine his reply, and the ways we might reply to that; and this may turn into a proper case of day-dreaming, where his reply and our next remark seem to form themselves, and the conversation develops and takes over an apparent life of its own. Thereafter, the next stage is actual dreaming, where the initial question 'what would happen if . . . ?' is not asked. Such an account seems very plausible. For Sartre, it has the advantage that he is able to retain for dream-images and hallucinations all the features which he listed as necessary for the image in general; and above all, he is not committed to the view that what we experience in dreams and hallucinations is a kind of perceptual object. It is rather that they *seem like* perceptual objects because we have no concept (or a very faint one) of actual perceptual objects, at the time when we experience the dream-objects.

Some of the cases cited by Jaspers may support some such account as has been sketched above. Jaspers is at pains to point out that there is a vast variety of different degrees of confusedness with regard to the relation of image or dream-experience to the world of reality. But broadly he distinguishes dream-states (day dreams or full dreams) from pseudo-hallucinations, and both from hallucinations proper. Proper hallucinations are defined as 'actual false perceptions which are not in any way distortions of real perceptions but which spring up on their own as something quite new, and occur simultaneously with and alongside real perceptions.'[1] Pseudo-hallucinations are those in which the images

---

[1] *General Psychopathology*, p. 66.

experienced are recognized as images, even though they may be to some extent projected into the outside world. Dream-states on the other hand are characterized by a quite different mode of presentation of the images. Dreams are intrinsically unlike waking experiences, because certain features of experience always present in any waking experience, however odd or confused, are absent. Above all, what is absent is the link between the experience as it occurs and the self, as a continuous subject of experience. In a dream there is no sense of the self, no sense of past, present and future, no awareness of that relation between things which is self-evident in waking life.

Obviously, whichever kind of experiences we are talking about, it is absolutely essential to the description of them that we use such terms as 'image'; and this fact in itself is worthy of remark since it is precisely with clarifying the *use* of such expressions that we are now concerned. One thing then that emerges certainly is that their use *is* unavoidable. But we may still ask what these images are—to what we should assimilate them. Jaspers argues that, even in the case of true hallucination, in which the hallucinatory world and world of reality are to some extent integrated, there are some features of the image which distinguish it from the real object even at the time when both are experienced together. For example, a patient described an hallucinatory vine which she began to see when she looked out of the window. Later, walking along the street, she saw the vine as a fog between the real bushes. On closer observation, real leaves could be distinguished from fictitious ones. 'The fantasy leaves were as if pasted on, while the natural ones stood out from the wall. Moreover when the eyes moved, the phenomena moved too. This was the criterion by which in the end the patient realized that they were not real objects.'[1] Here then the images seemed on *close* inspection to have an unreal character. They had a certain thinness, or two dimensionality; and they behaved differently in the presence of the observer.

In the case of what Jaspers classified as pseudo-hallucination, the images still more obviously had a character of their own, which made them different from true perceptual objects. A description of images induced by opium is considered.[2] The 'pictures

[1] *Op. cit.*, p. 72.
[2] *Op. cit.*, p. 68.

consisted of faces and figures seen during the day, old friends not seen for a long time, unknown faces, a yellow rose, and many others. These pictures were said to be projected outwards. They stood in front of the eyes, and yet despite this and despite the clarity and sharpness of their outline, they seemed to lack objectivity. The patient felt that though he undoubtedly saw these things with his eyes, it was not with his outward physical eyes that he saw them. His physical eyes saw nothing but a black visual field, flecked here and there with patches of foggy light. What saw the pictures were inner eyes, located somewhere behind the outer ones.' Such pseudo-hallucinations may change into proper hallucinations and the change will come about precisely according to the degree to which the objects of attention seem to occupy real space. One patient described what he saw as follows, 'The figures were there in space, but as if they had their own private space peculiar to themselves. The more my attention was diverted from its usual sensible objects, the more distinct grew this new space with its inhabitants. I could give the exact distance, but the figures were never dependent on the objects in the room, nor were they hidden by them; they could never be perceived simultaneously with the wall or the window. I could not accept the objection that I had only imagined these things. I could not find anything in common between these perceptions and my own imagination. I feel the figures of my imagination are not in space at all, but remain faint pictures in my brain or behind my eyes, while with these phenomena I experienced *a world*, but one which had nothing to do with the world of the senses.'[1]

From these descriptions, which could be multiplied, it seems to emerge that the degree of reality felt to belong to the images depends upon the degree to which they take over from ordinary perception. It is not that some images are more vivid, or intrinsically more life-like than others, but that as one's attention is caught by them and so diverted from real phenomena, so one ascribes more and more reality to them, and increasingly comes to be caught up in the belief that they have their own externality, their own space around them. The images themselves, whether visual or auditory, are representations of the real. But in some circumstances, with greater or less self-deception, we may be led

[1] *Op. cit.*, p. 71.

to take the representation for the reality, or at least to speak as though we do.

In general, then, there seems to be nothing in the cases we have considered to prevent our accepting some such view of images as Sartre proposes. Imagining, when that is carried out by images, is thinking of things through representations. One way of imagining an absent scene is to look at a photograph of it. Another way is to draw a picture of it. Yet another is to try to form a mental image of it, and still another is, whether we like it or not, to dream about it. But the crucial part of knowing that we have succeeded in imagining the scene is that, besides its visual appearance, we should also create, or revive, in ourselves some of the affective aspects of the scene, and feel in ourselves some of the emotions which the scene would produce in us if it were there in reality. In the case of *deliberately* imagining a scene this aspect of it may be the most important of all. We may claim to *be* imagining, let us say, the nave of Winchester cathedral, if we have the feeling, vague and hard to characterize though this feeling may be, which we would have if we were in fact standing, let us say, at the west end of the cathedral, looking towards the east.

Sartre has an elaborate example which brings out this point. He discusses the case of our recognizing an imitation as a representation of a particular person, and he takes as his example the actress Franconay, impersonating Maurice Chevalier.[1] 'The impersonator is small, stout and brunette; a woman who is imitating a man. The result is that the imitation is but an approximation. The object produced by Franconay is a feeble form which can always be interpreted in two distinct ways: I am always free to see Maurice Chevalier as an image, or a small stout woman who is making faces.' He goes on to describe in detail the case where first I apprehend conceptually that Franconay is going to imitate Chevalier, and then gradually begin to 'see' and 'hear' Chevalier *in* the performance. I first learn that Chevalier is intended by certain conventional signs, in this case a straw hat and a stick, which are the symbols of Chevalier. At first I do not *see* the hat of Chevalier in the straw hat on the stage, but I understand that the mimic's hat refers to Chevalier's hat. To decipher this sign is to produce the concept 'Chevalier'. Now Chevalier himself is not present, so if I am going to go further than merely to have the

[1] *The Psychology of Imagination*, p. 26 sqq.

concept, it can only be through the imagination. So from now on, Sartre says, it is a question of 'realising my knowledge *in* the material provided for me' (a Kantian role, after all, for imagination). I can do this first by seeing the woman on the stage as something indefinite. 'Her hair, her body are perceived as if they were indefinite masses, as filled spaces and no more. They have sensible opaqueness; in other words they are but a *setting*.' So there comes about in our actual perception of the woman on the stage a 'fundamental indeterminateness'. We do not concentrate on the actual qualities of what we see. They are all incorporated into the imagined object which we are beginning to see. As soon as we concentrate on the actual qualities, the imagined object disappears, just as the image disappears if we try to describe *it* rather than what it is an image of. But it is not only the appearance and gestures of Chevalier which we begin to superimpose on the appearance and gestures of Franconay. Chevalier himself has a certain affective quality. We may speak of his 'style', or, in a sense, his 'meaning' or his 'point'. It is this meaning which we now begin to see in the performance of the actress. It is this which unites all her actions on the stage into one object of our attention. The Chevalier-feeling, far more than the Chevalier-appearance is what makes us grasp the absent Chevalier imaginatively. But all the time it is still possible for our consciousness to glide from the level of imagination to that of perception. 'A hybrid condition follows, which is neither perception nor imagination. It is both.' In such a case, then, we are seeing Chevalier *in* Franconay, that is, we are seeing him in our imagination. The performance is, in Ryle's phrase, a 'stimulus to the imagination'.

Sartre seems to want us to conclude that if the imagination is thus stimulated, it is a matter of indifference whether we say that we are seeing Chevalier in our imagination or that we are creating an image of him. He wishes to assimilate the case where we should unhesitatingly say the latter to the former case. But even if we are willing to agree to this, would we be willing to go on to say that if the imitation is very good this is because the image it produces is very clear? We do not want to fall all over again into the trap of thinking that the image must be a kind of picture or representation. What seems to be clear or strong, in the case of a good imitation, is not a picture which is a good likeness, but a *feeling*. There seems to be no question of similarity, either more or less. A copy of something must be related to its original at least partly by similarity, however formal or conventional this may have become (though there is also a causal connexion between copy and original). But a good portrait is not good because it is extremely similar to its original, nor of course merely because it is causally connected with it. Still less is a good imitation good for this reason. It is rather that a good portrait or a good imitation is good because it has succeeded in its intention, which was to convey to the audience the *sense* or significance of the original. If we are successfully imagining something, then, this is what we are doing: either by means of physical or non-physical analogues we are calling up the sense or significance of something which is not present to us in fact. It is for us affectively as if the absent object were present.

The portrait and the imitation on the stage were supposed by Sartre to be physical analogues. The image is the non-physical analogue. Both Sartre and Ryle claim that the analysis of the former cases shows what kind of thing is happening in the latter. But neither suggests that it is possible to eliminate the word 'image' from the description of those cases, whether the exercise of imagination is normal or abnormal, where there is no physical analogue to hand. But have they at least succeeded in scotching the belief that the image we must refer to is a copy of an original?

Ryle has one more argument against the copy-theory which we should perhaps examine. He argues[1] that we cannot seriously hold images to be copies, that is to say objects like that of which they are copies, because of the case of smells. We may wish to say that we can smell something in our imagination or in our mind, but we know very well that there can be no such thing as copy-smells. There is nothing in the world that can function as an analogue to a smell in the way that a photograph or a portrait can function as an analogue to the visual appearance of an object. This argument does not seem to me to be conclusive as it stands, but it may nevertheless throw a little more light on the question what we are doing when we summon up an image of something. If we taste or smell something in real life (not in the mind's nose or palate) which reminds us of some past occasion, then, notoriously, we may be carried back to the whole sense or 'feel' of the past occasion by the smell or taste. The smell is then the physical

[1] *The Concept of Mind*, p. 252.

experience which acts as an analogue or representation of the original experience, just as a portrait does when, by looking at it, we give ourselves the sense or 'feel' of the sitter. When we have not the advantage of an actual smell to remind us, we may nevertheless try, more or less successfully, to produce an *image* of the smell we are seeking. The image-smell will be fugitive, vague, hard to concentrate on, in the very same way that an auditory or visual image may be. It may be true, as a matter of contingent fact, that in the case of smells and tastes we are more dependent on the existence of physical stimuli to help us 'smell' in the imagination the scenes of our past, or, say, of some fancied country life for which we hanker in the town, but it is only a matter of degree. We do not need the concept of the copy either more or less in such cases. By trying, we may be able to remember vividly the olfactory features of something, and we must describe the memory in terms of smell. That we do not readily speak of a 'copy' in such a case does not alter the fact that we need the language of smells to describe what we are recollecting.

In general, the image emerges as that which we create when we think imaginatively about something; and if this still seems (as well it may) to be circular or uninformative, then we can put it this way. We cannot speak of imagining without speaking of images. An attempt to analyse the concept expressed by the verb entails the use of an object-noun as an internal accusative. We cannot speak of real smelling without the internal accusative 'smell' for that which we smell; and in the same way we need the noun 'image' for that which we have before our mind's nose when we 'smell' in imagination. For 'image' is the generic expression of which 'mental smell', 'mental sound', 'mental appearance' are the species. But the image cannot be treated as an independent object which can be examined on its own, even though the word for it must occur in our accounts of imagining. We may need the noun; but to understand it we have to understand the verb. It thus becomes clear that the question how we are to describe an image as it presents itself to us, inevitably turns into the other question what we are doing when we imagine something. We cannot isolate the question of images and try to answer it by itself. Our aim in this part of the book was to throw light on imagination by examining the image. It has now become clear that the aim was misconceived. In order to understand the image, we need to understand the diverse but related functions of imagination.

Now to justify the claim that you are thinking about some particular thing, you must be able to call attention to at least some features of it. You may find that in this process of calling attention to features you need to 'reproduce' the features rather than describe them. (For example, in talking about a melody, it may be necessary to sing it or play it on the piano, and in any case, you will somehow have to 'hear' it, even if only in your head.) The images we form are necessarily incomplete, but they are ways of representing for ourselves some of the features of the object of our thought, those features which will identify what we are thinking of (though of course we may not successfully identify the object of our thought—that is, we may not be able to attach a name to it or connect it with other things). The image, that is to say, relates to the aspect of the object which we are for the time being concentrating on. If I conjure up the image of a man as he was yesterday, I may concentrate on what he looked like and think of him under his visual aspect. I may 'see' him. Or I may concentrate on what he said and the tones in which he said it trying, perhaps, to guess what he can have meant from the tones of his voice. Was it a threat? A promise? A confession? In that case I shall have, or try to give myself, auditory images. But all the time *he* is the object of my thought. The image *is* our attempt to reach the non-existent or absent object in our thoughts as we concentrate on this or that aspect of it, its visible appearance, its sound, its smell. We shall express ourselves relatively satisfied with our image when we can think clearly about the aspect of the thing in question. It is at any rate certain that we will *not* be satisfied unless we have also succeeded in producing in ourselves the particular, though probably inexpressible, 'feel' that the absent thing would have if we were actually in its presence.

There is one further qualification which needs to be made. So far the image has tended to appear as that which we create when we are trying to *do* something; and it may be thought that we always create images voluntarily. There are obvious counter-examples in dreams and hallucinations about which enough has perhaps been said. But often when one is indeed trying to think of something, there is a sense in which the imagery in which one thinks seems very much less than voluntary, or deliberately created. We seem to be subject to what images come, just as we are in dreams, although in these cases there is no suspension of our awareness of the outside world. I am referring to cases in which one may seem, in trying to think of something, to be waiting for an image to come, and then, when it comes, to inspect it. For instance, if I am asked whether someone was wearing a red shirt this morning, it may well be that I try to find out whether he was or not by thinking of him, and as it were waiting to see whether the image of him is of him in a red shirt or in one of some other colour. This is of course by no means an infallible procedure, but it seems to be one which we use. To take another example, there is a kind of musical puzzle sometimes set in quiz programmes on television, where a well-known tune is played on the wrong instrument, and one has to identify the instrument on which it should be played. In such cases, if one is extremely familiar with the melody, one may recognize it and ascribe it to its proper instrument without thinking, and probably without any auditory imagery at all. This looks like conceptual knowledge. But there are cases where the tune is familiar, but one cannot place it. One is distracted by the sound of it played, let us say, on the oboe and one has to try to 'hear' it as it should be played (in spite of what Ryle says, there does seem here to be almost a conflict between the actual sound and what one is trying to 'hear' in one's head. It is not that the present sound is too loud; it is that it conceals in itself the tones one is searching for.) Now if one succeeds in solving the puzzle, it seems appropriate to say that it is because one has managed to 'hear' the proper sound, and recognize it as right. But it may have taken several steps to reach the solution. One may first think 'it is too high', and then, 'it shouldn't have this reedy tone', and then finally one may 'hear' the 'cello, and the melody falls into place. The distinctive feature of this sort of case is that one feels 'I must wait for it to come', and then the image presents itself. The fact is that although we are *trying* to do something, namely to recall the melody as it should be, yet we seem not to produce the image voluntarily. Sartre pays only fleeting attention to this kind of case. He is concerned only with situations in which not only do we want to produce an image, but we construct it deliberately. He seems to overlook the fact that we are capable of thinking of two different things at the same time, of having at least two different trains of thought going.

Allowing an image to present itself is a case of this general kind, it seems to me. I think of 'how the melody ought to sound' as a question, and *also* I think of it as it is played here and now on the oboe, at the same time. The thoughts go on together. It is true, in a sense, that I construct the 'right' image; there is nothing magical about it, and of course I may hail it as right when it is wrong; but the point is that I am not aware of myself doing it. My imagination is working, but, as Kant said, below the level of consciousness.

The case we have considered so far is one of memory. But there are other similar situations in which the imagination produces images without my active intervention, and which have nothing specifically to do with trying to remember something. Obviously the case of dreaming may be thought to be one. But very often when one is awake one may, for example, be reading something which absorbs one's attention, and at the same time on the edges of one's consciousness, an image may form, perhaps quite disconnected from the subject one is reading about. It may be of some place, or it may be of some piece of music, or both. Are we aware of this image at the time? It is quite possible that it may not be until we happen to be in the place the next day that we realize, 'I was envisaging this yesterday all the time I was reading Cicero.' But possibly if one's reading had been interrupted and one had been asked what image was in one's mind one could have answered immediately, specifying a particular bit of a garden, or street in a town. (However, if one were questioned more closely and asked to say more about this image, then either it would fade, and one could not go on, or one would begin deliberately to construct it, putting in features which one knew independently were features of the place.) It seems to be the case that at the time of reading, one was thinking of two things at once, and in two different ways. It is in some such ways as these that images may be said to haunt one. But there is nothing particularly mysterious about it. It is like the case of driving a car when one is familiar with the techniques. One goes on driving while thinking of something different. One can recall one's attention to what one is doing, but one need not. But that one is not aware of one's movements in driving the car does not entail that somehow the car is driving itself or is being driven by magic. One *is* doing it, but unnoticingly.

Such examples as these, then, need not lead us to give up the proposition that images are our way of thinking of absent or non-existent things; they need only lead us to modify what seems to be Sartre's view, that such thinking always absorbs our attention while we are undertaking it. Moreover, if we do so modify his view, then the special cases of dreaming and hallucination do not appear so odd. They are only somewhat extreme cases of a kind of thinking that may go on for a large part of our life, in a lesser form. Sartre himself, it should be said, would not have liked this modification, because he was committed to the view that the mind is always open to its own inspection, whatever kind of thinking it is employed *in*. The notion of images being formed below the level of consciousness would seem to him to bring in a superstitious belief in the unconscious, a belief which it was a considerable part of the aim of phenomenology to overthrow.

In the course of expounding Sartre's views, I have fairly frequently overlooked or tried to eliminate what seemed to me to be minor inconsistencies or confusions of terminology. But there is one major distinction which he draws of which I have not yet spoken, but which cannot thus be pushed on one side, since it is both important to his theory and as it seems to me, wrong. This is the distinction between memory and anticipation on the one hand, and imagination on the other. It is true that in Part I of *The Psychology of Imagination*, where he is attempting to record the incontrovertible findings of introspection, he does not make the distinction. Images are lumped together, whether they are images of purely invented, or of past, or of anticipated things. But in the second part he says this: 'The problem of memory and of anticipation are two problems which are radically different from the problem of imagination.'[1] He goes on, 'If I recall an incident of my past life, I do not imagine it, I recall it. That is, I do not posit it as given-in-its-absence, but as given-now-as-in-the-past. The handshake of Peter of last evening in leaving me did not turn into an unreality as it became a thing of the past; it simply went into retirement; it is always real but in the past. It exists as past, which is one mode of real existence among others. But if I imagine Peter as he exists at this moment (and not as he was yesterday on leaving me) I grasp an object which is not at all given to me, or is not given to me as being beyond reach. There I grasp

[1] *Op. cit.*, p. 210.

nothing, that is, I posit nothingness. In this sense the imaginative consciousness of Peter is very much closer to that of a centaur (whose complete non-existence I proclaim) than it is to the re-collection of Peter as he was the day he left. What is common to Peter and the centaur is that they are both aspects of nothingness.' He then goes on to draw a parallel distinction between an imagi-nary future, and an anticipatory thought of the future, as for example when I am meeting someone off a train and am looking for him to appear at any moment. In the latter case, he says, 'All my actions and gestures are given significance by the expectation. I actually live the future in the present, and it is what gives sense to the present.' His further example of anticipation is that of a game of tennis. My opponent's act of hitting the ball makes sense in terms of my anticipation. I run up to the net, and this is a natural development of my opponent's act. Sartre is suggesting that in our interpretation of the present perceptual scene, there is always an element of awareness of the past and awareness of the future, and it is this which gives intelligibility to the present moment. But he insists that what makes us interpret the present as part, for instance, of a continuing game of tennis is not *imaginative* thought, but something different. Yet he himself, by drawing his examples in the introspective part of the programme indifferently from the images of memory, anticipation and fiction, has provided evidence that in *practice*, and as they actually occur, these modes of thought cannot be distinguished.

Let us consider in more detail the distinction he wants to draw. He allows that in perception there are many aspects of the object before us which are not perceived at any given time but are under-stood *in* the perception we have. To supply this kind of perceptual backing, if we may so refer to it, was the role of imagination in perception in the theories of both Hume and Kant. Sartre des-cribes the case of our looking at a patterned carpet, of which some parts of the pattern are visible to us, some are hidden by the legs of the furniture standing on it. 'The legs of the armchair', he says, 'conceal certain curves, certain designs. But never-theless I seize these curves as existing now, as hidden, but not at all as absent ... I do not try to present them by means of an analogue, but in the very way in which I grasp what has been given me of their continuation. I perceive the beginnings and endings of the hidden arabesques as *continuing* under the legs of the chair. It is therefore *in the way in which I grasp the real data* that I posit that which is not given as being real. . . . Likewise the successive tones of a melody are grasped . . . as that which makes of the tone now heard exactly what it is. To perceive this or that real datum is to perceive it on the foundation of total reality *as a whole*. This reality never becomes the special object of my attention, but is co-present as an essential condition of the existence of the reality actually perceived.'[1] The point he makes turns on his statement that we do not present the hidden parts of the carpet to ourselves by an analogue. To do this would be to form an image, deliberately to call up a mental picture of the hidden part, to match the part we can see. I *can* do this, Sartre says, but to do it is to perform a separate act. I *can* direct my attention to imagining the parts of the carpet which are hidden. But if I do this, I have to think of them specifically as *not* part of the perceptual data I have. 'I grasp them as nothing for me.' So the difference between merely expecting someone to arrive at the station, where my anticipation of his appearance makes sense of the present for me, and actually imagining, by means of a deliberately formed mental image, how he would look if he came, is a difference in degree of concentration, and in degree of isolation of the image from present reality.

In order to be a case of true imagining Sartre is here maintaining that one *must* form a mental picture, concentrate upon it, separate it from the world, recognize it as unreal, and, in his words, 'present it to oneself as a nothingness'. But his original analysis of images and image-forming goes against the distinction he is now drawing. For he has argued that we must not regard a mental image as something in itself which can be inspected and observed, in the way that an object in the world can be observed. The image, we were told, was nothing in itself but only our way of attempting to *bring* within our perceptual grasp, by means of an analogue, something which was *not* within our grasp. If this analysis is right, and we have been inclined to accept it, then when I look at a portrait of the Duke of Wellington, and see it as a portrait, I am grasping the Duke of Wellington imaginatively, through the portrait. But this does not entail that besides seeing the portrait I also see an image of the Duke, with which I can compare the canvas. The whole burden of the phenomenological

[1] *Op. cit.*, p. 209.

The Nature of the Mental Image

account of imagination, whether in Sartre's version or in Ryle's, was to deny this suggestion. I must in such a case be said to be imagining the Duke, but I certainly cannot be supposed to have, and isolate, a picture of him and 'grasp it as a nothingness'. The imagination comes into the account of my seeing the portrait as a portrait, precisely because I am seeing the Duke *in* the canvas. It is hard to see why one may not likewise be permitted to say that when I grasp the pattern *in* the parts of the carpet I can see, I am also using imagination, and not bare perception. It is certainly true that in order to interpret the pattern of the carpet I need to grasp parts of it which are not present to my eyes. And this does not entail forming an image of the absent part and as it were superimposing it upon the present part of the pattern. But then, seeing the Duke in the portrait does not entail superimposing a mental picture of the Duke on to the canvas either. And Sartre has allowed that the portrait case is an exercise of imagination. It cannot consistently be maintained therefore that for imagination to be at work, we need to isolate an image and present it to ourselves as an image of the non-existent. Indeed he has argued that no such image can be isolated.

Moreover there is an inherent lack of plausibility in the distinction Sartre attempts to draw between the absent as past (or future) and the absent as non-existent. We know quite well in practice how the thought of something which did happen may merge into the thought of something which might have happened; how we may slide imperceptibly from expecting someone to arrive to envisaging what he may do or say when he does; how easy it is simply not to know whether something is a remembered scene or not. There is a perfectly general objection to saying that things which are indistinguishable in practice are, deep down, totally different. Sartre's own analysis, then, and the observable facts, should both lead us in the same direction, which is to accept that imagination is what we use in interpreting our present experience in the light of past and future experience. We may entirely agree with him that interpretation by means of the past and future is what makes sense of the present. But he has provided no reason for separating such interpretation from the function of the imagination; and has indeed himself used a concept of imagination which makes sense of allotting to it this role among others.

When we considered Hume's view of the role of imagination in perception, it will be remembered, what made it implausible was his belief that the imagination works by forming images intrinsically similar to sense perceptions. Sartre, in the phenomenological tradition, insisted that even though we may need to talk of images, we must not think of them as *like* impressions. Thus the only difficulty in accepting the Humean theory of imagination's function has been removed. I certainly wish to assert, with Sartre, that in any intelligible experience there are elements of other experiences which, in his phrase, have 'gone into retirement'. These add up to an awareness of the past, the future and the hidden aspects of what we are now experiencing, and they can be said to be the thoughts about our present experience, though also forming a necessary part of the experience itself. But there is no reason so far to deny that these thoughts are brought to our present experience by the very same faculty which enables us to envisage the sitter in the portrait, or to frame a mental picture of the battle of Trafalgar, or of a mountain of gold.

It is perhaps worth raising the question why Sartre *did* want to deny this role to imagination, despite an analysis of imagination which would have made such a role intelligible. The answer, it seems to me, is that he wished to rescue imagination from the snare of necessity. His argument, indeed, once again, is reminiscent of Coleridge's against Hartley. He thought that if imagination were tied to the past, by being indistinguishable, in some instances, from memory, then one would have to say that the imagination was subject to causal laws. What images a man forms could in principle be explained by what he had previously experienced. Now Sartre believed that if he could find one area of human activity which was totally free from the possibility of a causal explanation, then it would justify his thesis of the essential freedom of man. Imagination, freed from the chain of associationism, or any other such explanatory system, was thought by him to furnish such an area. The power of envisaging what is not the case is, he argued, totally uncaused. And man's freedom of choice and action stems from this initial freedom to present to himself the non-existent, knowing it to be such. Man's freedom, then, lies in the imagination. Imagination thus has for Sartre a crucial role to play in the total metaphysical view of man, who is conceived as the only free item in a world otherwise wholly governed by necessary causal laws. In exercising imagination, Sartre argues, a man must start from the world he is in, but treat it as a world which does *not* contain the imaginary object. This is what is meant by saying that in imagining he thinks of the object as non-existent. A deliberate act of imagination entails saying, 'let me conceive of the world as containing *this* object, which it does not contain.' On this view, one cannot separate *consciousness of freedom* from *consciousness that one can imagine*. For in thinking, 'I can change this situation', I necessarily envisage the situation as containing some feature which it does not at the moment contain. Freedom of action and freedom to envisage the non-existent are the same. At the end of *The Psychology of Imagination*, Sartre argues that if consciousness is to be able to do what it manifestly can do, namely conceive what is not the case, it must be consciousness free. 'For consciousness to be able to imagine, it must be able to escape from the world by its very nature; it must be able by its own efforts to withdraw from the world. In a word it must be free.' He is here using a transcendental argument: the only way to account for the facts as we know them is to suppose a particular condition, and the condition essential to account for our ability to imagine is freedom. But he cannot plausibly say that our power to remember or to envisage a real anticipated future is totally free from psychological or other deterministic explanations. It is therefore essential for him to distinguish imagination proper (the conceiving of the non-existent) from memory or anticipation (the conceiving of the temporally absent). Unfortunately, as we have seen, such a distinction does not itself fit the facts.

However, if one does not share Sartre's commitment to an area of consciousness wholly outside the range of psychological determinism, then one need not follow him in the distinction he tries to draw. There is no reason why one should refuse to contemplate an imagination, the operations of which were explicable on psychological grounds (though of course this is not to suggest that an actual explanation of a causal kind could be found in practice for every operation of such an imagination). Associationism, it is true, was implausible in its crude mechanistic form; but this does not entail that we must try to find a way of freeing human consciousness, or any area of it, from any kind of causal system whatever. If we can rid ourselves of superstitious fear of necessitarianism, there is no reason to mark off imagination particularly from the rest of the human capacity to think about the world, whether in its presence or its absence, whether as existing or as not existing.

Let us return to Sartre's account of our perception of the patterned carpet. He speaks, as we saw, of our awareness of the whole pattern as 'co-present as an essential condition of the actually perceived'. What we have here is a description of perception exactly like that which was derived by Merleau-Ponty from Husserl. It is a description of present perception containing essentially a thought (a shadow-thought, perhaps) of that which cannot actually be seen or heard. It was this thought-element which I referred to, in the case of Merleau-Ponty, as constituting a gap into which the imagination might fit; it was indeed the same gap which was filled, in the theories of both Hume and Kant, by the imagination. We saw, in considering Kant, that the imagination here was not necessarily thought of as that which *did*, but merely as that which *could*, produce images. We were not bound to think of imagination furnishing us, in each act of perception, with a series of shadow-pictures or echo-sounds with which to fill out our present perception. It was rather that we could not understand our present perception unless it were *possible* for the imagination to fill it out, or supplement it, with images of aspects temporally or spatially absent. This account seems quite compatible with the account of images offered by Sartre, according to which images are our way of trying to render the absent present to ourselves. So far, then, the position seems to be this: there is no reason not to say that the thought-element in perception is the element supplied by imagination. We have found no satisfactory argument *against* adopting the terminology of Hume and Kant.

We are convinced that it makes no sense to say 'there are no such things as images', though it is clear that images are not strictly comparable to material objects. And the production of images is the work, *par excellence*, of imagination. But if we want to extend the function of imagination into perception itself, then we are committed to holding that there is a continuity of activity from 'seeing in our mind's eye' at one end, to seeing with our real eye and interpreting or understanding what we see at the other. If we use the name 'imagination' for both these functions, and for the creative function (the function of genius), as well, then we must be prepared to assert that these functions are identical in kind, if not in degree or in detail. Forming mental pictures, creating or understanding works of art, understanding the real world in which we live, are all of them to some extent dependent on the *same* mode of thought. Now it is one thing to say that there is no reason against making such an identification. It is another to find any positive arguments in favour of it. I want to conclude this section by trying to find such arguments, or rather, perhaps, to reinforce those arguments already suggested which lead towards such a wide interpretation of imagination.

Seeing, hearing, tasting; interpreting what we see, hear, or taste as of a particular kind; interpreting it as signifying something beyond itself, perhaps something other than the kind of which it is a member; creating it as symbolic; using symbols to suggest thoughts and meanings to others—all these activities can be quite readily seen to be related, and to form a sort of progression. Our problem is how this series of activities is related to 'seeing in absence' or 'seeing in the mind's eye'. In the *Philosophical Investigations* Wittgenstein has a famous discussion of 'seeing as' or 'noticing an aspect' at the conclusion of which he says that seeing an aspect is akin to having an image.[1] This is the clue that we must now follow. Let us, as a preliminary, consider a description of a perceptual experience, not, it is true, from Wittgenstein, but from Merleau-Ponty.[2] 'If I walk along a shore towards a ship which has run aground and the funnel or masts merge into the forest bordering on the sand dune, there will be a moment when these details suddenly become part of the ship, and indissolubly fused with it. As I approached, I did not perceive resemblances or proximities which finally came together to form a continuous picture of the upper part of the ship. I merely felt that the look of the object was on the point of altering, that something was imminent in this tension, as a storm is imminent in storm-clouds. Suddenly the sight before me was recast in a manner satisfying to my vague expectation. Only afterwards did I recognize as justifications for the change the resemblance and contiguity of what I call stimuli, namely the determinate phenomena seen at close quarters and with which I compose the "real" world. "How could I have failed to see that these pieces of wood were an integral part of the ship? for they were of the same colour as

---

[1] p. 213.   [2] *The Phenomenology of Perception*, p. 17.

the ship, and fitted well enough into its superstructure". But these reasons for correct perception were not given as reasons beforehand. The unity of the object is based on the foreshadowing of an imminent order which is about to spring on us a reply to questions merely latent in the landscape.' The phenomenon Merleau-Ponty here describes is exactly that of the dawning of an aspect, the dawning recognition, with which Wittgenstein is also concerned, though his examples are rather different.

Wittgenstein in the *Philosophical Investigations* starts[1] with the illustration of a box which can be interpreted in various ways.

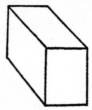

'You could imagine the illustration appearing in several places in a book. ... In the relevant text something different is in question every time: here a glass cube, there an inverted open box, there a wire frame of that shape, there three boards forming a solid angle. Each time the text supplies the interpretation of the illustration. But we can also *see* the illustration first as one thing, now as another. So we interpret it and see it as we interpret it.'

The question now arises whether we can separate *what we see* from our interpretation of it. One feels that it ought to be possible somehow to describe the actual visual experience (what Merleau-Ponty, in the passage quoted above, referred to as 'the stimuli') first, and then add on an account of the interpretation as an extra. But in fact it is impossible to do this. If one were to try, one would feel inclined to say 'what I actually saw was this', and then draw exactly the same picture again. Or one might attempt an analysis of the picture into its component lines and angles before saying how it was that one interpreted it (for example as a box). But it may be extremely difficult to describe the lines and angles once one has seen the drawing in a particular way. Analogously, if one has interpreted a sound as a voice calling one's name, one may not thereafter be able to describe it as *pure* sound, nor reproduce it as such.

[1] p. 193.

In order to shed more light on the relation between seeing something and seeing it as something, Wittgenstein next[1] introduces the trick picture of the duck-rabbit. If I see this picture without even realizing that it could be taken to represent a duck, it seems that what I see is a picture-rabbit. Someone else who knows that it is a trick-picture, open to a different interpretation, may report of me, 'she sees it *as* a rabbit'. But this is not the form

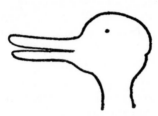

of words I should use myself until the alternative interpretation has been pointed out to me. As soon as the trick is shown to me, I can see the picture either as a duck or a rabbit, and the question becomes, 'What in my perception changes when I see it first as one and then as the other?' Wittgenstein says, 'I describe the alteration like a perception, exactly as if the object had altered before my eyes.' But I know that it has not altered. The whole point of the example is that I am, and I know I am, seeing the same thing but seeing a different aspect of it when I see it as something else. 'The expression of a change of aspect is the expression of a *new* perception and at the same time of a perception being unchanged.'[2] Wittgenstein then tries to determine how I might be able to explain the phenomenon of *seeing as*, or seeing an aspect, in two stages. I might say, 'If I saw the duck-rabbit as a rabbit then I saw: these shapes and colours (I give them in detail), and I saw besides something like this: and here I point to a number of different pictures of rabbits. This shows the difference between the concepts. "Seeing as" is not part of perception. And for that reason it is like seeing and again not like.'[3] Just so one can incidentally imagine Hume breaking up my perception of, let us say, a particular dog into stages, 'I had the following impressions, brown long shaggy etc., and at the same time I had, besides, some

[1] *Op. cit.*, p. 194.   [2] *Op. cit.*, p. 196.   [3] *Op. cit.*, p. 197.

ideas like this' . . . and I produce some pictures of dogs from out of my store-house imagination which became available as the word 'dog' suggested itself.

Wittgenstein goes on to explore the meaning of such expressions as 'being struck by an aspect' of something. He comes up to examples of this by way of examples of quite ordinary perceptions. When I look, for example, at a cupboard in my room, am I aware of its spatial character, its depth, all the time that I see it, do I feel it all the time, or do I become aware of it only when I think about it? Can we make sense of saying that someone who sees the cupboard is aware of its depth just occasionally, or when he thinks about it only? These are the aspects of the cupboard which in Sartre's language have 'gone into retirement', and there is no kind of ordinary perception in which there are not numbers of such 'retired' features. It is the connexion between the ordinary case of perception and the case which we should more readily describe as 'seeing an aspect of something' which makes philosophers since Wittgenstein describe as 'a philosophical cliché' the proposition that *all* seeing is *seeing as*. Wittgenstein goes on to raise the question, 'Is being struck by an aspect, or some likeness in what we see, looking *plus* thinking?', and to this he answers that one ought rather to suppose that the concepts of looking and thinking cross in the case of being struck. We have already seen that conceptual analysis becomes difficult where concepts 'cross'. And perhaps to say that they cross is only to say that they are at this point inextricably connected—that one cannot discuss the one without reference to the other.

Suppose that I am looking at an object which is in fact a rectangular pink piece of blotting paper, lying on the desk before me, and in the course of looking at it, it strikes me as looking like something else (perhaps it looks like a kind of dress material, or like some kind of synthetic pink pudding spilled out on my desk). About this case, Wittgenstein seems to want to draw a sharp distinction between the part of my experience which is seeing, and the part which is seeing an aspect. 'The colour of the visual impression corresponds to the colour of the object (this blotting paper looks pink to me and is pink); the shape of the visual impression to the shape of the object (it looks rectangular to me and it is rectangular); but what I perceive in the dawning of an aspect is not a property of the object, but an internal relation between it and other objects. It is almost as if "seeing the sign in this context" were the echo of a thought. "The echo of a thought in sight" one would like to say.'[1] This expression, 'the echo of a thought in sight', might have been the very expression we would have chosen to sum up the passage from Merleau-Ponty which we quoted above. But whereas Merleau-Ponty was talking about the recognition of an object as what it was, Wittgenstein is talking about seeing an aspect of something, seeing, that is, a likeness between it and something which may be quite different from it. And so far he does not seem to wish to extend this way of speaking ('the echo of a thought') to other cases which are mere cases of seeing a thing as what it is.

But, as we have suggested, there is a tendency which arises from the contemplation of such cases to assimilate all perception to the perception of aspects; and we may well come to feel an extreme difficulty in drawing any line between the 'aspect' case and the rest. Is there any real justification for making the distinction? As a move towards answering this question, let us notice one fact, namely that in our exposition of Wittgenstein so far the word 'imagination' has not occurred, neither has the word 'image'. There are, however, passages in this part of the *Investigations* where Wittgenstein does connect images with the twin concepts of seeing an aspect and interpreting what we see in a particular way: and he also describes a particular *kind* of aspect-seeing as requiring imagination. To bring out the contrast between those cases where he wants to say that we need imagination and those in which we do not, it is necessary to introduce two further diagrams. Take as an example, Wittgenstein says, the aspects of a triangle. This triangle can be seen as a triangular hole, as a solid, as a geometrical drawing; as standing on its base,

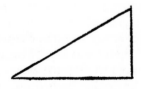

as hanging from its apex; as a mountain, as a wedge, as an arrow or pointer; as an overturned object which is meant to stand on the shorter side of the right-angle as a half parallelogram, and as various other things. The question then is, 'How is it possible to *see* an object according to an interpretation? What is the connexion between seeing and interpreting?' After several totally different examples, including the example of children saying that a chest is a house and seeing it as a house ('a piece of fancy is worked into it'), Wittgenstein returns[1] to the case of the triangle and says, 'It is as if an image came into contact, and for a time remained in contact, with the visual impression.' This then seems to be what seeing according to an interpretation is. It is to have an image and to bring this image to bear upon the immediate impression, the 'stimulus'. Once again it is easy to see how the language of Hume could be made to fit this account. The imagination will come up with a particular idea or image and apply it to the present impression, thus enabling us to go beyond the mere impression considered on its own.

But Wittgenstein contrasts this case with a different kind of aspect-seeing. Take the example above, which he calls the double-cross. It may be seen either as a white cross on a black ground or as a black cross on a white ground. The two aspects of the double cross can be reported either by drawing a white cross on its own, or drawing a black cross on its own, and saying in each case, 'What I saw was this, against a particular ground or standing out against a ground.' That is to say, in explaining what we saw in seeing an aspect of the double cross, we point to actual parts of the original figure and say, 'That part stood out.' He concludes, 'It is possible to take the duck-rabbit simply as the picture of a rabbit, the double cross simply for the picture of a black cross, but not to take the bare figure for the picture of an

[1] *Op. cit.*, p. 207.

object that has fallen over. To see this aspect of the triangle demands *imagination*.'[1] Is the difference that the triangle seen as a picture of a fallen object is seen as a *picture* of something three-dimensional, while itself considered as lines on the page, is two-dimensional? Is imagination needed, that is to say, to enable us to see the triangle as a *picture* rather than as a diagram? This certainly seems to be an important difference between the triangle regarded in this light and the double cross. But what about the duck-rabbit? We are not supposed to need imagination to see it as a rabbit; yet to do so involves taking it as a two-dimensional representation of something three-dimensional, not merely as lines on the page. Or do we know from a long habituation to the convention, that it is meant as a picture, whereas in the case of the triangle it might be meant as either a diagram or as a picture? Wittgenstein does not answer these questions. But he goes on to consider the related question of how much I need to know (how many concepts I need to have available for my use) before I can be said to see certain aspects of a thing. 'In the triangle I can see now *this* as apex, *that* as base—now *this* as apex, *that* as base. Clearly the words "now I am seeing *this* as the apex" cannot so far mean anything to a learner who has only just met the concepts of apex, base and so on. "Now he is seeing it like this, now like that" would be said only of someone capable of making certain applications of the figure quite freely. The substratum of this experience is the mastery of a technique.'[2] But it may seem very odd to suggest that the logical condition of someone's having a particular experience should be that he is capable of doing certain things. We would never say, Wittgenstein argues, that a man could have toothache only if he was capable of doing particular things and not otherwise. But this merely goes to show, he thinks, that there is a distinction between *seeing* (the experience in the case of the triangle) and such experiences as having toothache. 'It is only if someone *can do*, has learned, is master of such and such, that it makes sense to say that he has this experience. And if this sounds crazy, you need to reflect that the concept of seeing is modified here.'[3] But our question is, how much is it modified? Do we need to add something *more* to the notion of seeing, when we talk of a man's seeing the triangle under a certain aspect?

The next example which Wittgenstein uses brings out more

[1] *Loc. cit.* [2] *Op. cit.*, p. 208. [3] *Op. cit.*, p. 209.

clearly than ever the difficulty of drawing any such distinction (the distinction, that is, between the seeing and the 'more'). Suppose that I am looking at an animal with its neck stretched out, its ears forward, sniffing at something. I see that the animal is in an enquiring, a hesitant posture. 'How could I see', Wittgenstein asks, 'that this posture was hesitant before I knew that it was a posture and not the anatomy of the animal?' (The animal's neck just was elongated, his ears fixed forward as a matter of structure.) The suggestion may be that I cannot use the concept of hesitance to describe a purely visual experience, because the concept has necessarily more than a purely visual application; it refers essentially to how the creature feels, and only derivatively to how it looks. But Wittgenstein objects, 'Might I not for all that have a purely visual concept of a hesitant posture or of a timid face?' That I can see hesitance or timidity *in* the object, he is suggesting, does not necessarily mean that I can be said to be doing 'more' than seeing. More exactly, we should say that my seeing hesitance in the object, a quality, that is, which cannot be thought of as referring, like shape, to merely visual aspects, does not entail that I can separate what I am doing into two parts, the seeing and something else. Wittgenstein compares the visual case with the auditory case of hearing major and minor in music. There is no doubt that my use of these terms to describe what I hear (and I may use them absolutely unreflectingly) both presupposes a certain knowledge, and may entail also a certain emotional value attached to each. But all the same I simply hear them. What I actually hear can only with great difficulty be separated from the concepts and values introduced into my account of what I hear.

Summing up what he has said about seeing an aspect Wittgenstein says, 'The concept of an aspect is akin to the concept of an image. In other words: the concept "I am now seeing it as . . ." is akin to "I am now having *this* image." Doesn't it take imagination to hear something as a variation on a particular theme? And yet one is perceiving something in hearing it.'

We are now in a position to raise again the question we left before. Can there be a clear distinction drawn between seeing and seeing an aspect, between hearing and hearing as . . . ? Or are we to go along with those who say that *all* seeing is seeing as . . . ? There are certainly some passages (including some which I have already quoted) where Wittgenstein himself seems doubtful whether such a distinction can be made. Seeing an aspect at least in some cases involves having certain techniques by which one can distinguish one aspect from another. But so does seeing itself, or so it seems. If I hear a minor chord, or see a triangle resting on a certain line as base, I want to say that that is what I see or hear *immediately*. I do not want to say that I receive certain stimuli and interpret them afterwards. I do not *first* hear something and *then*, in the light of my knowledge, recognize it as a minor chord. When Wittgenstein says that the concept of seeing is *modified*, we feel like replying that if so, it is always modified; that there is no essential difference between these and other cases of seeing and hearing. (But perhaps that is what being modified means. Modification could be thought of in the way that qualities used to be. There is no substance which does not have *some* qualities; so, there is no case of perception which is not modified in some way or other.) The fact of the matter is that Wittgenstein's phrase 'the echo of a thought' seems appropriate in *all* cases if in any. And he himself is sometimes inclined to extend the use of imagination, to cover not only a few special cases of aspect-seeing (the triangle as a picture of a fallen object) but cases of recognition as well.

Having just said this, 'The flashing of an aspect on us seems half visual experience, half thought', he goes on to illustrate it as follows: 'I meet someone whom I have not seen for years: I see him clearly, but fail to know him. Suddenly I know him, I see the old face in the altered one.' Now here is surely a description which invites us to say, as he said of the triangle, 'It is as if an image came into contact, and for a time remained in contact, with the visual impression.' Of this recognition, Wittgenstein asks is it a case of both seeing and thinking, 'or an amalgam of the two as I should almost like to say?'[1] And again at the very end of the long discussion of seeing an aspect, he says, 'Do I really see something different each time, or do I only interpret what I see in a different way? I am inclined to say the former. "I am seeing this figure as a . . . " can be verified as little as (or in the same sense as) "I am seeing bright red". So there is a similarity in the use of seeing in the two contexts.' But he leaves it open in the end how far this similarity can take us. 'We find certain things about seeing

[1] *Op. cit.*, p. 197.

The Nature of the Mental Image

puzzling because we do not find the whole business of seeing puzzling enough.'[1]

The puzzle we ought to feel is this. How far can we separate thought from seeing, concept-using from sensing? And if we cannot separate them, how far must we allow not only that concept-using enters into perception, but also that the power of *re*-perception, of presenting to ourselves perceptual objects in their absence, also enters into concept-using? Not separating these things entails both that we must think of perception as containing a thought-element, and, perhaps, that we must think of thinking as containing a perception-element.

Let us try to see, then, what Wittgenstein has suggested. In concentrating on the particular kind of seeing which he calls seeing an aspect he has done two things. First he has linked at least *this* kind of seeing (or hearing) with knowing or having concepts; and in some cases he has linked it as well with the use of the imagination. Secondly, he has connected the actual use of images with some cases of aspect-seeing and has strongly suggested their use in cases of recognition. We have seen some evidence to suggest that Wittgenstein himself had doubts about sharply distinguishing seeing an aspect from seeing in general. We may therefore quite legitimately argue that he has raised again the question raised by Hume and Kant as to the role in *all* perception (not just aspect-seeing) of the imagination; and that the connexion between perception and imagination is through the image itself (for the notion of aspects and that of images are, as he says, akin). Wherever seeing and hearing seem to take us beyond the actual immediate object of the senses (the stimulus, if we can separate it out) there it looks as if Wittgenstein (unlike Merleau-Ponty) has left room for the imagination. Now all the questions raised by Wittgenstein about aspect-seeing were thought by him to be of interest primarily because they might cast light on the phenomenon of understanding language. He speaks of the connexion between 'seeing an aspect' and 'experiencing the meaning of a word'. This suggests that at least some part of our perceptual experience must be described in terms of the significance which we attach to what we perceive. That I may take a certain object to be such and such, or recognize a face as the face of a friend, is a fact to be laid alongside the fact that when you

[1] *Op. cit.*, p. 212.

utter the word 'march' I may take it as an order or as the name of a month. I attach significance to it as I hear it. We are reminded that Husserl proceeded from the significance of words in a language to the significance of perceptions in the world. Our perceptions are taken by us to mean, or to point to, certain objects in the world.

It may well be said that we are hopelessly distorting the views of Wittgenstein if we suggest that in some ways he did not want to mark off seeing an aspect from seeing in general; and that we are foisting on to him a dogmatic view which he never held about the role of imagination in perception as a whole. And there would be a good deal of justice in this complaint. Perhaps the most we can say is this. What Wittgenstein says about aspect-seeing is quite explicitly connected by him with the imagination, in its image-forming sense. It is also explicitly connected with the fact that, in perception, we often go beyond what is merely sensory into the region of interpretation, and that very often these two parts of perception cannot be separated. He has left room for doubt whether what he says about aspect-seeing may not be extended, at least in part, to seeing, and perception, at large. If we do so extend it, then a kind of continuum in our experience begins to suggest itself, a continuum which runs from (1) envisaging things when they are not there before us, through (2) having a certain vision, and imposing it upon what we *do* have before us (noticing an aspect), to (3) perceiving things in general, and recognizing them as familiar, in the cases when we do indeed know them, or know things like them, of old. And it is precisely this continuum which is our concern.

Wittgenstein does say one thing which supplies a reason for his usually linking imagination with seeing an aspect, and separating both from ordinary perception. He says, 'seeing an aspect and imagining are subject to the will. There is such an order as "imagine this" and also "Now see the figure like this" but not "now see this leaf green".'[1] But this criterion of distinction does not seem to me wholly satisfactory. Neither the imagination, nor, I suspect, the seeing of an aspect is always subject to the will. The fact that both are sometimes subject to the will (and that therefore Wittgenstein's commands make sense) is not enough

[1] *Op. cit.*, p. 213.

to show that in the cases where they are *not*, there may not be more important links between ordinary seeing and seeing an aspect than Wittgenstein is willing wholeheartedly to allow.

But the connexion between seeing an aspect of something and having an image at least is clear. In seeing the duck-rabbit as a duck I might complete it as a duck in my mind's eye. I might mentally project the rest of the duck to the right of the now duck-head and put webbed feet underneath; and I might even draw this into my copy of the *Philosophical Investigations* and thus fix the trick picture in one of its looks for ever. On the other hand, if I wish to see it as a rabbit facing right, I may project on to the picture some whiskers or a mouth on the right of the picture itself. This example in turn relates to the more complex case of seeing a painting as a portrait, that is seeing the original in the painting and perhaps conjuring up other aspects of him, to complete the portrait-painter's image, as the likeness dawns. It relates also to recognizing an imitation as an imitation of Maurice Chevalier or Edward Heath. In these cases we cannot separate the interpretative function of the imagination from its image-forming function. Moreover, we have found no reason to suppose that we can sharply separate those cases of perception which call for interpretation from those which do not (an attempt rather half-heartedly made by Plato,[1] which he did not wholly succeed in making clear, not to our surprise). We cannot draw a hard line between perceiving the world as familiar, as where we live, as full of remembered objects, and perceiving a portrait of a familiar face, of recognizing the Duke of Wellington *in* the canvas. Into both these kinds of perception it seems that imagination enters.

We have come then by a long and circuitous route to the place where Wordsworth led us. Imagination is our means of interpreting the world, and it is *also* our means of forming images in the mind. The images themselves are not separate from our interpretations of the world; they are our way of thinking of the objects in the world. We see the forms in our mind's eye and we see these very forms in the world. We could not do one of these things if we could not do the other. The two abilities are joined in our ability to understand that the forms have a certain meaning, that they are always significant of other things beyond themselves.

[1] *The Republic,* 523b1.

We recognize a form as a form *of* something, as Wittgenstein said, by its relations with other things. It seems to me both plausible and convenient to give the name 'imagination' to what allows us to go beyond the barely sensory into the intellectual or thought-imbued territory of perception.

PART V

Conclusion

Imagination and Education

I make no absolute claims for the interpretation of imagination which I have tried to expound and illustrate in these pages. On the one hand, there may well be failures in the connexions I have attempted to demonstrate, and on the other hand, there are quite certainly totally different ways of looking at imagination. All I would claim is that my interpretation is *possible*, even if I have not expounded it in the clearest possible way. If this claim is accepted, then it follows that we can intelligibly state the case like this: there is a power in the human mind which is at work in our every-day perception of the world, and is also at work in our thoughts about what is absent; which enables us to see the world, whether present or absent as significant, and also to present this vision to others, for them to share or reject. And this power, though it gives us 'thought-imbued' perception (it 'keeps the thought alive in the perception'), is not only intellectual. Its impetus comes from the emotions as much as from the reason, from the heart as much as from the head.

The expression 'power in the mind' may quite properly be found objectionable. It is very hard to find a substitute for the vocabulary of faculty psychology. It seems to me in fact that such vocabulary is steadily becoming more innocuous as we more and more clearly recognize it as metaphorical. But what I am claiming could be put in a different and possibly less objectionable way. I am claiming the intelligibility of finding *similarities* between certain aspects of intelligent perception, and thinking of things in their absence, and so on. My thread of connexion can be conceived just as a series of similarities; and the name of the whole series is 'imagination'.

On this matter, on the question, that is, of how widely the name is to be used, it is necessary to return to Sartre. In his view, the ability to imagine is identical with the ability to detach ourselves from our actual situation, and envisage situations which are *non-actual*. Thus, in looking at a picture and seeing it as a portrait, we are detaching ourselves from what might be described as the brute facts of vision. The facts are that we are standing before a canvas object, of a certain dimension and coloured in a certain way, and looking at it. We detach ourselves from total immersion in these facts when we choose to see *in* the canvas the subject of the portrait, who is not present, but whom we feel to exist in the canvas. The portrait is, Sartre says, 'conceived as a material thing *visited* from time to time (any time the spectator assumes the imaginative attitude) by an unreality, which is precisely the painted object'. That which we judge when we consider the canvas from an aesthetic standpoint, that which moves us if we are moved by the picture, is essentially unreal. What is real, both for the artist and the spectator, is the canvas, the colours, and so on. But the artist has constructed out of these real elements an analogue of his own mental vision. He has constructed an analogue such that anyone can be aware of it as an analogue. And it has sense, and can be judged and enjoyed, only in so far as it is an analogue of something other than itself. Even non-representational painting, Sartre says, must be seen and appreciated in this way (and here he is surely right); 'the real object no longer functions as an analogue of a bouquet of flowers or a glade. But when I contemplate it, I nevertheless am not in a realistic attitude. The painting is still an analogue; but what manifests itself through it is an unreal collection of new things.' One of the incidental merits of this formula seems to me to be that it could be adapted to fit the case of music, a rare benefit in the discussion of the aesthetic. The creative artist, then, constructs an external form which is to be interpreted as signifying something which does not, in the same sense, exist. Both artist and spectator have to detach themselves from the world in order to think of certain objects in the world in a new way, as signifying something else.

This, in our view, is the function of imagination whenever it is exercised. For we need not lay down that a particular artist need have meant a particular thing in order for us to see the object before us as significant. We can, after all, easily conceive a situation in which, like Valéry's man with the sea-shell, we did not know whether an object was or was not made to be an analogue in Sartre's sense. Yet we may come to the sea-shell in an imaginative mood, and see in it something other than itself. We may see it as embodying a form, as exemplifying a sense which is in some way universal . . . Here, then, we come upon a use of the imagination which is not identical with its use in the contemplation of a portrait, but is akin to it. But Sartre himself would deny that it is imagination that is in question here. In *Being and Nothingness* (part IV, chapter 2, section III)[1] he introduces a series of descriptions of the world seen as symbolic or significant, which are precisely of the kind to illustrate the imaginative perception illustrated also in some of Coleridge's Notebook descriptions, which formed a crucial link in our chain of connexions. But he is, as we saw in Part IV above, determined to rule imagination out of perception of all kinds in order to preserve its unique conceptual identity with the thought of the non-existent (in order, in turn, to preserve its supposed total freedom). In this part of *Being and Nothingness* he speaks admiringly of a book by Bachelard entitled *Water and Dreams*, which, he says, is an attempt at a 'psycho-analysis of things' (i.e. an analysis of some meanings which are necessarily attached by us to things). He says, 'The author has made a great discovery in his material imagination. Yet in truth this term *imagination* does not suit us, and neither does the attempt to look behind things and their gelatinous, solid or fluid matter for the "images" which we project there. Perception . . . has nothing in common with imagination; on the contrary, each strictly excludes the other. To perceive does not mean to assemble images by means of sensations; this thesis, originating from the association theory in psychology, must be banished entirely. Consequently, psychoanalysis will not look for images but will seek to explain the meaning which really belongs to things.'[2] Sartre seems here to want to exclude imagination from perception out of a fear that if he does not he will fall into the trap of treating perception as a matter of having a series of images, after the Humean model. He wishes very properly to insist on the contact, in perception, with the real, not the imaginary world. This is the other aspect of his insistence, noted above, that imagination is exclusively concerned with the *un*real. But his view is over-simplified. We may agree that imagination is the

[1] Translated by Hazel Barnes (N.Y., 1956). [2] *Op. cit.*, p. 600.

image-forming faculty; but even if it is conceded that interpreting the world, seeing it one way rather than another, involves this very image-forming faculty, it does not follow that *what* we see is an image, rather than the real thing. When we look at the lines on the page which represent the duck-rabbit, and interpret them as a duck, we may indeed do this by means of an image of a duck, that is by the *visual thought* of a duck; but to say this is not to say that we are *not* seeing actual lines on an actual page. 'Material meanings', Sartre says, 'the human sense of needles, snow, grained wood, of crowded, of greasy etc. are as real as the world, neither more nor less, and to come into the world means to rise up in the midst of these meanings.' But to 'rise up in the midst of meanings' is to rise up equipped with imagination in our sense. And Sartre in this same chapter proceeds to descriptions of the viscous, that sticky sliminess of the world, which he thinks of as revealing the nature of the world; and these very descriptions precisely demonstrate the capacity we have been considering for taking things as significant, for seeing more in them than would meet the purely sensory eye.

The qualities of things we perceive are necessarily taken by us, Sartre says, as symbolic of the real being, being-in-itself, of the objects which possess the qualities. Sartre argues that unless such properties as oiliness, sliminess, viscosity, had actual significance as they are perceptible by us in the world, we should never be able to use the names of these properties metaphorically as we do, with the certainty of being understood. Therefore, he argues, perception of the properties must be perception of *real* characteristics, and cannot be ascribed to imagination. And if the perception is not the work of imagination, neither is the interpretation of it. But we may reject this line of argument. For to say that perception is perception of real properties of things is *not* to say that imagination does not enter into it: and if we allow that imagination is at work in the perception, then we may certainly allow that it is at work also in the interpretation of what is perceived. Indeed, it is impossible to draw a sharp line between the two. So we may read Sartre's account of the perception, for example, of the viscosity of some things in the world, and the disgusting character of this viscosity, as an exercise of the imagination in perception, or, if we prefer to put it so, of the perceptual or material imagination.

Conclusion

A few lines of this description, still from the same chapter of *Being and Nothingness*, may serve to show how natural a way of putting it this would be. 'The honey which slides off my spoon onto the honey in the jar first sculptures the surface by fastening itself onto it in relief, and its fusion with the whole is presented as a gradual sinking, a collapse which appears at once as deflation and as display, like the flattening out of the full breasts of a woman who is lying on her back ... the slowness of the disappearance of the drop in the bosom of the whole is grasped first in softness, which is like a retarded annihilation and seems to be playing for time, but this softness lasts up to the end; the drop is sucked into the body of the viscous substance. ... If an object which I hold in my hands is solid I can let it go when I like; its inertia symbolises my total power. ... Yet here is the viscous reversing the terms. I, the conscious being, am suddenly compromised. I open my hand. I want to let go of the viscous object and it sticks onto me, it draws me, it sucks at me. Its mode of being is neither the reassuring inertia of the solid nor a dynamism like that in water, which is exhausted in fleeing from me. It is a soft yielding action, a moist and feminine sucking. It lives obscurely under my fingers. ... At this moment I suddenly understand the snare of the viscous; it is a fluidity which holds and compromises me. ... The viscous seems to lend itself to me, it invites me; for a body of viscosity at rest is not noticeably different from a body of very dense liquid. But it is a trap. The viscous is like a liquid seen in a nightmare, where all its properties are animated by a sort of life and turn back against me. Viscosity is the revenge of Being in-itself. A sickly-sweet feminine revenge which will be symbolised at another level by the quality "sugary". ... A sugary viscosity is the ideal of the viscous; it symbolises the sugary death of consciousness, like the death of a wasp which sinks into the jam and drowns.'[1]

The reader of this kind of description may willingly grant that it is imaginative. Yet he may still feel doubts. To what extent is the imagination, as we have described it, just a form of sensibility, a kind of openness to the feelings, perhaps an avenue of sentimentality? Hume stated that a powerful imagination was the ability to turn ideas into living impressions, to arouse actual

[1] *Op. cit.*, p. 608.

passions and to experience them, in areas, such as reflection on past experiences or the doings of other people, where one might expect only reason, or the most pale and unimpressive ideas, to be in charge. The thread which I have attempted to trace may be seen, not so much as a thread, as a stream of incoherent *feelings*, running from its most minute beginnings in the recognition of objects about us (as a dog, as a familiar dog, our friend; a hill, a familiar hill, and thence a hill with unspecified threatening or moral significance in our life) ending, in its final form, as a flood of associations and random interpretations of the world. And the flood may be seen to carry along with it a flotsam and jetsam of confused and unverifiable statements about nature, the world and Being, such as we find in Fichte and Schelling, and indeed in the pages of *Being and Nothingness*, even though Sartre denied that imagination was either what he was talking about, or what he was employing. There may well be justice in this charge. For it could be said that what I have elaborately and confusedly done in the preceding pages is to trace the development of the romantic concept of imagination. Fichte, Schelling, Coleridge, Wordsworth, Sartre . . . all these are partakers, however different from each other in some respects, of the romantic spirit.

I would not try to deny this. But my justification would be that it is impossible to understand the concept of imagination without attempting to understand the romantic version of this concept, even if it is not the only possible version. More than that, I would argue that there is some sense in which the romantic version is true, and fits the facts. It fits the facts in this way. There is in all human beings a capacity to go beyond what is immediately in front of their noses. Indeed there is an absolute necessity for them to do so. That they are able to use language is sufficient proof of this, since, to speak in truisms, that we describe things and classify them entails that we look beyond the immediately present, by relating the present to the past and future, to what we have experienced before and expect to experience again. What I have tried to do is to bring together some of the ways in which this capacity to look beyond the immediate and the present manifests itself. The interest of the subject seems to me to lie precisely in the degree to which an identity or close similarity can be shown to exist between what I have thought of as the various uses of imagination.

The fact is that we all of us use language; and we all of us can form images, well or less well, of what we are not experiencing at this minute, but we might experience in the future, or have experienced in the past, or would like to experience in an ideal world. Moreover, we all of us, all the time, attach some significance to the form which our experience takes, even if it is only to hail it as familiar, or sink back in it as, roughly, predictable. We are therefore in my view, inevitably exercising imagination in our daily conversation and in our practical uses of things in the world. If the continuity of function for which I have argued exists, then one must recognize the universality of the imaginative function both in that it belongs to everyone and in that it is exercised by each over all of his experience. But besides its universal employment, the imagination has emerged, in addition, as necessarily connected with our emotions. And this is of the greatest importance. For if we think of imagination as a part of our intelligence, universally, then we must be ready to admit that, like the rest of human intelligence, it needs educating; but this will now entail, if we are right, an education not only of the intelligence, but, going along with it, of the feelings.

Quite independently of the present argument and on other grounds I am inclined to regard the emotions as part of the proper territory of education, the emotions, that is, if they are thought to include taste and sensibility. And it now looks as if this is not mere sentimentality. For if the link which I have tried to establish is established, then various apparently different things in fact go together . . . are more like each other than at first might appear. Imagination is necessary, on the one hand, for the application of thoughts or concepts to things, and without such application no human discourse and no goal-directed activity would be possible. But it is also that by which, as far as we can, we 'see into the life of things'.

The belief that there is more in our experience of the world than can possibly meet the unreflecting eye, that our experience is significant for us, and worth the attempt to understand it . . . this kind of belief may be referred to as the feeling of infinity. It is a sense (rather than an item in a creed) that there is always *more* to experience, and *more in* what we experience than we can predict. Without some such sense, even at the quite human level of there being something which deeply absorbs our interest, human life becomes perhaps not actually futile or pointless, but experienced as if it were. It becomes, that is to say, boring. In my opinion, it is the main purpose of education to give people the opportunity of not ever being, in this sense, bored; of not ever succumbing to a feeling of futility, or to the belief that they have come to an end of what is worth having. It may be that some people do not need education to save them from this; my claim is only that, if education has a justification, this salvation for those who do need it must be its justification.

There is nothing new in such a view; it is, roughly speaking, Wordsworth's. In the fragment of 'The Pedlar' which Dorothy copied immediately after 'The Ruined Cottage', and which was later incorporated, with alterations, as part of the second book of 'The Prelude', the following lines occur.

> . . . there would he stand
> Beneath some rock, listening to sounds that are
> The ghostly language of the ancient earth,
> Or make their dim abode in distant winds.
> Thence did he drink the visionary power.
> I deem not profitless these fleeting moods
> Of shadowy exaltation: not for this,
> That they are kindred to our purer mind
> And intellectual life; but that the soul
> Remembering how she felt, but what she felt
> Remembering not, retains an obscure sense
> Of possible sublimity, at which
> With growing faculties she doth aspire,
> With faculties still growing, feeling still
> That whatsoever point they gain, there still
> Is something to pursue.'

More explicitly, he speaks of the function of the image-forming aspect of the imagination, at the end of the seventh book of 'The Prelude', where he argues that education among the 'forms perennial of the ancient hills' gives to one so educated a means, by referring back to and reflecting upon these forms, to retain 'among least things an under-sense of greatest' and to 'see the parts as parts, but with a feeling of the whole'. The same thought has its grandest statement in the conclusion of 'The Prelude':

'Yet compassed round by mountain solitudes,
Within whose solemn temples I received
My earliest visitations, careless then
Of what was given me; and which now I range
A meditative, oft a suffering man . . .
Do I declare . . .
That, whatsoever falls my better mind,
Revolving with the accidents of life
May have sustained, that, howsoever misled,
Never did I, in quest of right and wrong,
Tamper with conscience from a private aim;
Nor was in any public hope the dupe
Of selfish passions; nor did ever yield
Wilfully to mean cares or low pursuits
But shrunk with apprehensive jealousy
From every combination which might aid
The tendency, so potent in itself,
Of use and custom to bow down the soul
Under a growing weight of vulgar sense.
And substitute a universe of death
For that which moves with light and life informed
Actual divine and true. To fear and love,
To love in prime and chief, for here fear ends,
Be this ascribed; to early intercourse
In presence of sublime and beautiful forms.'

And finally, as we have seen, he identifies this love and fear with the power of the imagination itself.

Because of the vastness of the claims for imagination here, and perhaps particularly because of the specifically moral function which is ascribed to it, it is easy to write off what Wordsworth says as the private creed of a moralistic visionary, or even as simply words, the manifestation of a kind of verbal inflation. But the whole purpose of the foregoing arguments has been to suggest that, quite soberly considered, there is something in the connexion he makes between the imaginative ability to perceive and recreate the 'forms of the ancient hills' and 'salvation from the universe of death'. If imagination will save us, it is the very same imagination which enables us to grasp the forms in the first place and then to visit and revisit them in our mind's eye thereafter.

The most famous witness to the possibility of such salvation and by such means is of course John Stuart Mill. Mill, it will be remembered, records in his *Autobiography* his period of depression in the 'melancholy winter of 1826–7'. The depression arose out of an increasing dissatisfaction with the practical result of the kind of Hartleian associationism on which he had been brought up. He discovered that the feelings of pleasure, which were supposed to have been associated by habit with the thought of the increasing well-being of mankind as a whole, did not in fact occur. He began to reflect that such pleasures were only artificially annexed to the things which were supposed to give rise to them, and therefore such an association of idea with feeling could not withstand the power of analysis, the whole purpose of which is to separate things which are different. 'All those to whom I looked up were of the opinion that the pleasure of sympathy with human beings, and the feelings which made the good of others, and especially of mankind on a large scale, the object of existence, were the greatest and surest source of human happiness. Of the truth of this I was convinced, but to know that a feeling would make me happy if I had it, did not give me the feeling.' The consequence of these thoughts was that Mill began to place more reliance, for human happiness, on the cultivation of feelings themselves. 'I ceased to attach almost exclusive importance to the ordering of outward circumstances, and the training of the human being for speculation and for action.' At the worst stage of his depression, the thought which tormented him was that pleasures are not inexhaustible. Even music, from which he had always got the greatest pleasure, seemed to him now to be liable to come to an end. 'The octave consists only of five notes and two semi-tones, which can be put together in only a limited number of ways: most of these it seemed to me must already have been discovered, and there could not be room for a long succession of Mozarts and Webers to strike out as these had done entirely new and surpassingly rich veins of musical beauty.' It was at this stage that he first read Wordsworth. He was predisposed in favour of Wordsworth's poetry in that it addressed itself to his own natural love of scenery, and particularly of mountain scenery. 'But Wordsworth would never have had any great effect on me if he had merely placed before me beautiful pictures of natural scenery. Scott does this still better than Wordsworth, and a very second-rate landscape does it more effectually than any poet. What made Wordsworth's poems a medicine for my state of mind, was that they expressed, not mere outward beauty, but states of feeling, and of thought coloured by feeling, under the excitement of beauty. They seemed to be the very culture of the feelings which I was in quest of. In them I seemed to draw from a source of inward joy, of sympathetic and imaginative pleasure, which could be shared by all human beings; from them I seemed to learn what would be the perennial sources of happiness, when all the greater evils of life shall have been removed. And I felt myself at once better and happier as I came under their influence.' When Mill speaks of the cultivation of the feelings it becomes clear that what he is really referring to is the cultivation of the imagination. A few pages further on in his *Autobiography*, he discusses the character of John Arthur Roebuck with whom he disagreed about Wordsworth. 'He saw little good in any cultivation of the feelings, and none at all in cultivating them through the imagination, which he thought was only cultivating illusions. It was in vain that I urged on him that the imaginative emotion which an idea, when vividly conceived, excites in us is not an illusion but a fact, as real as any other qualities of objects: and far from implying anything erroneous and delusive in our mental apprehension of the object is quite consistent with the most accurate knowledge and most perfect practical recognition of all its physical laws and relations. The intensest feeling of the beauty of a cloud lighted by the setting sun is no hindrance to my knowing that the cloud is vapour of water, subject to all the laws of vapours in a state of suspension; and I am just as likely to allow for, and act on, these physical laws whenever there is occasion to do so, as if I had been incapable of perceiving any distinction between beauty and ugliness.'

'The imaginative emotion which an idea when vividly conceived, excites in us' is, as Mill says, a fact; and furthermore it has intrinsic value. We can be certain that the pleasure of this feeling will not wear out, or be exhausted, because it is not a pleasure just attached arbitrarily to certain limited experiences. It is part of the actual creation of the experience. If we create the idea vividly, then *in so doing* we experience the imaginative emotion. It is in this sense, then, that we may agree with Mill that the feelings should be cultivated. Children cannot be taught to feel deeply; but they can be taught to look and listen in such a way that the imaginative emotion follows. As in the Victorian nursery story, Eyes and No-Eyes differ *in what they see*; and it is No-Eyes who lives in the universe of death.

On this matter of educational policy, perhaps a few further words would be in place. For there are two possible misconceptions which I wish to avoid. The first is that, in suggesting that the education of children should be directed to their imagination, I am suggesting that they should be specially encouraged to be 'creative' or to express themselves. I do not believe that children exercise imagination more by having a set of hand-bells put before them, or a glockenspiel, and being told to make their own music than by listening to music with a receptive ear. I do not believe that there is anything uniquely valuable (though it may have value) in getting children to write or draw things which are to be *original*. On the contrary, they may be deprived if they are not encouraged to read and to look at the works of other people . . . grown-ups, or the works of nature. The fact is that if imagination is creative in all its uses, then children will be creating their own meanings and interpretations of things as much by looking at them as by making them. And this leads to the second possible misconception. I do not hold that children should be told *what* interpretation to place upon their experience, what, if it is taken as symbolic, it is symbolic of. In so far as they begin to feel the significance of the forms they perceive, they will make their own attempts to interpret this significance. It is the emotional sense of the infinity or inexhaustibleness of things which will give point to their experience, not a body of doctrine which they might perhaps extract from it, if they were doctrinally inclined. (That this is true perhaps explains my feeling that those critics who wish to pin the Wordsworth of 1798 to a belief or lack of belief in pantheism, Christianity or what not are missing something.)

Perhaps enough has now been said in support of my thesis, which is that meanings spring up round us as soon as we are conscious. The imagination is that which ascribes these meanings, which sees them *in* the objects before us, whether these are the ordinary three-dimensional furniture of the world, diagrams in a text book, pictures, music, or images in the mind's eye or ear. At an everyday level we must use imagination to apply concepts to things. This is the way we render the world familiar, and therefore manageable. At a different level, and sporadically, we may also use it to render our experience unfamiliar and mysterious. If, below the level of consciousness, our imagination is at work tidying up the chaos of sense experience, at a different level it may, as it were, untidy it again. It may suggest that there are vast unexplored areas, huge spaces of which we may get only an occasional awe-inspiring glimpse, questions raised by experience about whose answers we can only with hesitation speculate.

A study of this use of imagination, not by poets or painters, but by ordinary, perhaps uncreative, even 'unimaginative', people has been made by Michael Paffard in his recent book *Inglorious Wordsworths*.[1] He sets out in the book to explore the territory of what James Joyce called 'epiphanies'. He boldly sent out a questionnaire to a number of undergraduates and sixth formers, based on a description of such an 'epiphany' from W. H. Hudson's autobiography, *Far Away and Long Ago*. He asked his respondents whether they had ever had experiences of a comparable kind, and, if so, to describe them. The replies he received make it very clear that such experiences are common, especially in childhood and adolescence, tending, as Wordsworth knew, to become less frequent with age. Perhaps the best account of such experiences is to be found in C. S. Lewis's autobiography, *Surprised by Joy* (and I owe this example to Michael Paffard, too,[2] though I had had it dimly in my memory since I first read it). There he describes three moments of extreme imaginative intensity, all from his childhood. I quote, as an example, the second of his memories. 'The second glimpse came through Squirrel Nutkin; through it only, though I loved all the Beatrix Potter books. But the rest of them were merely entertaining; it administered the shock, it was a trouble. It troubled me with what I can only describe as the Idea of Autumn. It sounds fantastic to say that one can be enamoured of a season, but that is something like what happened; and the experience was one of intense desire. And one went back to the book, not to gratify the desire (that was impossible—how can one *possess* Autumn?) but to reawaken it. And in this experience also there was the same surprise, and the same sense of incalculable importance. It was something quite different from ordinary life, and even from ordinary pleasure; something they would now say "in another dimension".' In writing of these early experiences, Lewis is quite explicitly writing about what he refers to as 'the

[1], [2] M. Paffard, *Inglorious Wordsworths*, Hodder and Stoughton, 1973.

highest sense' of the word 'imagination'. He goes on to pick out the common qualities of the three moments. 'I will underline the quality common to the three experiences; it is that of unsatisfied desire which is itself more desirable than any other satisfaction. I call it Joy, which is here a technical term, and must be sharply distinguished both from Happiness and from Pleasure. Joy (in my sense) has indeed one characteristic and only one, in common with them; the fact that anyone who has experienced it will want it again. Apart from that, and considered only in its quality, it might almost equally well be called a particular kind of unhappiness or grief. But then it is a kind we want.'

Lewis himself, in the end, minimizes the importance of such experiences, on the grounds that in themselves they are not religious, at most a kind of image or reflection of religious experiences. But he is wrong to play them down. The faculty of producing such feelings, such 'love and fear', is quite literally what gives value to our world. It is a matter for universal congratulation if it is true, as I have tried to argue, that each of us necessarily possesses this faculty.

Index

ς

Jˈ